COFFEE AND DEMOCRACY IN MODERN COSTA RICA

Coffee and Democracy in Modern Costa Rica

Anthony Winson

Assistant Professor, Department of Sociology and
Anthropology, University of Guelph, Ontario

MACMILLAN

First published 1989

Published by
THE MACMILLAN PRESS LTD
Houndmills, Basingstoke, Hampshire RG21 2XS
and London
Companies and representatives
throughout the world

Printed in the People's Republic of China

Winson, Anthony, 1952–
Coffee and democracy in modern Costa Rica.
1. Costa Rica. Coffee industries, 1950–1978.
Socioeconomic aspects
I. Title
338.1'7373'097286
ISBN 0–333–47269–1

For my mother, Dorothy,
for the memory of my father Robert,
and for Devin

Contents

Contents

List of Tables

List of Figures

Preface

Of all the Central American countries, Costa Rica has been perhaps the most accessible and frequently visited by North Americans and by Europeans. Ironically, less is known today about the roots of Costa Rica's present situation by the peoples of these metropolitan countries than is known about Nicaragua, for instance, or El Salvador, or possibly even Guatemala. This is unfortunate because the historical experience of Costa Rica, especially after the Second World War, offers rich insights to students of politics, economic development, and to those with a more general concern with the prospects of progressive change in countries and regions traditionally mired in the usual legacies of underdevelopment.

Costa Rica is regularly hailed in the Western press as possibly Latin America's most vibrant democracy and frequently compared favourably with its sister republics for its pacifist traditions and absence of a professional army, in a region that has become somewhat of an armed camp in the 1980s. Certainly, in the Latin American context the longevity of this country's experiment with liberal democratic political processes is a very commendable achievement. A serious analysis of the socio-economic and political circumstances that produced and sustained this experiment is, I believe, long overdue. This book is first and foremost an effort to help fill this gap. However, the development model inaugurated by José Figueres and his forces through armed struggle in 1948 had more than just unique political dimensions. A further objective of this work has been to examine the economic and sociological dimensions of this model through an analysis of a sector that was traditionally, and continued to be, a cornerstone of this society – the coffee economy. Indeed, I believe that it has been at this level that the real weaknesses and inequities of the Costa Rican development model have become evident. The accelerated concentration of land and capital which have fuelled the resurgence of powerful economic interests in Costa Rican society are only part of the story. The other side of the coin has been the progressive marginalisation of the poorest sectors in the countryside and the cities. It has taken the world recession of th early 1980s and the 'Contra' war against Nicaragua to bring the contradictions inherent in the Costa Rican model of development to a head.

I was tempted to write at least a summary chapter dealing with the current crisis in Costa Rica, which is arguably not only socio-economic but also political. I have resisted this temptation, for I believe that the economic and geopolitical circumstances that this nation has faced since the late 1970s are sufficiently complex to require a separate study of their own. It is hoped, in any case, that this book as it now stands will not only make Costa Rica's present situation a little more comprehensible, but also suggest some insights to those with a more general interest in the dilemmas of Third World development, particularly in contexts where a class of large agriculturalists have left their mark on society.

In bringing this long project to completion, a number of acknowledgements are due. For his encouragement to undertake my studies of the Central American countries well before they had attracted the academic attention they presently enjoy, I am very much indebted to Miguel Murmis. In challenging my interpretations in a forceful yet always constructive way, he has made this study better than it would otherwise have been. Harriet Friedmann and Richard Roman have also left their mark on this work, in different ways. Anton Allahar and Peter Meier provided intellectual support and comradeship when it was needed, and Jaime Tenjo was helpful on some of the more economic dimensions of this study. Robert Brym has shown a genuine interest in my manuscript and I am very grateful to him for the assistance he has provided.

In Costa Rica I must thank Dr Daniel Camacho, former Secretary General of FLACSO, for the generous assistance he was able to provide, and Dr Edelberto Torres Rivas for our brief but useful conversations. I am grateful to Ing. Alvaro Jimenez Castro, former Executive Director of the Coffee Office, for making available to me the resources of his institution, and thanks are also due to Drs Martin Piniero and Eduardo Andrade of the Instituto Interamericano de Ciencias Agricolas, to Sn. Guitierrez of the Ministry of Agriculture, and Sn. Gerardo Barquero of the Central Bank of Costa Rica for their generous assistance. A considerable debt is also owed the staff of the National Library in San José.

Acknowledgement is made to Cambridge University Press for permission to use a map first published in its volume edited by I. Rutledge and K. Duncan titled *Land and Labour In Latin America* (1977).

Finally, the support of the Social Sciences and Humanities Research Council of Canada in the early stages of this project, and more recently that of the Department of Sociology and Anthropology at the University of Guelph, have been invaluable.

ANTHONY WINSON

1 Introduction

The attention of the world in recent times has been continuously focused on the Central American isthmus. This interest was initially sparked by the revolutionary tide in Nicaragua, just as it had been with progressive changes in Cuba and, more recently, in Allende's Chile. However, in the last few years, concern with the region has been maintained more because of the backlash of American foreign policy intent on stemming progressive change. On the edge of the Central American cauldron, yet not entirely out of the spotlight, has been Costa Rica. This republic historically has had much in common with its sister Central American republics. But in today's highly charged political climate, Costa Rica's peculiarities as a country stand out more than its shared heritage.

If Costa Rica is known to the student of Latin America today, it is probably for one particular reason. This country has for some time now followed a political path that has distinguished it from both its other Central American neighbours, and from patterns of many South American republics as well. This path has entailed the successful transition from the kind of liberal oligarchic state still present elsewhere in Central America, to a liberal democratic politics similar to that of the advanced capitalist economies. And though conservatives today increasingly point to Costa Rica as an alternative political model to revolutionary change in the region, little attention has been given to the question of how liberal democratic politics did emerge in Costa Rica. An answer to this latter point would seem to be essential before we can assess the possibilities of 'transplanting' this model elsewhere. One of the basic objectives of this book is precisely to offer a provisional interpretation of the emergence of Costa Rica as a liberal democracy.

The economic development of this country has been tied up with the establishment of a national coffee economy. Consequently, an examination of the social organisation of coffee production, processing and commercialisation, and of the class relationships associated with this activity, necessarily forms an integral part of this study. To begin we examine the *ancien régime* that characterised Costa Rican society up until the 1940s and then proceed to an interpretation of the peculiar form of transitional State that emerged at the end of

1

this decade to inaugurate a new era in the life of the republic. This study also considers in some detail State policies that were elaborated after this crucial transitional period had been superceded. These policies were not only to change the economic organisation and the class structure associated with the nation's vital coffee economy. They also played a significant role in ensuring the viability of the State-sponsored programme to reform the economy and public sector of the country.

The new era heralded by the expansion of coffee production in Central America was inaugurated first in Costa Rica. Even before 1850 agrarian based capitalists – many of recent European origin – began planting coffee here as a new and promising source of accumulating wealth. In time, the most powerful economic interests engaged in the spheres of production and commercialisation of this commodity typically sought to consolidate their operations integrating the production, processing and commercialisation activities within a single enterprise. Those who successfully did so came to form the core of what may be called the coffee oligarchy. It was this group that was to determine the fundamental structure of the national economy for almost a century after 1850.

Historically, large agriculturalists organising the production and commercialisation of export crops destined for the metropolitan powers have constituted a most powerful, and often the leading, fraction of the dominant class in post–colonial Latin American societies. Argentina's *estancieros* controlling wheat farming and beef ranching, Brazil's *fazenderos* who dominated the world's premier coffee economy, and the influential *hacendados* located in Chile's fertile Central region all suggest the importance of such a class for the development of Latin American societies.

Lately, historical scholarship has come to pay much closer attention to the internal structure of the commercial agricultural estates that supported this class, and also to the relationship of these estate owners to other classes, and to the State.[1] This work has begun to show the importance of the social organisation of capitalist estate agriculture for structuring the wider economy and political society. A few studies have indicated that the peculiar organisation of commercial estate production placed limits on the expansion of a home market for manufactured goods. Indeed, for many decades in these societies the agrarian bourgeoisie managed to keep in place a liberal free trade policy that favoured their own class interests, at the expense of local manufacturers who required protection to resist the onslaught of cheap industrial goods coming from the advanced capitalist countries. This study will explore these themes in the Costa Rican context, during the era when a coffee oligarchy left its formidable mark on this society. However, we are also interested in more recent times, when this oligarchy lost power to other class forces in Costa Rican society intent on reshaping the national economy and political life in this country. This important transition was, of course, not a development limited to this nation alone.

As yet, the fate of this agrarian bourgeoisie in the socio–economic and political restructuring of Latin American societies during and after the Second World War has not been well studied. However, it is fairly clear that the Great Depression of the 1930s, and to some extent the War itself, weakened the hegemony of this group and set the stage for a challenge to their longstanding political dominance. It then became possible to modify the economic policies that had favoured this oligarchy to the detriment of other social classes, among them those interests that would benefit most from industrial expansion and further modernisation.

In most of Central America, for instance, this challenge to the crisis of the export–oriented landowners, where it occurred, was relatively shortlived. The recent history of Guatemala is illustrative. In this country after 1945 the Government of Juan José Arevalo, and later that of Jacobo Arbenz, spearheaded attempts to lay the groundwork for popular participation within a liberal democratic framework. This period was marked by the rapid growth of political parties among the small but influential urban and rural petit bourgeoisie and the limited urban artisan and working–class population. The flourishing of these parties was accompanied by a strong pressure to expand the political arena into the rural areas and thereby incorporate the very oppressed but potentially mobilisable mass of workers involved in commercial estate agriculture. The attempt ended in disaster. A combination of geopolitical factors that predisposed American sponsored intervention, and the immaturity of the political forces favouring economic and social reforms prevented the successful displacement of the oligarchy and a successful transition to a form of liberal democratic politics. Recent decades have been characterised by the further intensification of capitalist agriculture, and a first phase of import substituting industrialisation, with the traditional oligarchy and foreign capital appropriating most of the benefits that were to be had. A politics of barbarism infamous throughout the world has replaced the earlier tentative moves towards liberal democracy. Meanwhile, the revolutionary struggle has come to the fore as reforms that could achieve a more equitable distribution of national wealth have been continuously thwarted.[2]

In some of the more economically developed countries, considerably greater success was had in challenging the dominance of powerful landowning interests, for a time at least. Their experience would seem to have some vital lessons for students of contemporary Central America. In Argentina, for example, the crisis of the agro–export economy after 1930 stimulated local industry, once imports of industrial goods were substantially curtailed. By the early 1940s the social weight of the urban working class was quite significant, while industrialists were coming to play a much more influential role in orienting State policy. With the establishment of the Perón government, the demands of these classes came to receive much more attention. In good part this was at the expense of the large agrarian interests who had hitherto been in a position to appropriate a large part of the social surplus. The policy of this regime was oriented almost entirely towards drawing surplus out of the agrarian sphere to urban activities, without attempting to restructure agriculture in order to strengthen its performance within the national economy. The freezing of agricultural rents in particular hit the rentier fraction of the agrarian bourgeoisie hard, and served to redistribute wealth to industry and the working class.[3] Thus, while curtailing some important economic privileges of the powerful landowners, the Government did not eliminate large landed property as a major economic, and political, fact within Argentine society.

Eventually the continued monopolisation of the nation's best land by a small group of powerful agriculturalists was to hamstring attempts to raise agricultural productivity in this vital economic sphere. As viewed by some observers the root of the problem lay in the landowners' ability to appropriate speculative rents that were more lucrative than income to be gained through productive investments.[4] Later, agricultural price support policies, by aggravating the deteriorating economic situation induced by a stagnating agriculture, helped to undermine the social bases of support for Perón in the cities.[5] When the basically redistributionist politics of Perón's regime faltered and social tensions mounted, Argentine politics entered a phase of increasing polarisation as various class interests attempted to resolve, one way or another, the crisis provoked by the inherent contradictions of the Government's economic policy. Indeed it has been argued that the failure of the 'middle class' and its political representatives to define an alternative to the political and economic model of the oligarchy by this time meant that it was at a loss to see the solution to this crisis in anything but the terms defined by the oligarchy.[6] The rightist military coup of 1955, in which the participation of the landowners was central, verified the correctness of a warning given by one contemporary observer – 'either the Government destroys the oligarchy' he noted, 'or the latter will finish off the Government'.[7] The first alternative had been largely precluded, because of the unwillingness or inability to perceive the oligarchy as at the root of the problem.

The Argentine experience is not the only one to demonstrate that the displacement of the large agrarian interests from their longstanding dominance in politics does not, by itself, terminate their influence in society. Indeed, Brazilian history during the populist period of Vargas that ended with the 1964 military coup against his successor, Goulart, (finishing the populist political period for good) tends to confirm this view. Brazil's economic system and social structure was based on export production of a few agricultural commodities organized on an estate basis, and 'the estate was still the basic social and economic institution of the country.'[8] The failure to undermine the economic base of the large agrarians through structural reforms – once politics took on a national and popular character after the Second World War – not only determined the subsequent structure of industrial development in Brazil. It also jeopardised the movement from liberal oligarchic to bourgeois democratic state structures, in no uncertain terms. For here as well, the influence of the landowning oligarchy cannot be viewed in economic terms alone. As Celso Furtado has written, 'since the process of industrialisation has not involved conflict with the old vested interests in the sector of agricultural exports, the country did not give rise to an industrial ideology favouring effective political expression.'[9] And to the extent that the ideology of the large landowners imbued the rest of society, it limited the possibilities for the elaboration of a distinct political project that could be oriented towards solving the structural problems posed by the organisation of agriculture.

One important lesson derived from this historical experience is the centrality of the dialectic between redistribution and production during the conjuncture in which the agrarian bourgeoisie is weakened and a new relation of political forces emerges. Historically, governments which promulgated redistributionist measures without attempting to modernise a backward agriculture before long ran into structural obstacles to further economic growth. Eventually this provoked a crisis that put into jeopardy emergent forms of liberal democracy. Another lesson indicated is the importance of ideological hegemony. Given that the economic superiority of the landowning oligarchy typically entails the dominance of its political culture and economic doctrine, a successful challenge to the old agro–exporting system will require of the opposing forces the ability to approach the longstanding problems this system imposed on society in new ways.

Costa Rica has followed neither the trajectory of the other Central American countries, or that of populist Argentina and Brazil. In Costa Rica, a class of estate owners emerged in response to demand for coffee on the European market – a class which later came to control the processing and exporting of coffee. Coffee exports provided a primary impetus behind important infrastructural development. However, the internal organisation of the estates – and the relationship of agrarian capital to the small coffee growers – constituted a structural obstacle to the development of local manufacturing and a more diversified and dynamic economy. This experience was shared with its sister republics in the isthmus.

In the post Second World War period, however, Costa Rica represents one of the few successful challenges to the longstanding dominance of the large agriculturalists, within a fully capitalist social framework. Much of this study, then, is concerned with understanding how the kinds of problems traditionally associated with a type of agrarian development where large landowners predominate have been 'solved' in the Costa Rican context. Among these problems, one of the most important is the obstacle that landowners potentially pose for the development of economic sectors outside their own domain, notably industrial activities. In the following chapters I argue that the Costa Rican experience demonstrates a landowning oligarchy may indeed be successfully subordinated to a strategy for a broader-based economic development, without it actually being eliminated as a fundamental social sector of society.

This study also deals with what has been historically a more problematic question – the role large landowners have typically played in blocking the establishment of a democratic form of politics. In Costa Rica the political power of the coffee bourgeoisie had been in decline for some years by the time the Junta of 1948 brought an end to the oligarchic state. This study contends that the establishment of the Costa Rican variant of liberal democracy is closely related to the question of how, after 1948, the State came to have a degree of autonomy in Costa Rica that proved to be lasting. I refer to autonomy from both the oligarchy, and from the *Partido Vanguardia Popular* on the left and the organised and periodically influential popular sectors it represented.

Specific conjunctural factors in 1948 gave José Figueres and his rebel army the opportunity to disarm and disorganise the major party on the Left and its well-organised cadres. This was one key factor that provided the subsequent regime led by Figueres with political manoeuvring space. However, this new political project was not long in meeting resistance from the chief beneficiaries of the long established social order – the traditional coffee interests – who threatened to block the programmes envisaged by the new government. Initially this resistance was focused around the question of the surplus generated by coffee production, and the State's attempt to control a much greater share of this wealth. This study is therefore also concerned with understanding why in Costa Rica the oligarchy was not successful in bringing about a return to the *status quo ante*. In this regard, it is argued that credit must be given to Figueres as a political figure and his ability during the struggle over the wealth generated by the coffee economy to blunt the attack of the coffee oligarchy, while at the same time winning over a politically important sector of rural smallholders to his programme for change.

Especially notable in establishing the relative independence of the State at this time was the fact that the forces led by José Figueres who took power by force of arms in 1948 did have a well articulated alternative to the old estate economy of the coffee bourgeoisie. Indeed, Costa Rica during the 1940s had witnessed intense debate among intellectuals over alternative models of economic development. The successful implementation of a political project envisioned in earlier years was in good part due to the efficacy of the forces grouped around Figueres in waging an ideological battle against the laissez–faire world view of the agro–export oligarchy, and in winning over the population to a programme of aggressive state intervention.

This study argues that the longer term success of the political project fostered by Figueres and the Junta was in large part secured by a decision to plough back this surplus captured by the State into rural development projects that secured the economic prosperity of the country in the short and medium term. This was to give the State critical leaway in elaborating redistributive social programmes that were the foundation for Costa Rica's variant of welfare capitalism. The first and most ambitious of these development projects was the revitalisation of the coffee economy itself, and in later chapters I discuss in some detail the components of this strategy to redevelop coffee production, and the impact it had on the economic and social structures in the countryside. In this regard, it is argued that while the initial programmes to restructure the economy had to be imposed on a landowning class adamantly opposed to any such change, in the longer term the most powerful elements of this oligarchy were to be substantially strengthened in the process of modernising the coffee sector. Moreover, this group, together with new entrepreneurial sectors in the countryside outside the coffee sphere, have been considerably more successful in appropriating State funds directed towards rural revitalisation than have the rapidly growing number of marginal smallholders in Costa Rica.

In summary, this study suggests that by achieving a lasting degree of political autonomy from the traditionally dominant class, and by capturing for the State an important share of the national wealth generated by coffee, it was possible for Figueres to maintain a workable balance between (i) the imperative to effect a redistribution in wealth and (ii) the need to stimulate productivity and rationalise the nation's foremost economic activity – coffee production. This balance between the imperatives of redistribution and production would seem to be one of the keys underlying Costa Rican 'exceptionalism'.

In order to provide the necessary context for understanding this challenge to oligarchic power in Costa Rica, it will be useful to first consider the chief characteristics of the old social order, its historical beginnings in the nineteenth century, the era of expansion and consolidation of the coffee economy after the turn of the century, and the period of crisis, decay and political turmoil that set in with the Great Depression and continued through the Second World War and afterwards. It is these matters that I turn to in the first two chapters.

Notes

1. Several notable examples of this recent literature are to be found in a valuable collection of essays edited by K. Duncan and I. Rutledge, *Land and Labour in Latin America*, Cambridge University Press, 1977). Some other recent examples of note are Juan Martinez-Alier, *Haciendas, Plantations and Collective Farms*, (Frank Cass, 1977); Edelberto Torres Rivas, *Interpertación del Desarrollo Social Centroamericano* (San José: Editorial Universitaria Centroamericana, 1973); Warren Dean, *Rio Claro: A Brazilian Plantation System, 1820–1929*, (Standford: Standford University Press, 1976), and Marco Palacios, *Coffee in Colombia* (Cambridge University Press, 1980).

2. Works dealing with the Arevalo and Arbenz period in Guatemala's history are by now quite numerous, although few penetrate beyond a superficial analysis of American foreign policy decisions in explaining the demise of Arbenz's government. A few that do include Robert Wasserstrom's 'Revolution in Guatemala: Peasants and Politics under the Arbenz Government', *Comparative Studies in Society and History*, vol.17, no.4 (1975); Jim Handy, *Gift of the Devil: A History of Guatemala* (Toronto: Between the Lines, 1984) and Richard Adam's classic *Crucifixion by Power* (Austin: Univesity of Texas Press, 1970). Also see by 'The Formation of Capitalist Agriculture in Latin America and its Relationship to Poltical Power and the State', *Comparative Studies in society and History*, vol.25, no.1 (1983).

3. See Guillermo Flichman, *La Renta del Suelo y el Desarrollo Agrario Argentino* (Mexico: Siglo Veintiuno, 1977).

4. For instance, Murmis 'El Agro Serrano y la Vía Prussiana de Desarrollo Capitalista', in Miguel Murmis (ed.) *Ecuador: Cambios en el Agro Serrano* (Quito: CEPLAES, 1980) and Flichman, ibid.

5. José Nun, *Latin America: The Hegemonic Crisis and the Military Coup* (Berkeley: Institute of International Studies, University of California, 1969), p.40–1.

6. Nun, ibid.

7. Cited in Flichman, *La Renta*, p.162.

8. See Celso Furtado, 'Obstacles to Political Development of Brazil', in C. Veliz (ed.) *Obstacles to Change in Latin America* (New York: Oxford University Press, 1969) and Nun, *Latin America: The Hegemonic Crisis*.

9. Furtado, 'Obstacles', p.152–3.

2 Estate Economy in Costa Rica: Class Formation, Politics and Underdevelopment

INTRODUCTION

Prior to the establishment of coffee cultivation in the nineteenth century, the economy of Costa Rica was little developed despite earlier cycles of economic activity during previous centuries. There had been some efforts by descendants of the early *conquistadores* to carry on cocoa cultivation with local Indian labour, for example, but high colonial tariffs, the expenses of transportation and labour shortages had never permitted such an activity to thrive.[1] To this must be added the absence of an indigenous population of any size that could have formed the basis for a pre-capitalist hacienda economy, as in Guatemala and Mexico.

The marginality of Costa Rica from the powerful beneficiaries of the colonial economy – large landowners, the Church and State functionaries – undoubtedly facilitated experimentation with new economic activities in the early nineteenth century. After several failures, some limited successes were achieved with the export of coffee beans to Europe in the 1830s, via Valparaiso, Chile and Cape Horn.[2] There was little real prosperity however, until a firmer linkage with the English market was established with the efforts of the merchant captain Lacheur in 1845. Thus, by the mid nineteenth century, coffee cultivation to supply the expanding markets produced by the industrial revolution in Europe was becoming established in Costa Rica, decades before coffee production was organised elsewhere in Central America. Cardoso, for instance, writes that

> By the time of Independence from Spain, strongly entrenched interest groups had developed in both Guatemala and El Salvador. The liberal reforms demanded by the expansion of commercial coffee cultivators were only put into effect by the decline of the

10

Figure 2.1   Coffee regions and railway construction, circa 1900

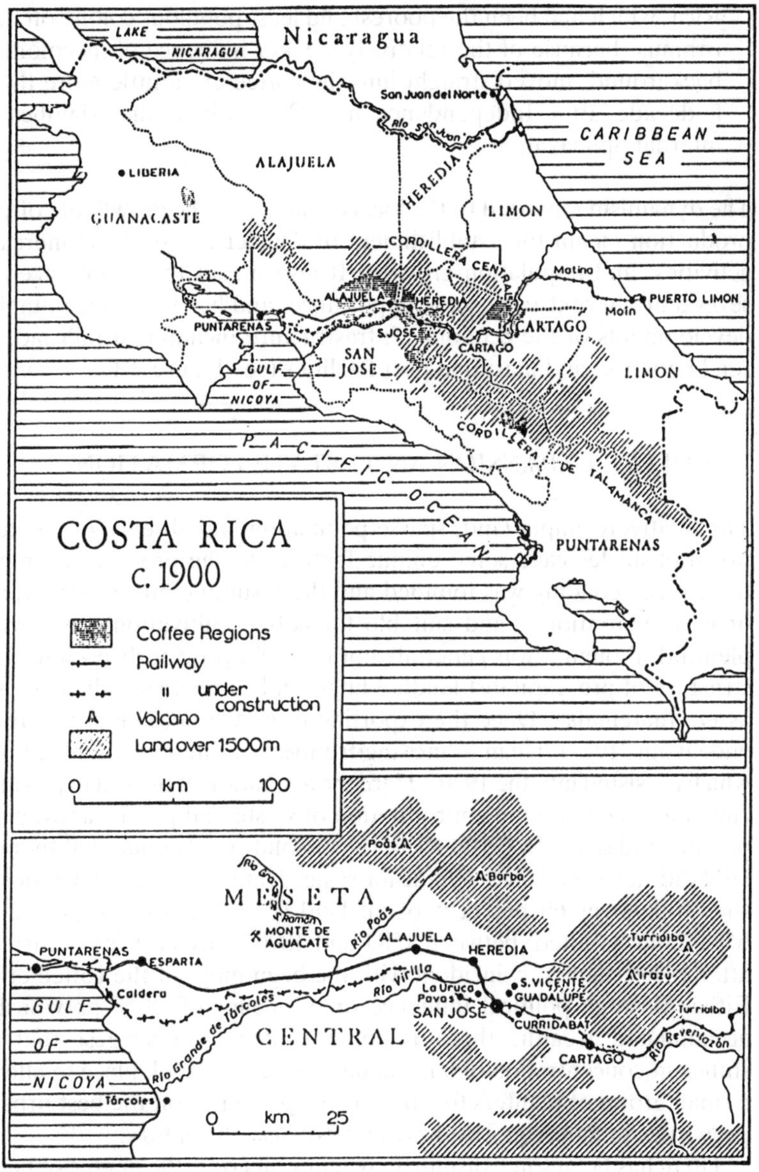

Source: C. Cardoso (1977), p.166

world market for dyestuffs during the 1860s and 1870s, and after a bitter struggle between rival groups in Guatemala in the 1870s and in El Salvador between 1881 and 1886. In the meantime Costa Rica, which had been the poorest and least populous colony on the isthmus, because of the relatively weaker influence of its colonial background, moved straight into the coffee era a little more than a decade after Independence in 1821, without any significant internal upheavals.[3]

The dynamism imparted to the local economy by the growth of coffee production meant the establishment of a wider range of commercial activities, and population growth.[4] It also meant the emergence of several urban centres of some importance, and by 1900 some notable developments of the economic infrastructure including a railroad, a road network, and maritime port facilities (see Figure 2.1).

2.1 COFFEE EXPANSION AND ESTATE FORMATION

The relatively empty land, sparse population and absence of institutional obstacles gave some unique features to the process by which the coffee economy was founded and the resulting internal structure of its organisation. Land suitable for coffee cultivation was never plentiful, though it was generally not part of a previously established structure of pre–capitalist landholdings, and communal Indian lands, as in Guatemala[5]. Once the exporting of coffee became a lucrative endeavour, there began a 'moving frontier' of internal colonization, which persisted into the 1920s. Here the alienation of the soil to private cultivators entailed the appropriation of waste and public lands, and private land sales. In Costa Rica, the dissolution of communal Indian land did not occur on a significant scale. Data provided by Cardoso show that over 60 per cent of all land sold and over 80 per cent of all land 'granted' between 1584 and 1890 in Costa Rica occurred after 1840[6], that is, coincident with the beginnings of the coffee era. Either through political influence or by means of some previously accumulated wealth, there is some evidence to suggest that a sufficient concentration of land suitable for coffee took place to allow a small group of planters to construct large houses on the best urban properties in San Jose,[7] even by mid-nineteenth century.

There has been some dispute in recent years over the degree of land concentration in this period and its effects on the rural population, with one side arguing that an early tendency to proletarianisation existed in the *Meseta Central*, the other disputing this and pointing to evidence of a substantial mass of smallholders in the coffee zones.[8] While Hall and Cardoso for instance, have criticized Moretzsohn de Andrade who tends towards the former position, their objections are not always convincing. Hall[9], for example, takes issue with the latter's claim that the concentration of land had produced a class of landless peones in the 19th century, by arguing that data show the preponderance, numerically and in terms of area in farms, of small and medium farms in the *Meseta Central*, owned by *campesinos*. This does not necessarily contradict the argument of Moretzsohn de Andrade, in my view, for the establishment of commercial estates does not usually require the elimination of small parcelised property. On the contrary, the persistence of a mass of formally independent smallholders can be seen as a central precondition for the reproduction of the estates, at least during the early phase of their development. The real point, at least for this early period, is not so much whether the developing estates are eliminating smallholders (and it is fairly certain that they were not in Costa Rica) but rather, what kind of structural relationship existed between the mass of small farmers and the large coffee haciendas.

Astaburuaga, an early observer gives some idea of the type of linkage that did come to be established in Costa Rica when he notes that the smallest farmers in the *Meseta*, once finished with the work on their own plots, went to work on the large haciendas, especially during the harvest period. Indeed, this practice apparently became more common once small producers no longer processed their own coffee, thus reducing the capacity of the smallholding to absorb labour.[10] I shall return to this matter below.

In any case it is clear that large properties, created in the nineteenth century represented 'the greatest concentration of land compatible with the specific circumstances of this and other factors of production in the country'.[11] On the other hand, relative to the great coffee estates of this era elsewhere, such as the massive Brazilian *fazendas*, Costa Rican coffee haciendas were modest in size.[12] It should be added that even by the 1930s, the coffee census of that time shows large estate owners had, as a group, less of the coffee land than did the mass of small and medium growers. The former, who were typically processors as well, had approximately 10000 of the 40000 *manzanas* of land devoted to coffee.[13] Nevertheless, the large agriculturalists were not entirely dependent upon a monopoly over the control of land to secure their dominant position in society. In Costa Rica there were other material bases from which this class could establish its influence. Cardoso, for example, has argued that what essentially constituted a coffee bourgeoisie in Costa Rica never depended entirely, or evenly mainly, on the control of land to achieve a high degee of economic, social and political dominance.

> Rather their dominance lay in their ability to manipulate and combine the three basic monopolies which were fundamental to the coffee trade: the control of rural credit and the processing and marketing of the crop. These monopolies were secured and maintained by an early and close association with British capital. . . . Thus the particular demographic, historical and ecological conditions of the country permitted the survival and even the expansion of the smallholding property structure, at the same time as the control of rural credit and the processing and marketing of coffee underwrote the economic, social and political supremacy of the small ruling group.[14]

Finally, Moretzsohn de Andrade was correct to argue that the very existence of what has been variously termed a coffee aristocracy or oligarchy implied the appearance of a rural labour force – a class of *peones* – in the coffee growing areas. Several factors are indicated as responsible for the growth of this landless rural population. Moretzsohn de Andrade notes repossession of the land of small holders unable to pay debts during the periodic slumps of the world coffee market, and the excessive fragmentation of landholdings passed down from one generation to the next. To this should be added the historically high price of land on the *Meseta*. This land had undergone a dramatic process of valorisation since at least 1840, so that land prices near San Jose which seldom exceeded 100 pesos per *manzana* in 1840 was changing hands at 200 to 300 and occasionally 500 pesos a *manzana* even by 1850.[15] As this trend likely continued, it is clear that before long it was exceedingly difficult for those without substantial capital, whether immigrants or prospective local farmers, to form viable farms in the *Meseta*. The absence of an indigenous population made for a chronic labour shortage,[16] which was never completely solved, as coffee growers had elsewhere, by attracting masses of European migrants. Why this was not attempted on a substantial scale is not clear, though the scarcity of land may have been an obstacle, since Europeans migrating to such countries as Brazil to

Figure 2.2   Coffee exports from Costa Rica, 1854–1936

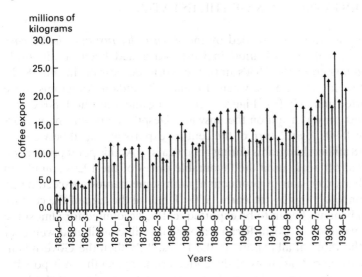

Source: Revista del Instituto de Defensa del Cafe, IV, no. 25, 1936, p.385,

work on agricultural estates could usually count on receiving plots for themselves as well.[17] It must have been largely through demographic increase, in conjunction with the above mentioned structural factors, which enabled estate owners to secure a labour force and thereby carry on their cultivation and processing activities. In 1886 Joaquin Bernardo Calvo wrote that while a chronic labour shortage persisted, the data from an earlier census (1883) showed the existence of some 18278 *jornaleros* employed in the countryside, in addition to 7479 'estate–owners', out of a total population of 182073.[18]

A sizeable, if not massive, landless labour force, a mass of small and medium farmers, many of whom engaged in commercial coffee production, and a very reduced group of large coffee planters – the *cafetaleros* – these were the basic social groups constituting rural society in this largely agrarian economy. In the next sections I shall attempt a more detailed examination of the structure of the Costa Rican coffee economy as it existed before the Great Depression of the 1930's. This will help to clarify the manifold relations which linked these three main social sectors within a complex structure which determined the dominant position of a few, and the subordination of the many.

2.2 LANDHOLDING STRUCTURE AND THE ORGANIZATION OF THE ESTATES.

According to data provided by the *Revista del Instituto de Defensa del Café* coffee cultivation in Costa Rica had been continuously expanding from the 1850s until the world depression in the 1870s. By the latter date between 10 and 12 million kilograms were exported annually (see Figure 2.2). During and after the 1880s coffee production was again on the upswing. Despite some very poor years in the 1890s, by the turn of the century exports averaged between 16 and 18 million kilograms during good years.[19] At this point production levelled off again until the favourable prices of the 1920s stimulated another expansion of production, with some harvests exceeding 25 million kilograms by the early 1930s. Up until the turn of the century when bananas began to be exported, coffee accounted for almost the total value of all Costa Rican exports and still contributed well over half the value of all exports in the 1930s.[20] By then the Government had carried out a census of the coffee economy, so that it is possible with this and some additional sources to get some idea of the basic features of this activity.

There were some 25477 farms or *fincas* producing coffee in Costa Rica as of the early 1930s, with over 73 million coffee trees occupying 68578 manzanas of planted land.[21] Though coffee would have been the most valuable product on the majority of these farms, it occupied only 24% of the land of coffee producing enterprises. The remaining area in these farms was occupied by pastures, wasteland and other cultivations, principally sugar cane, corn and beans. A population of 144 thousand persons were found to live on coffee *fincas*, or about one quarter of the country's total population. Of this, 21,576 'owners' of coffee *fincas* were listed, along with 25,472 'persons that work'. The great majority of the latter group were farm labourers or peones (21,424), the rest being administrators, chauffers and servants. Almost all coffee farms, and hence the bulk of the population, were concentrated in the provinces of San Jose, Cartago, Alajuela and Heredia. In Costa Rica the fact that a very substantial group of smallholders has participated in the nation's most important economic activity as producers, has often been used for ideological purposes and principally by the main beneficiaries of this activity. When a survey of the distribution of coffee trees among all producers was undertaken in 1940, for example (see Table 2.1), the fact that the great majority of farmers had under 2000 trees each

Table 2.1   Costa Rica: distribution of coffee trees, circa 1935

Coffee Trees	Number of Farms	%
1– 1000	12049	55.74
1001– 2000	4290	19.85
2001– 3000	1609	7.44
3001– 4000	865	4.00
4001– 5000	595	2.75
5001– 6000	410	1.89
6001– 7000	204	0.94
7001– 8000	257	1.19
8001– 9000	163	0.75
9001– 10000	158	0.73
10001– 15000	371	1.72
15001– 20000	169	0.78
20001– 25000	100	0.46
25001– 30000	77	0.36
30001– 35000	53	0.25
35001– 40000	29	0.14
40001– 45000	24	0.12
45001– 50000	24	0.12
50001– 60000	37	0.17
60001– 70000	17	0.08
70001– 80000	20	0.09
80001– 90000	22	0.10
90001–100000	13	0.06
100001–125000	21	0.09
125001–150000	8	0.04
150001–175000	6	0.03
175001–200000	7	0.03
200001–250000	5	0.02
250001–300000	6	0.03
300001–350000	1	0.05
350001–400000	—	—
400001–450000	1	0.05
450001–500000	3	0.01
500001 plus	3	0.01

Source: *Informe Sobre la Situacion del Café* (San José: Instituto de Defensa del Café, 1940).

was used by the offical journal of the coffee industry to argue that in Costa Rica, smallholders were the mainstay of the nation's primary agricultural industry.[22] In his well known thesis on the Costa Rican economy, Rodrigo Facio, the nation's foremost modern economist, indicated some of the ideological connotations of this kind of facile argumentation (residues of which are still found in more recent studies of the coffee economy). Without elaborating on his point too much, Facio was probably the first to suggest that data such as that found in this early survey show the importance of large property in the country's agrarian economy. In fact, an examination of the data in this survey allows one to make an approximation of the concentration of production, at least, in this sphere. In this regard, it is apparent that 75 per cent of producers, the 16319 farmers with less than 2000 trees each, controlled roughly 12.5 million trees. Less than 1 per cent of the growers, the 170 haciendas with 50000 trees each, had about 20 million trees in all.[23] Thus, considering only one aspect of the coffee economy, the coffee trees belonging to producers, we have some indication of the economic power of the *cafetalero* group, relative to the mass of small–holding coffee growers.

While there are few early studies of these large haciendas where much of the nation's coffee production was carried on, a few sources give some idea of the features of these large enterprises. A special supplement to the journal *La Tribuna* entitled 'Homenaje al Café de Costa Rica'[24] is one especially noteworthy source. This survey of the haciendas of 30 of the country's leading coffee growers provides some insight into the organization of the large estates, including some production and social data.

The landholdings of the estate owners surveyed were relatively modest in size compared to large estates in other Latin America countries, averaging about 371 hectares. The largest estates though, were over 1000 hectares. What is notable is the high proportion of each of these estates that was under cultivation. Except for the very largest farms, over half of total farm acreage was generally planted with coffee, and in a number of cases this proportion was over two thirds.[25] In other words, these estate owners were clearly producers and not mainly landlords with income based primarily on rents. The importance of cultivation organised by the estate owner was confirmed by the substantial numbers of permanent workers located on these landholdings. Of those landowners reporting, the number of permanent estate workers ranged from 50 to in excess of 300, the average being over 200 regular workers per estate. This worked out to roughly 1 permanent worker for every 2 manzanas in coffee, for those growers providing information on their labour force. In addition to this, however, estate owners hired large number of "temporary" workers during the harvest season. The data provided by landowners indicated that the estate labour force would swell to about four to five times its normal size during this period.

From this survey, together with historical data provided by Hall it is possible to surmise a few aspects of the social organization of coffee estates in Costa Rica. The most prevalent system it seems, was to have permanent workers and their families living on the estates in houses provided by the owner.[26] The survey of large landowners indicates it was not uncommon to provide resident workers with a small plot of land as well, and schools and dispensaries existed on some of the remoter haciendas, according to Hall. Estate formation in much of the *Meseta Central* took place where smallholding property was already established and therefore the large haciendas here tended to be quite fragmented into a number of smaller units.[27] Consequently the settlement pattern of the resident estate labour force was dispersed, a factor conducive to personalistic labourer–employer relations. In addition to a domicile and possibly a plot of land, resident *peones* were remunerated with a fixed wage. This was also the case with those haciendas which did not have their labour force living on the estate, but rather in nearby villages or towns. This latter type of situation existed on haciendas formed relatively later and in more remote areas where labour supply was always a difficult problem for landowners.[28]

The heavy dependence on temporary labour during the harvest season described in the survey of estate owners points to another central feature of the Costa Rican coffee estates. This is the structural relationship between the haciendas and the numerous smallholders that populated the Central Valley. Historical data are as yet unavailable to indicate how estate owners incorporated the labour of smallholders. It is fairly certain that they were the labour reserve of the large grower, though some growers were apparently able to secure temporary labour in the larger towns, also.[29] There is little evidence to suggest peak seasonal labour demands were met any other way, such as with migrant labour. Certainly in this respect, coffee estates in Costa Rica differed from those elsewhere in Central America (Guatemala, for example) where a migrant labour system involving highland subsistence farmers was integral to the reproduction of the large commercial estates in this period.[30] In any case, Hall's detailed study of one hacienda in the eastern margin of the Central Valley shows that estate–owners met at least part of their peak labour requirements with the labour of women and children.[31] This suggests that the entire family of the smallholder constituted a labour reserve for the estates then, as indeed has been the case in more recent years. The fact that climatic conditions tended to produce an uneven maturation of the coffee fruit in much of Costa Rica, would seem to have been an important factor in making the chronic labour shortage somewhat less acute, since only a part of the annual crop would be ripe at any time.

As for the employment of capital on the estates, it appears that productive investment in cultivation was comprised largely of expenditures on labour power, and of course, land and infrastructure.[32] Relatively little was spent on the agricultural inputs such as fertilisers, herbicides and pesticides, compared with contemporary times. This is not to say that estate owners were not employing scientific agricultural practices known at this time, for there is evidence to indicate they were. None the less, advanced agricultural techniques were employed within the framework of a productive process that remained labour, rather than capital, intensive. Despite having the country's most productive enterprises, the large *cafetaleros* rarely managed to produce more than 15 *fanegas* of coffee per *manzana* of land (Homenaje al Café, 1933) a far cry from the productivity of the large farms after the Second World War, when much more intensive cultivation was introduced (see Chapter 6).[33]

The organisation of production within the capitalist estates thus incorporated the following characteristics. The scale of production was considerably greater than anything that had existed before it, while rational agricultural practices were disseminated and employed by estate owners. In addition, 'the process of production has become the process of capital itself', as Marx put it. The labour process is here subsumed under capital – the capitalist is the organiser of production, and is not principally an intermediary between the producer and the market as was the case with the merchant.[34] Of course, he may also play this role in his function as exporter. However, the low technical composition of capital, the still archaic forms of productive relations employed, and the purely quantitative character of accumulation suggests that we are speaking of what Marx referred to as the formal subsumption of the labour process by capital. With this form of capitalist economic organization conditions do not yet exist to enforce the complete and constantly repeated technological revolution in the productive power of labour that some have argued is the *sine qua non* of a full–blown capitalist economy.[35] Rather, Costa Rica's coffee estates at this time might be best understood as having constituted a *transitional* form of agrarian development.[36] This would only be superceded in the years after the Second World War, when major changes in the structural organisation of the estates propelled a transformation of the technical level of production. In this earlier period, low and even declining levels of productivity determined by the relatively constant composition of capital were the norm on the large coffee estates. Before too long, this situation was to become a serious problem for the big growers, particularly once a longterm downturn in the world market price for their coffee became established. This is a matter to be addressed in a later section.

2.3 ESTATE OWNERS AND THE ORGANIZATION OF PROCESSING, CREDIT AND MARKETING

The fact that a small group of powerful agrarian capitalists controlled the nation's coffee processing facilities in Costa Rica has been of considerable significance historically and in several ways. Unlike other coffee economies, such as Brazil, Costa Rican coffee has traditionally been processed by the so–called 'wet–method', which has allowed it to produce coffee of the highest quality. Since the development of more sophisticated machinery in the nineteenth century, this process has required a substantial capital investment on the part of prospective processors[37] so that it rather quickly became the monopoly of those of considerable financial means. This meant either large coffee growers or, not infrequently, foreign capitalists who established processing plants, called *beneficios*, and only later became agriculturalists. By the mid 1930s there were 220 *beneficios* of various sizes scattered through the *Meseta Central*.[38] The coffee processor or *beneficiador* would typically process the coffee of the smaller coffee farmers in his vicinity in addition to his own production. Frequently the amount of coffee produced by clients would substantially exceed the *beneficiadores* own production. Small, and many medium growers were thus dependent upon the beneficio to process their coffee, not only because coffee processed by primitive manual methods was not as valued in the international markets, but also (one could surmise) because the *beneficiadores* monopolized the export business and were therefore in a favoured position to regulate what coffee got sold abroad.[39] Thus, the processing activity entailed another aspect of the relationship between estate owners and smallholders. In fact this has been the most important one historically. It has been around the matter of the price coffee growers would receive from the *beneficiador* that has brought to the fore the class antagonisms integral to the organization of the coffee economy. Around this issue coffee growers – large and small – could make common cause against the processors. The potential of these groups as a political force became apparent in the 1930s when growers were hit especially hard by the abrupt decline of the price of coffee in the world market. Thus, at the onset of the Great Depression,

> Coffee producers established the *Asociacion Nacional de Productores de Café*, whose stated purpose was to pressure for government intervention in the relationship between producer and exporter (Barrenechea, 1956:6). They achieved success in 1933 when, in the depths of the economic depression, the government for the first time decided to intervene in the coffee industry, thus ending its century old policy of laissez–faire. The *Junta de Liquidaciones* (Settlement Board) was established...to set the price that each *beneficio* was to pay the producer; it based its calculations on the quality of the coffee and set a maximum profit for the *beneficio* at 12 percent.[40]

In addition to the control of land and the processing of coffee for export, the small nucleus of producer–processors also had a prominent position in the commercialisation of coffee as exporters and were the only real source of the credit which coffee growers required to get from one productive cycle to the next. Cardoso has provided a succint summary of the mechanisms by which the provision of credit became another buttress of the economic and social domination of the *cafetaleros*:

> The coffee bourgeoisie, which controlled exports and consequently the inflow of foreign exchange, also paid in advance part of the value of the coffee crop that the small farmers who used their *beneficios* promised to sell them after the harvest. This – and the frequent requirement of written contracts – enabled them to lay down certain quality levels for the coffee beans from the small *fincas* and allowed them to exercise a high degree of pressure and social control over the small farmers, which was necessary to

guarantee them the additional labour needed on a large scale for the harvesting and processing of their own coffee. It also permitted the large growers to transfer part of the losses they might suffer to the peasants: since they advanced to the owners of small parcels only a part of the payments for the beans that they would deliver at harvest time, leaving the final reckoning until after the harvest and export of the product, it was always possible for them to claim that they had made a loss and to pay less than they had promised.[41]

Finally, it is apparent from the *Homenaje al Café*, among other sources, that the business affairs of the large *cafetaleros* not infrequently went beyond the coffee industry and other agricultural pursuits, such as sugar cane production and livestock farming. Felipe J. Alvarado, for instance, was described as being involved with banking, transport agencies, steamship lines and industry, in addition to his coffee *beneficio* and 400 *manzanas* of land in production. Another estate owner is noted to have been an important merchant in San Jose, while involvement in banking was mentioned for several other important *cafetaleros*. The Tournon family was involved in a major brick manufacturing company, gold mining activities and was the agent of a major European shipping line. Thus by the 1930s and probably much earlier, a small group of a few hundred individuals had attained a dominant position in the nation's most important economic activity, as major coffee cultivators, as the sole proprietors of processing facilities and through a monopolistic control over agricultural credit and the exporting of coffee to Europe. In addition, a small nucleus in this group apparently had considerable influence in those few other economic activities that had emerged in this still primarily agrarian based economy. At the economic level, there was no propertied group that compared with the influence of the *cafetaleros* in the business affairs of the country. And in political terms, the large coffee producer–processors were very conspiciously represented by their control of the most important positions of the State. A further consideration of the last point is in order at this time.

2.4 COFFEE, POLITICS AND THE LIBERAL STATE

With the organisation of coffee production and its export to European markets came new political structures in Central America, which might be most accurately termed modernising dictatorships. Especially in the northern countries, these relatively centralised and interventionist States were basically a political expression of the need of a coffee bourgeoisie, in formation' to free up land and labour power so that coffee cultivation could be organised on an extensive and rational basis. Where these two factors of production were still enmeshed in a pre–capitalist communal economy, as in Guatemala for example, the need for a forceful State intervention of this kind was concomitantly greater.[42]

The emergence of such a State structure occurred first in Costa Rica, however, under the firm control of the dictator Braulio Carillo in 1841. As in neighbouring countries, the political affairs of this emerging nation–state were organised on a highly exclusionistic basis. A number of 'controls' acted to restrict politics, not only to an educated elite, but to owners of means of production in particular. Thus, in addition to the requirement of being literate, holders of major political positions (electors, representatives, magistrates, ministers, president and vice–president) had to possess a considerable amount of 'capital' and a money income that was also substantial for those times. The bourgeois inspiration in the organisation of political life was indicated by the fact that it was 'capital' that was a key prerequisite to important political office, and not immovable property, such as land, as had been the case until the 1840s.[43]

A further effective 'control' once direct suffrage was introduced in 1913 was the requirement of casting verbally one's vote for political representatives. This system was especially intimidating for the *peones* on the coffee estates, who might jeopardise their positions should they not vote for the candidate favoured by their *patron*.[44]

Stone's detailed study of the social and political organisation of the influential families related to the coffee economy indicates the predominant position of this fraction of the propertied classes in the nation's political life since the 1850s.[45] This early consolidation of their political influence was certainly related to the fact that commercial agriculture was well established in Costa Rica long before it was in other coffee economies of Latin America. Furthermore, the weakness of a conservative Church establishment and influential landowners related to a pre–capitalist senorial economy gave the *cafetaleros* a more or less fee hand in the orientation of State policy, unlike in other Central American countries such as Nicaragua. The State of this period in Central America is often characterized as being 'liberal' and 'oligarchic'. Considering this latter aspect, I have mentioned above the controls that served to underpin the reproduction of an oligarchy in national politics. Zamosc has captured this aspect of the Costa Rican State during this epoch. Though he refers to El Salvador, his description would seem to be more or less accurate for Costa Rica, at least up until the turn of the century and possibily for some time afterwards.

> The political regime which came to prevail . . . was republican from the formal point of view, but authoritarian, exclusionist and personalistic from the point of view of its content. The political scene was not articulated by the relations among parties which expressed the particular interests of the classes and fractions. What we had were ephemeral parties or factions, which were organized in electoral times on the basis of personalities and not of political platforms. Generally the nomination of a president was the result of an agreement among the dominant groups about a suitable candidate, whose eventual election was ensured through the manipulation of the polls. The same procedure regulated the election of local authorities and of representatives to the legislative assembly.[46]

The rise of a modernising coffee bourgeoisie brought with it the emergence of new ideological currents – by the turn of the century positivism and liberal political and economic doctrines structured the world view of an important section of the local intelligencia. As Gutierrez has noted, these ideas profoundly influenced the so–called 'generation of 88', the 'Olimpo', who were central in organising teaching and scientific institutions, the beginnings of more open and popular discussions in the national press, and the diffusion of democratic ideals.[47]

The impact of the social reforms molded by these positivist and liberal currents introduced around the turn of the century, were particularly significant in Costa Rica. The early development of a more broadly-based educational system meant high rates of literacy especially relative to neighbouring Central American countries, even in these early years. This, in turn, stimulated a pressure for direct suffrage and opened up the possibility of further reforming the exclusionistic oligarchic State. Prior to this politics had consisted largely of intra–oligarchic rivalries between powerful personalities who typically represented the leading coffee families.[48] It was in the context of one of these personalistic political struggles that in 1909, Ricardo Jimenez Oreamuno, a presidential candidate and *cafetalero*, was instrumental in broadening the existing political process. Jimenez offered to decentralise the central government by giving municipal governments greater autonomy and having local leaders popularly elected, rather than being appointed by the executive power. By so doing, he was able to bring into the political process for the first time an influential middle strata of peasants that had developed with the spread and growth of coffee cultivation. These *gamonals* supported such a proposal because it would basically grant them more say in the direction of municipal affairs. It also opened the way for the direct participation in national politics of this better off section of the rural population.[49]

Reforms such as this and the secret ballot introduced in the late 1920s did not in themselves seriously threaten the dominance of the *cafetaleros* in national politics. Even by the 1930s it was clear that any real challenge to electoral candidates of the oligarchy were usually deflected by a well developed system of fraud and corruption. Moreover, the *coup d'état* directed against Gonzalo Flores in 1917 demonstrated the oligarchy's ability to handle leaders who, once in power, were so bold as to place the economic well being of other sectors, or the society as a whole, above that of the coffee oligarchy.[50] The real importance of these reforms only became apparent in subsequent years, in the historical opening they provided for the initiation of a broader range of popular political involvement and agitation in the decades after 1900. Politics had begun to take on a less exclusive character, as Monge describes

> In these years . . . the political parties were no longer simple circles of friends, but consisted of large formations – of a personalistic and non–ideological kind certainly – in which were grouped vast sectors of the population. *Campesinos* and workers intervened in politics with the same right as the economically powerful sectors. The parties chose their candidates . . . in huge conventions in celebrated theatres of the capital.[51]

Soon, politics was no longer only the domain of the traditional parties either, as Vega Carballo notes of the period following the First World War.

New organizations of popular and nationalist orientation emerged, such as the *Liga Civica* that struggled against foreign companies that, propelled by the expansion of North American capitalism, increased their control over the country's resources. The Communist Party was founded in 1931 and, already by 1934 organized an important union struggle against the United Fruit Company with the support of about 10000 workers. Innumerable strikes were organized and in 1937 the Cultural Association of Law Students was formed. This was the seed of the later Centre for the Study of National Problems, which contained an important sector of young liberal and social democratic intellectuals[52]

Moreover, the agitation of the small coffee growers in 1930 for greater controls over the exploitative practices of the producer–processors, and the concessions they received from the State was a further indication that the grip of the *cafetaleros* over national politics was not absolute; indeed it was on the wane.

In Costa Rica then, limited forms of popular participation were established at an early period and with them the respect for certain political rights. This development inevitably gave some legitimacy to other kinds of political expression in later years – union activity, non–traditional political associations and pressure groups – which tended to dominate the political scene in the 1920s and 1930s. The *differentia specifica* of the oligarchic state in Costa Rica, relative to its Central American neighbours, would seem to be this development. In the latter countries, political rights were either undeveloped or not respected in reality. This may be a key to understanding why popular organisation and protest was more consistently met with repression in the latter contexts.

By the 1930s the political scene was less exclusive and a broader range of groups were making their interests known to the State and society at large. The response of the coffee bourgeoisie was to seek a more formalised relationship with the State through stable institutional channels. The creation of the *Instituto de Defensa del Café* at this time offered precisely these kinds of channels. Through the *Revista* of the Institute, *cafetaleros* could not only put forward their concerns in a public fashion but more importantly they could further strengthen their class identity, as new threats to their hegemony began to loom on the horizon.

2.5 THE COFFEE COMPLEX AND THE WIDER ECONOMY BEFORE 1940

Despite the sketchy historical studies presently available on the structure of the rest of the economy, and notably the character of local manufacturing and the impact of the coffee monoculture on its development, it is sufficiently important to warrant a preliminary assessment. In general terms, I take the view argued by Palacios in his important study of coffee in Colombia as my point of departure on this subject. He notes that understanding the linkage between the organization of commercial export agriculture and economic development

> implies shifting the emphasis of one's analysis from the loss of political sovereignty and from the terms of trade and from the different elasticities in the demand for coffee or manufactured goods. One has to look at the structure of coffee production, and how coffee is financed and traded, and one has to understand the formal and informal mechanisms that concentrate income from coffee.[53]

The expansion of coffee production in Costa Rica since the 1850s did provide an early stimulus to other spheres of production, that is certain. The problem was that these opportunities were quite limited, and the possibility of broadening the productive structure of the local economy were largely curtailed by those private interests who were the main beneficiaries of the agro–exporting system.

To begin with, it was inevitable that the various requirements of the large coffee farmers would give some initial impetus to local commerce and industry. Coffee cultivation could not be profitably exploited without a transportation and communications systems. Such major infrastructure projects as the Atlantic railroad begun in 1871 by Henry Meiggs[54] and the Pacific railroad later on would have provided a demand for local machine shops and other small industries to provision construction crews, though rail and rolling stock were imported. Port facilities at Limon, streetcar systems in San Jose and Cartago, bridges, telephones, telegraphs, electric street lighting and a road network were other projects underway before the turn of the century.[55] However, it must be added that a good part of this infrastructure, notably the coastal railways and the port facilities, was constructed under the aegis of foreign capitalists interested in developing massive plantations for banana production on the eastern littoral. As an enclave development, the benefits it provided for the national economy were minimal. The companies' operations were largely self contained. Workers wages were siphoned off by company commissaries (reducing their effect in generating local demand) and the monopoly had sufficient influence in governing circles to thwart almost all measures aimed at transferring part of its massive revenues to the State.[56] Moreover, through its control of the Atlantic railway, United Fruit was able to charge monopolistic rents to local capitalists dependent upon this artery to US and European markets. Coffee expansion in Costa Rica entailed an important agro– industrial development, the *beneficios*. The more than 200 plants operating by the 1930's required purchase and subsequent maintenance of considerable machinery, much of which was purchased in Europe in the early days. Later on, however, local machine shops had grown up to supply some of the machinery and parts for the *beneficios* and also for the local sugar mills.[57] Some other industrial establishments existing by the 1930s are described in an early study by Quijano. Especially noteworthy was a large brewing and bottling plant, owned by the Lindo brothers who were also leading *cafetaleros*; garment factories, at least one of which employed over 100 operatives and utilised modern equipment for that time; a factory making steel furniture; a soup and candle factory; a pharmaceutical plant; a large and modern bakery; a factory producing wines and processed food products; and a large textile factory employing several hundred workers.[58]

In terms of its structure, manufacturing in Costa Rica was still, up until the Second World War, limited to industries processing agricultural products, ancillary industries servicing the requirements of the former, and a small non–durable consumer goods industry. Most of these enterprises dated from after the turn of the century – at least this is the impression given by Quijano's study. This meant that all goods produced by heavy and intermediate industry, including durable consumer goods and machinery and many items produced by light industry, had to be imported.[59]

My purpose so far has been to indicate the possibilities offered by the organisation of the coffee complex for an initial growth of local manufacturing. However, it is also important to understand how the organisation of the coffee economy, at the level of production and at the political and ideological levels, mitigated the broadening and deepening of this initial industrializing process.

Costa Rica became a monoculture economy with coffee expansion, though it did not start out as one. At one time the producer of a broad range of agricultural produce, the valorisation of land in the *Meseta Central* that came with this country's insertion into the world market brought with it the steady elimination of other cultivations in favour of coffee. This process led to the severe rise in the cost of subsistence goods later on when many articles had to be imported.[60] Of more significance was the way it left a great part of the population dependent on coffee and those interests that controlled this activity. The possibilities for accumulation among the mass of small coffee producers in the *Meseta* were severely restricted by the hold the *cafetaleros* had on the agrarian surplus, through their monopolization of processing, credit facilities and the exporting houses. The internal structure of the coffee estate allowed owners to keep money wages at very low levels, while the personalistic nature of *patrón–peon* relations made collective organisation of these labourers to raise incomes all but impossible. It is instructive to note that even on the coastal banana plantations, infamous for their exploitive conditions, labourers were paid at around 10 times the rate of a coffee *peon* in the 1930s.[61] Despite the fact that most of the population was integrated into a commodity economy (pure subsistence producers were relatively unimportant) the social organisation of coffee kept the material standards of much of the rural population at a level too low for it to have contributed much to the expansion of a home market for consumer goods.

As for the local market for production goods, two points should be noted. Firstly, coffee cultivation was carried on by extensive methods, whereby production increases were attained by additional increments of land and labour. In this stage of the formal subsumption of the labour process by capital, productive investments in cultivation were minimal – for the most part simple infrastructure and rudimentary tools.

In the processing sphere, productive consumption by agrarian capitalists was much more substantial. However, the demand for machinery utilised by the *beneficiador*, together with any fertiliser, tools and other goods he might use in his role as cultivator, had a very reduced impact on the national economy. These goods could be procured from the more advanced economies at a price well below that which would have been the case had they been produced by relatively backward local industry. The coffee oligarchy was therefore adamant in its support for free trade and espoused the doctrine of comparative advantage achieved by an international division of labour. They maintained that,

> Costa Rica must stimulate and protect the production of coffee, and not be preoccupied with the production of other articles. Given the quality of its coffee, renowned in the world market, it was more productive to acquire these articles in the exterior with the gold imported through the sale of coffee, than to produce them in Costa Rica itself.[62]

When, by the 1930s, non–coffee related agricultural interests and a few local industrialists had gained some modest concessions from the State in the form of a tariff on specific imports, the *cafetaleros* took to propagandising the evils and waste of any move towards protectionism. The statement by one of their leading ideologues of the time summarised their position.

> The growth of the rural population in the cities is the effect . . . of a badly understood policy of protection for non– agricultural industry. It is precisely industrialism which creates social problems in agricultural countries. . . . There is no room for transformation industries in countries where capital is so scarce and with a low aquisitive power. The social argument, that is the employment opportunities offered in these industries for labour, is a sentimental one because, firstly, these workers are badly paid and secondly, they would be better off in the countryside.[63]

This polemic hints at another fear of the large *cafetaleros* – that more industrial development would attract labour away from the countryside. Clearly, with the chronic labour shortage still persisting in the 1930s, the coffee estate owners were wary of any development that would affect their labour supply, a supply dammed up in the countryside by the lack of opportunities in the cities.

To this must be added two points. First, the *cafetaleros* were not infrequently closely integrated with local commercial capital that had fared well by its concentration of the import trade in few hands.[64] Therefore, influential coffee growers, as well as those who were strictly merchants, stood to lose should protection restrict the flow of goods into the country in favour of local manufacturing. Most of the owners of manufacturing enterprises in these years appeared to be foreign capitalists recently arrived in the country.[65] Those few major industries owned by *cafetaleros* were specialised in areas such as brewing which was little threatened by imports and hence needed no protection.

Secondly, the foreign owners of the United Fruit Company that monopolised the massive banana plantations on the Atlantic littoral were also beneficiaries of a free trade situation. Neither did they lack the means to block any State policies that might have restricted their ability to import production and consumption goods for their operations. Along this key dimension, the interests of the agrarian bourgeoisie controlling the coffee economy largely corresponded with the foreign banana monopoly and together they constituted, historically, a formidable barrier to a serious reorientation of State policy.[66]

The old liberal agro–exporting model had reached the zenith of its development in the halcyon years of the 1920s, and with it peaked the influence of the coffee bourgeoisie in the economic and political affairs of the nation. This system was remarkably successful as long as external conditions upon which it was so dependent did not change. The problem for the *cafetaleros* and indeed for most of the rest of society, was that in the 1930s these external conditions did change, abruptly, and much for the worse. In the following chapter, I wish to devote some space to a discussion of the impact of the world economic crisis on the coffee bourgeoisie, and the peculiar features of the political conjuncture of the 1940s, provoked by the Second World War.

Notes

1. See Murdo J. MacLeod, *Spanish Central America* (Berkeley: University of California Press, 1973), ch. 18 and Samuel Stone, *La Dinastíia de los Conquistadores* (San José: Editorial Universitaria Centroamericana, 1975), p.60–1.
2. Stone, p.80.
3. Ciro Cardoso, 'The Formation of the Coffee Estate in Nineteenth Century Costa Rica' in Duncan and Rutledge (eds) *Land and Labour in Latin America* Cambridge University Press, 1977), p.168
4. Stone, *La Dinastía*, p.92.
5. Hall, *El Café y el Desarrollo Historico-Geografico de Costa Rica* (San José: Editorial Costa Rica, 1978), p.27.
6. Cardoso, 'The Formation of the Coffee Estate', p.172–3,177.
7. See Hall, *El Café*, p.75.

8. In an earlier paper, Moretzsohn de Andrade argued the former position, while more recently Hall and Cardoso have disputed his thesis. See ibid. and F. Moretzsohn de Andrade, 'Decadencia do Campesinato Costarriqhenho' *Revista Geografica* no. 75 (1967) and Carlos Monge *Historia de Costa Rica* (San José, Trejos, 1974, 16th edition), ch.9.
9. Hall, *El Café*, p .88.
10. Cited in Moretzsohn de Andrade, 'Decadencia de Campesinato', p.141.
11. Cardoso, 'The Formation of the Coffee Estate', p.192.
12 500 hectares would have been a very large estate in Costa Rica's coffee zone in these times, according to Cardoso, 'The Formation of the Coffee Estate', p.192. A special report on the country's leading coffee growers in the 1930s reported that a very few of the country's largest estates at this later date were over 1000 hectares. By comparison, in more recent times Haarer reported that in one Brazilian state (Sao Paulo) about two dozen coffee estates had 1300 hectares or more, and that the largest one covered an area five times this figure. Haarer, A.E., *Modern Coffee Production*, (London: Leonard Hill Books, 1962), p.418.
13. Hall, *El Café*, p.88.
14. Cardoso, 'The Formation of the Coffee Estate', p.192–3.
15. Ibid., p.175.
16. See the *Revista del Instituto de Defensa del Café* (hereafter R.I.D.C.) no.141 (1946), for example.
17. Thomas H. Holloway, 'The Coffee Colono of Sao Paulo, Brazil: Migration and Mobility, 1880–1930' in Rutledge and Duncan (eds) *Land and Labour in Latin America* (Cambridge University Press, 1977).
18. Cited in Cardoso, 'The Formation of the Coffee Estate', p.178.
19. Due to biological characteristics of the coffee plant, a good harvest one year is normally followed by a poorer one the next. Figure 2.2 illustrates this phenomenon graphically.
20. R.I.D.C., no.86 (1941), p.553.
21. R.I.D.C., no.14 (1935), p.58–60 and *passim*.
22. Cited in Rodrigo Facio, *Obras de Rodrigo Facio* , vol. 1 (San José: Editorial Costa Rica, 1972), p.104. See also Carlos Merz, 'Estructura Social y Economica de la Industria de Café en Costa Rica' *R.I.D.C.* no.32–3 (1937), p.293.
23. Facio, *Obras*, pp.103–5 and Perez Brignoli, 'The Economic Cycle in Latin American Agricultural Export Economies (1880–1930)'. (*Latin American Research Review, XV*, 1979) p.23–4). Since these are not categorized by the absolute number of trees they control, but only by a numerical range, I have taken the mid point in each range and multiplied this average figure by the number of farms found in each particular range.
24. *La Tribuna*, 'Homenaje al Café de Costa Rica' (October, 1933).
25. This contrasted with coffee estates in Colombia, for instance, which Palacios describes as generally having two-thirds to three- quarters

of their total land area put to other uses. Palacios, *El Café en Colombia*, p.95.

26. Also see Hall, *El Café*, p.99,110–12.

27   Gertrud Peters S., 'La Formacíon Territorial de las Grandes Fincas de Café en la Meseta Central: Estudio de la Firma Tournon (1877–1950)' unpublished thesis for the degree of Licenciatura, University of Costa Rica (1979), p.123.

28. *R.I.D.C.*, no.141 (1946),p.83; Stone, *La Dinastía*, p.110; and Hall, *Formación de una Hacienda Cafetalera* (San Jose: Editorial Universidad de Costa Rica, 1978b), p.36.

29. See Raymundo Amerling, *Estudio Sobre las Condiciones Agricolas del Distrito Cafetalero Uruca* (San Pedro: Facultad de Agronomia, 1939), p.22. and Peters, 'La Formación', p.23.

30. See Edelberto Torres Rivas, *Interpretación del Desarrollo Social Centroamericano* (San José: EDUCA, 1973); Lester Schmid, 'The Role of Migratory Labour in the Economic Development of Guatemala' (unpublished Ph.D. dissertation, University of Wisconsin, 1967) and C. Bataillon and I. Lebot, 'Migración Interna y Empleo Agricola Temporal en Guatemala' *Estudios Sociales Centroamericanos* no. 13 (1976) and my 'Class Structure and Agrarian Transition in Central America', (*Latin American Perspectives*, 5, 4, 1978).

31. Carolyn Hall, *Formación de una Hacienda*, p.38. On the hacienda studied by Hall, the most important expenditures on infrastructure was on the *beneficio*, followed by roads, drainage canals, carts to transport coffee, tools, etc., ibid., p.6.

32. *R.I.D.C.* no.141 (1946), pp.75–6 and *La Tribuna*, 'Homenaje al Café' (1933).

33. The coffee census notes that even on the farms of those using fertiliser, which was a very small percentage of all coffee farms in these times, the average productivity was only 9.26 fanegas per *manzana* (R.I.D.C., no.14,1935:59)

34. Karl Marx, 'Results of the Immediate Process of Production', appendix to *Capital*, vol.1 (New York: Vintage Books, 1977), p.1020,1035.

35. The view that a revolution in the productivity of labour was the essential feature of capitalist development in the countryside finds its most sophisticated contemporary expression in Robert Brenner's 'The Origins of Capitalist Development: a Critique of Neo–Smithian Marxism', (*New Left Review*, no. 104, July–August 1977).

36. The notion that estate agriculture or 'landlord capitalism' represents a unique path of capitalist development in the countryside (the so-called Prussian or Junker path) has become increasingly accepted in recent years, especially in the Latin American context. See, for example, Roger *Bartra Estructura Agraria y Clases Sociales en Mexico* (Mexico: Era, 1974); Agustin Cueva *El Desarrollo del Capitalismo en America Latina* (Mexico: Siglo Veintiuno Editores, 1977); Alain de Janvry, *The Agrarian Question and Reformism in Latin America* (Baltimore: Johns Hopkins University Press, 1981) and Miguel Murmis, 'El Agro Serrano y la Via Prussiana de Desarrollo Capitalista' in *Ecuador: Cambios en el Agro Serrano* (Quito: FLACSO/CEPLAES, 1980). For a more detailed

theoretical discussion of estate agriculture as a model of agrarian development, see my 'The "Prussian Road" of Agrarian Development: A Reconsideration' (*Economy and Society*, *11*, 4, 1982).

37. *R.I.D.C.* no.45 (1938), p.569. The basic features of this process were as follows: coffee being delivered to the *beneficio* are processed by different mechanical apparatuses which removes the pulp from the coffee bean. The mucous or 'honey' that remains covering the bean is removed by fermenting the beans in large tanks with water, for up to 36 hours. After fermentation has occurred, the beans are washed and agitated to remove the remaining mucous, and then dried on large concrete terraces or 'patios' in the sun, or else by mechanical dryers, which were in use before 1940. Once dry, the beans are classified according to quality, and at this point the 'parchment' still covering the bean may be removed.

38. Cardoso, 'The Formation of the Coffee Estate', p.193 and *R.I.D.C.* no.45 (1935), p.60.

39. This is indicated by the lists of *beneficiadores* and *exportadores* found in various issues of the R.I.D.C. Also see *Homenaje al Café*.

40. Mitchell A. Seligson, *Peasants of Costa Rica and the Development of Agrarian Capitalism* (Madison: University of Wisconsin Press, 1980), p.36.

41. Cardoso, 'The Formation of the Coffee Estate', p.193.

42. Eric Wolf and E. Hansen, 'Caudillo Politics: A Structural Analysis', *Comparative Studies in Society and History*, vol. 9, no.3 (1967). See also Augusto Cazali Avila, 'El Desarrollo del Cultivo del Café y Su Influencia en el Regimen del Trabajo Agricola: Epoca de la Reforma Liberal (1871–1885)', *Anuario de Estudios Centroamericanos*, no.2.

43. Capital valued at several thousand pesos, depending upon the position, was required in 1841. Later in the century this was reduced to 500 pesos for most important political offices, but the additional requirement of an income of 200 pesos annually was stipulated. Stone, *La Dinastia*, p.216–217.

44. Ibid., p.221.

45. Ibid., ch.5.

46. Leon Zamosc, 'The Definition of a Socio–economic Formation: El Salvador on the Eve of the Great World Economic Depression' (Department of Sociology, University of Manchester, mimeo, 1977), p.98.

47. Cited in Stone *La Dinastía*, p.268. See also Jose Luis Vega Carballo, 'Etapas y procesos de la evolucion socio–politico de Costa Rica' *Estudios Sociales Centroamericanos* no.1, (1972).

48. Monge, *Historia de Costa Rica*, p.226).

49. After 1920 many more individuals from the rural areas besides the wealthy coffee growers were to be found in the National Assembly. See Stone, *La Dinastía*, p.223.

50. See Jorge I. Romero, *La Social Democracia en Costa Rica* (San José: Editorial Universidad Estatal a Distancia, 1982), ch.1. The best known source detailing the corrupt practices of the oligarchic parties in these years is Carlos Luis Fallas' *Mamita Yunai* San José: Libreria Lehmann, 1978). Before becoming one of the country's

best known writers, Fallas was himself a political activist for many years.

51.   Monge, *Historia de Costa Rica*, p.255–6.
52.   Vega Carballo, 'Etapas y procesos', p.58.
53.   Marco Palacios, *Coffee in Colombia, 1850–1970* (Cambridge University Press, 1980), p.200.
54.   The contract was later taken over by a relative, Minor Keith. After many delays the railway was completed, but not before the government had been forced to cede the railroad for a period of 99 years to Keith, in addition to 800 thousand acres of land along the right of way. This land later formed the basis for the development of extensive banana plantations in subsequent years, in which Minor Keith played a leading role. Tomas Soley Guell, *Compendio de Historica Economica y Hacendaria de Costa Rica* (San José: Editorial Solley y Valverde, 1940), p.63.
55.   Ibid., p.65–9.
56.   D. Kepner and J. Soothill, *The Banana Empire* (New York: The Vanguard Press, 1935) and Seligson, *The Peasants*, ch.3.
57.   The *Revista del Instituto de Defensa del Café* regularly carried the advertisement of these workshops.
58.   Alberto Quijano, *Costa Rica de Ayer y Hoy (1800–1930)* (San José: Editorial Borasse, 1939).
59.   Soley Güell, *Compendio*, p.72 and Facio, *Obras*, ch.5.
60.   As Facio, noted, Costa Rica imported many foodstuffs, processed foods and non-durable consumer items that could easily have been produced locally *Obas*, p.142. See the figures provided by the British consul, F.N.Fox, (1934:30) on the value of the principal imports into Costa Rica for 1928–9. About half of the value of these imports comprised textiles and foodstuffs. See Dept. of Overseas Trade, *Economic Conditions in the Republic of Costa Rica* (London: HMSO, 1934), p.30.
61.   Quijano, *Costa Rica de Ayer*, p.487.
62.   Merz, 'Estructura Social y Economica', p.93–4.
63.   Ibid.
64.   Facio, *Obras*, pp.54–5 and Peters, 'La Formacíon Territorial', ch.1.
65.   Quijano, *Costa Rica de Ayer* and *R.I.D.C.*, no.32–3 (1937), p.292.
66.   In many respects a power unto itself, United Fruit had for a long time a special relationsip with the ruling oligarchy. As an example, contracts between the State and the Company were drawn up by the executive branch of Government, not Congress, and were therefore of a special, almost extra–legal nature. This allowed the company to regularly revise the terms of their contracts, without being subject to legal sanctions. Seligson, *The Peasants*, p.62.

3 Economic Decline and Political Crisis

INTRODUCTION

The events of the 1940s, in the field of politics especially, are fascinating in their own right, though my purpose in this chapter will be limited to examining how they set the stage for the new era that began in 1948. The world depression of the 1930s induced a structural crisis for estate producers that made more tenuous their control over the State. The disorganisation in the world economy with the initiation of World War II exacerbated the economic crisis for estate owners dependent upon European markets. There was at the same time an upsurge of popular unrest having a definite organisational expression in the Communist Party. Together they produced a unique political development destabilising the old oligarchic system of domination, and set the stage for a new era of capitalist development.

3.1 THE ECONOMIC DECLINE

Between 1926 and 1929 Costa Rican coffee producers were getting record high prices for their product, averaging over US $.50 per kilo. In 1930 and 1931 this price plumetted to US $.39 per kilo and by 1932 it was less than half the 1926–9 average at US $.26 per kilo.[1] This price decline translated directly into a dramatic fall in the incomes of coffee growers. The value of the coffee crop had in fact declined from almost US $10 million in 1928 to slightly more than US $4 million as of 1932, a drop of 60 per cent (see Figure 3.1). A price depression of this magnitude could not but have had deeply felt consequences for Costa Rican growers, as indeed was the case for primary commodity producers dependent upon foreign markets faced with similar price declines throughout the whole world.

    To some degree Costa Rican producers were more insulated from the falling prices after 1930 than were coffee producers elsewhere for whom prices dropped even more dramatically. Historically Costa Rica had a special position in the London coffee market. In the early 1930s Costa Rica supplied over 40 per cent of English consumption.[2] This meant that her coffee consistently fetched the highest prices there, and that these prices served to establish the price for Costa Rican coffee sold in other European markets as well (see Table 3.1).[3]

As about 40 per cent of the nation's coffee arriving on the London market was re–exported, principally to Germany, a major problem developed when the latter decided in 1934 on a policy whereby the value of commodities of foreign countries in Germany had to be matched by the purchase of German goods of equal value. It was not possible for Costa Rica to purchase from Germany goods of a value equal to her coffee exports there, without seriously dislocating indigenous industry. This, in turn, meant that a substantial proportion of her annual crop had to be diverted to another market where, inevitably, competition from other 'milds' producing countries was much fiercer and prices lower.[4]

While the devalorisation of coffee in the 1930s had repurcussions for all producers in Costa Rica, different kinds of growers were affected, and could react, in specific ways. Peasant smallholders on the one hand, could weather the worst year by at least partial return to a subsistence economy. Indeed, Palacios has argued that the predominance of peasant producers in Colombia was a key to understanding why the Depression did not produce as much disruption for its economy as it did in countries where large capitalist

Figure 3.1   Coffee production and value of exports

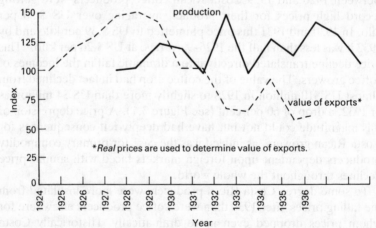

Table 3.1   Coffee prices on the London market Nov. 1936

Country and Class of Coffee	Price (Shillings/quaintal)
KENYA	
Good to fine	130
Regular to good	90
COSTA RICA	
Good to fine, 1st size	115
Good to fine, 2nd size	70
Regular quality, 1st size	65
MYSORE	
Good to fine	100
Regular to good	60
MOKA	
Short bean	95
Large bean	65
TANGANYKA	
Good to fine	90
Regular to good	60
COLOMBIA	
First size	60
Second size	45
PERU	
Good to fine	57
GUATEMALA, EL SALVADOR AND MEXICO	
Good to fine, 1st size	55
Good to fine, 2nd size	45
Regular quality, 1st size	52
COORG	
Good to fine	55
Regular to good	53
SANTOS (Brazil)	
Superior	50
ROBUSTA	47

Source: *R.I.D.C.* vol.5, (Jan–Feb.) 1937.

haciendas dominated.[5] Even so, it is clear that such a price decline affected Costa Rica peasant producers negatively, if not disastrously, since it was precisely at this time that they became the most militant in pushing for controls on the processors.

The larger *cafetaleros*, on the other hand, did not have the option of pursuing an autarchic economy. They could only counter the decline in their revenues by expanding the area in production, while attempting to force down wages – their major production cost. Annual production in Costa Rica was in fact higher in the mid 1930s than it had been 10 years previously and did not show a tendency to decline at that time, despite substantially lower prices. Large producers, however, faced additional problems which reacted on their costs, for which solutions were not easily found. One of these was the high cost of land. The role of this factor in determining high costs of production in Costa Rica appeared to be well known by the 1930s.[6] This situation placed definite limits on a strategy of combating low prices through a substantial increase in the area under cultivation.

Further aggravating growers' costs were the monopolistic rates they were charged for the transport of their coffee to the coast and the use of port facilities by the US banana monopoly owning these facilities. By 1940 the Coffee Institute was protesting to the President about the monopolistic rates charged to producers, which it noted were some 400 per cent per kilometre more than rates charged Colombian producers, despite the fact that the railway in the latter country traversed much more difficult terrain.[7]

Inflation, which developed towards the end of the 1930s, and especially after 1940, was another problem for the capitalist growers. While the value of agricultural exports was less in 1940 than in 1936, the value of most imported items was generally higher. In response to this, the cost of living rose gradually but steadily until 1940, and then accelerated rapidly in the following years. Higher living costs exerted a pressure on wages, of course, which had oscillated around 1.50 colons per day before 1935, but had been fixed by law at a minimum of 2.50 by 1942. The stimulation given to local industry during the 1930s apparently exacerbated the historical labour shortage in the countryside, and probably prevented growers from having more success in resisting the pressure on wages.[8] Though the increase of the latter was marginal in real terms for labour, it nevertheless represented an additional burden on capitalist farmers plagued by low coffee prices determined in the exterior, prices that showed little inclination to increase until the end of Second World War.[9]

The initiation of the Second World War dealt something of a *coup de–grâce* to the coffee economy, and notably the producer–processor group. Unlike some other exporters of 'mild' coffees, such as Colombia, Costa Rica was very dependent upon the European market, and especially the privileged position it had in the London market. The loss of this market meant a further devaluation of its coffee,[10] which now faced the prospect of competing with other producers in the American market. A more serious price decline was avoided once the US organised the Inter American Coffee Agreement and fixed prices to its allies.[11] This development, however, seriously dislocated the numerous local exporters – who were usually the producer–processors – with their large established European clientele. The 193 exporting firms in business in 1938 had been reduced to 81 during the 1940–1 season. By 1943–4, only 19 exporting firms were registered and six of these, mostly American, controlled over 80 per cent of all Costa Rican exports.[12]

In sum, the 1930s saw a weakening of the leading *cafetaleros* who, despite their favoured niche in the world coffee market, were facing a cost–price squeeze throughout the decade. The further price decline and the loss of much of the exporting business with the beginning of war in Europe was responsible for a further deterioration of their economic position. And as could be expected, the economic crisis eventually brought social contradictions to the fore. By 1940 the contradictions of this agro–exporting economy coincided with critical conjunctural events. The interaction of them had major consequences for national politics.

3.2 THE ORGANIC CRISIS OF THE OLIGARCHY

Until recent times it has not been the mass of rural labourers on the coffee estates that has left an indelible stamp on Costa Rican history – rather, it has been the proletariat, found both in the largest urban centres, and especially in the banana enclave. Moreover, the Communist Party exercised hegemony over this work force. As a result the organised elements of the proletariat moved beyond a simple awareness of their economic corporate interests to the development of a collective political consciousness. At this point the organised proletariat could, and eventually did, become a major force in national politics.

The organisation of banana plantations in the first decades of this century had created a classical proletariat on the Atlantic coastal plain – a homogeneous mass of landless wage workers numbering thousands who worked year–round under a single corporate employer and within an enterprise organised along modern capitalist lines. By contrast, the coffee estates of the *Meseta* were much smaller and the predominance of a differentiated and fragmented work force favoured the development of personalistic ties with the employer. The absence of common economic circumstances among the estate labour force (notably the differences between permanent and seasonal labour) prevented them from making common cause against the *patrón*.

In the early 1930s the United Fruit Company reacted to the Depression by a ruthless cutting of its workforce to reduce its losses, a policy which stimulated an upsurge of labour militancy in the banana zones. It was the mass strike of 1934, however, involving some 10000 labourers that marked a vital turning point. Arguably the most important strike in Central America to that date, it demonstrated that the banana monopoly was not entirely omnipotent, while the leading role of Communist Party militants in this action gave the Party a legitimacy that years of patient organising could not have achieved. By the 1940s, the Communist Party influence among the banana workers and the urban proletariat was further strengthened, and it had made inroads into national politics in previous years through the election of several of its candidates as congressional deputies.[13]

The pressure on the ruling oligarchy of commercial capitalists and large *cafetaleros* for an accommodation with the demands of the popular classes were thus considerable by the late 1930s, precisely at a time when the already weakened export dependent oligarchy turned to face the additional international crisis occasioned by the outbreak of War in Europe. It was increasingly apparent that the old system of domination had to be modified. What was not clear was whether the coffee and commercial bourgeoisie had the desire or ability to organise a process of change that would serve their own favoured position over the longer term.

The regime of Calderon Guardia, which came to power in 1940, illustrated the extreme pressures that were then being placed on the State, and by extension on the oligarchy's ability to rule. Initially a regime as favourable to the *cafetaleros* interests as any other,[14] within two years Calderon had alienated much of the propertied class, and many professionals and intellectuals as well.[15]

Calderon's response to the deterioration of his social base was to broaden his popular support through the promulgation of various social reforms – the so–called Social Guarantees.[16] Not only did this find a resonance with wide sectors of the population, but perhaps more importantly, it was a policy direction which the Communist Party – then having considerable legitimacy and popular appeal –

could welcome and actively encourage. In part this laid the ground-work for a *rapprochement* between the old party of the oligarchy led by Calderon – the National Republican Party – and the Communists. On the other side, the reorientation of Comintern policy after 1940 in favour of the formation of national popular fronts wherever possible encouraged the local Communist Party to more actively support progressive Government initiatives.[17]

The precariousness of Calderon's support as the 1944 elections drew near and the boldness of forces now opposing his Government forced Calderon to seek a strengthening of his ties with the Communists. The Communist leader Manuel Mora Valverde was open to such a process, particularly since there was evidence that some *cafetaleros* and financial interests were planning a *coup d'etat*. Mora went so far as to make public overtures to the reform-minded Archbishop of these days, Victor Sanabria, soliciting the support of the Church for Calderon's candidate as the guarantee of a Government interested in progressive social legislation.

In this fashion emerged the unlikely alliance between the old party of the oligarchy and the Communists with the support of the Church hierarchy.[18] In the remainder of this chapter I would like to focus on two basic consequences of this political development, consequences which I believe lie at the roots of more contemporary political developments in Costa Rica.

Calderon's move to secure Communist support in a more for-mal way signalled, among other things, the seriousness of the rupture between the old bourgeoisie, led by the *cafetaleros*, and the traditional party of this class. It was a classic example of that phenomenon noted by Gramsci, where 'the traditional parties in their particular organisational form, with the particular men who constitute, represent, and lead them, are no longer recognised by their class (or fraction of a class) as its expression'.[19] At this point the bourgeoisie was disorganised, internally divided and without a political expression that could have rebounded from the advances made by the Left, organised its constituency to overcome internal differences and confront the impending threat to their general class interests.

As one source unsympathetic to both Calderon's Government and the old oligarchy noted, the role of the big capitalists within the opposition forces opposing Calderon in 1944 was weak and tactless. Moreover, 'the constant fear of possible Government reprisals has kept the capitalists at the margin, cornered and withdrawn.

Undoubtedly now these capitalists cannot pretend to be the ruling class in Costa Rica, as they were in past times.'[20]

It was evident that in the future the old ruling circles could no longer rely on their old system of patron–client relations in the countryside, together with systematic electoral fraud and corruption, to maintain their influence over the State. The strength of new forces on the national political scene would require them to form alliances with other classes and groups as a minimal strategy to rebuild their former political influence.

The demise of the old oligarchic politics where one class, or more precisely one class fraction – the *cafetaleros* – had a privileged access to the State was one result of the developments of the 1940s. There was another long–term consequence of these events, however. This concerns the impact of these events in restructuring the composition and alliances of the subordinate classes in Costa Rican society.

3.3 THE RISE OF NEW SOCIAL FORCES

Several observers have noted that already by 1942, and definitely by the time of the alliance with the Communist Party, Calderon and his coterie within the National Republican Party had done much to discredit themselves through mismanagement, 'unusual' political practices, rampant nepotism and just plain corruption.[21] Adding to anti-Government sentiments was Calderon's action to curb political liberties in response to the violence that accompanied the 1943 election campaign.[22] In any case, when the Communist Party and its important following went to the side of the government, other groups – the progessive petit bourgeoisie, many intellectuals, professionals and students who had been alienated by Calderon's old style of politics and links with the corrupt practices of the past, were left behind. This in turn, provided the basis for an historic schism of the Left.

The *Centro Para el Estudio de Problemas Nacionales* (hereafter, the *Centro*) formed in 1940 was an early manifestation of the non Communist Left in Costa Rica of the 1940s. Initially it was formed by a group of young intellectuals oriented to the analysis of the nation's political malaise and the urgent social and economic problems of the day. Through their journal *Surco*, the *Centro* propounded an analysis of society that was at once anti–oligarchic and anti–imperialist in orientation,[23] and opposed 'Manchester liberalism', but did not incorporate the Marxist view of class conflict being integral to the private appropriation of the means of production under capitalism. Though several notable figures were associated with the *Centro*, the economist Rodrigo Facio was to play the most outstanding role in criticising the old order, and plotting the reforms that were to come in later years.

Towards 1944 the *Centro* was becoming increasingly partisan in its public statements through *Surco*, and had become a leading critic of the Government and a proponent of the necessity for a cleansing of the political scene, despite its initial qualified support for Calderon's social legislation. In addition, its stance was now markedly anti-Communist.[24]

After the turmoil of the '44 election, which was plagued by fraudulent practices on both sides, the *Centro* abandoned its previous 'neutrality' and publicly sought to form an 'ideological party' oriented to national reconstruction. By 1945 it had joined forces with another group, *Accion Demócrata* led by a young agriculturalist, José Figueres Ferrer which, though opposing the Government, was not entirely compromised by ties with the oligarchy.[25] Out of this union emerged the *Partido Social Demócrata* – a new force in an ever more complex political landscape.

The orientation and programme of the new party were formalised in *Surco* some time later. Given the future significance of this movement, it will be useful to expand on the items contained in this first programmatic statement. Most notable were *Social Demócrata's* support for (i) the development of natural resources through protection from foreign capital and the stimulation of small rural property and small industry; (ii) the defence of the *campesino* by means of the co-operative organisation of agriculture and technical aid provided by autonomous institutions; (iii) the defence of the salaried population through non–political union organisations and legal protection of their economic interests; (iv) the creation of an efficient and honest administration, the scientific organisation of public finances, the establishment of a Civil Service and the development of autonomous technical institutions and; (v) the promotion of social welfare by means of education, health care, public works and co-ordinated economic planning.

These postulates denoted an orientation that was of a decidedly reformist and popular character, though even in these early days there was little to indicate the elements forming *Social Demócrata*

were antithetical to existing property relations – but only to some
of the inequalities that these had produced. This may be viewed
as a fundamental contradiction of their thinking, the implications
of which cannot be dealt with until later chapters. It will also be
necessary to return to a discussion of the implementation of their
programme, once the opportunity to apply their views in practice
presented itself. The importance of other conceptions largely absent
from the *Social Demócrata* platform, notably the emphasis on State
interventionism, only later emerged as integral to the ideology of this
movement, though such matters had already been broached by the
Centro years earlier. For now, it is necessary to continue with the
historical narrative.

After 1944, the political landscape crystallised even further, as
the new *Partido Social Demócrata* solidified ties with the main
opposition forces. The latter were led by Leon Cortes, an ultra
conservative who had been President before Calderon Guardia,
and Otilio Ulate, publisher of the newspaper *Diario de Costa
Rica*, an organ vociferous in its criticism of the Government.
This developing Opposition alliance brought together figures that
represented the interests opposed to social progess and linked to
important economic circles, with a young group comprised of
intellectuals with advanced ideas and little sympathy for the pre-1940
political order.[26] Nevertheless, despite the absence of a strong
ideological glue, a working alliance emerged as all parties looked
towards the 1948 elections.

The months leading up to this election were characterised by
declining moral authority of the Government and the growing
willingness of the Opposition to destablise the *status quo* by any
available means short of civil war. Even this latter was threatened
by *Social Demócrata's* José Figueres, and by Ulate, now the leader
of the Opposition alliance.[27] Intent on securing more control over the
electoral process, the Opposition organised an employers' lockout,
the famous *Huelga de Brazos Caidos*, in which even the banking
institutions were involved.

As a pressure tactic, the employers' lockout proved effective and
demonstrated that capital was, if not entirely with the Opposition,
then at least largely against the Government alliance. The Government, without the support of the Communist Deputies this time,
conceded to the Opposition its demand for a tribunal, organised
by the latter to oversee this electoral process. The tribunal's
decision on the final results was not to be subject to appeal.

This condition, among the several conceded by the Government, proved to be the most dangerous; for it did not provide either side with peaceful mechanisms through which to seek recourse in the event that one party felt that wrong doings had taken place. Given that electoral fraud was hitherto commonplace in Costa Rica,[28] given the tension of the previous months and the demonstrated lack of authority on the part of the Government, it is apparent with hindsight that the conditions had become especially volatile and most propitious for the resolution of this longstanding struggle by extra–legal means. Not surprisingly, this is precisely what occurred.

I do not wish to enter into the complicated details concerning the dispute over the 1948 elections, and the aftermath. These are ably discussed elsewhere and I wish to note only the most outstanding events before proceeding with a more detailed analysis of the developments of the post-1948 era.[29]

The 1948 elections were again marred by fraud, this time accompanied by administrative foul–ups. Because of this the Calderonistas called for the nullification of the election, when it became apparent they had lost the vote for the Presidency. With the Communist deputies, they still controlled the Congress however, and Congress still had the power to nullify the elections, which it did. Not long afterwards, an armed rebellion broke out under the initiative of José Figueres. Several weeks of fighting eventually produced some strategic defeats for the Government forces, among which was included an important contingent organised by *Vanguardia Popular*. These defeats, together with the force of external pressures led to the capitulation of the Government. On the 8th of May, the Founding Junta of the Second Republic was established, with Figueres at its head accompanied by leading members of *Social Demócrata*. At this point, it is necessary to add one additional detail. Figueres and his comrades in arms had come to power with the support, and also the legitimacy, provided by Ulate and his followers. Therefore, there was considerable pressure on Figueres to come to an agreement with this group on how to proceed. The pact that was reached between Figueres and Ulate had the Junta governing the country without Congress for a period of 18 months, after which it was to hand over the Government to Ulate. In the meantime, the Junta was to organise elections for the Legislative Assembly and draw up a new constitution for the nation. These terms would seem to have severely circumscribed the future actions of Figueres and his forces. In fact, to some extent they did, but in other ways they did not.

Notes

1. *R.I.D.C.* no. 12 (1937), p.606.
2. *R.I.D.C.* no.2, (1934), p.107.
3. See the letter of the *Instituto de Defensa del Café* to the President of the Republic, of March 19, 1940, published in the *Informe Sobre la Situacion del Café*, (1940), pp.34–8). Costa Rican coffee was still trading in 1936 at prices double those of other Latin American producers of 'mild' coffees, such as Guatemala, El Salvador, Mexico and even Colombia. See *R.I.D.C.*, Jan.–Feb., (1937), p.525.
4. *R.I.D.C.* no.1, (1934), p.61.
5. Palacios, *El Café*, ch.10.
6. Instituto Interamericano de Ciencias Agricolas, *El Café en 1931 y 1932: Cuestiones Economicos y Tecnicos* (Rome: 1935), p.67.
7. *R.I.D.C.* (1940), p.14.
8. *R.I.D.C.* no.141 (1946), pp.74,94 and 97. The State intervened for the first time to fix wages for coffee workers in 1935, an event which undoubtedly contributed to the general rise in wages in these years.
9. Stone, *La Dinastía*, p.297, Table IX–6.
10. Between September 1939 and May 1940, prices fell some 39 per cent (Instituto de Defensa del Café,1940:10).
11. As Palacios writes, 'the German invasion of the Low Countries aggravated the position of producers when it became clear that the United States could not consume all of the coffee supplied. For Latin America, coffee was the principal item of her total exports, and in many countries political stability depended directly on the conditions of the coffee market. It does not seem at all illogical to conclude that the Pan American solidarity sought by the United States in confrontation with the Axis powers led to the Inter-American Coffee Agreement.' *El Café en Colombia*, p.222.
12. See *R.I.D.C.* nos.39,86 and 121 (1938,1941,1944).
13. Seligson, *Peasants*, P.20 and 21.
14. With the coffee interests in deep crisis by 1940, Calderon moved quickly to implement legislation exonerating producers from most of the existing taxes. At the same time he planned to guarantee a minimum price for coffee, thus cushioning producers from the worst of the price decline, at the expense of the rest of society.
15. In part this was assuredly due to his move against the local German community, and the incarceration of individuals and confiscation of property this entailed. Some of the leading producer–processors and coffee exporters were German, while the connections with German financial capital were longstanding. Stone, *La Dinastía*, p.300. The Government also seemed to receive blame for the chaos and hard times produced by the War, though its growing reputation

for corrupt administration ultimately proved more serious. *Surco* no.44 (1944), p.3.

16. Ibid.

17. Stone, *La Dinastía*, p.300.

18. Stone notes that the Costa Rican Communists were openly denounced by other Latin American parties of the Third International for their open alliance with the National Republican Party, a party that had often been denounced by the Communists for its longstanding tradition of fraud, corruption and political chicanery. *La Dinastía*, p.305.

19. Antonio Gramsci, *Selections From the Prison Notebooks* (New York: International Publishers, 1971), p.210.

20. *Surco* no.44 (1944), p.6.

21. Ibid., pp.1–7 *passim* and Stone, *La Dinastía*, p.299–304.

22. Oscar R. Bulgarelli, *Costa Rica y sus Hechos Politicos de 1948* (San José: Editorial Costa Rica, 1969), p.96.

23. Ibid., p.56 and Jacobo Schifter, *La Fase Oculta de la Guerra Civil en Costa Rica* (San José: Editorial Universitaria Centroamericano, 1979), p.68.

24. The Centro was most vehement in its criticism of the Vanguardia Popular for its purported disrespect of individual liberties, and its willingness to abandon political principles if this would further strengthen the governing Party. *Surco* argued, for example, that the Communists abandoned their support for land reform because this disturbed landowners still supporting Calderon. *Surco* no.40,(1943), editorial.

25. Bulgarelli, *Costa Rica y sus Hechos*, p.77 and Stone, *La Dinastía*, p.308.

26. Bulgarelli, ibid., p.119.

27. Ibid., p.122.

28. One of the better known statements in this regard was made by Vanguardia Popular leader, Manuel Mora, who noted that 'In Costa Rica electoral fraud has come to be a type of sport. Our politicians manage it with complete naturalness – here there is a school of fraud and professionals in fraud the likes of which there are not in any other place in America' (cited in Bulgarelli,1969:150).

29. The best documented source is that of Bulgarelli, but also see Schifter's work and that of Ameringer for differing interpretations of these events. Charles D. Ameringer, *Don Pépé: A Political Biography of José Figueres of Costa Rica* (Albuquerque: University of New Mexico Press, 1978).

4 Emergence of the Interventionist State

> In reality, it was the only form of government possible at a time when the bourgeoisie had already lost, and the working class had not yet acquired, the faculty of ruling the nation.
> (K.Marx on the regime of Louis Bonaparte.)[1]

INTRODUCTION

The following discussion will attempt to establish that the political events of the 1940s resulted in a stalemated struggle between two major class forces in Costa Rican society – one basically reactionary, the other more progressive in its political content. Further, that this conjuncture opened a breach for a third force to capture State power and maintain a degree of autonomy from the traditional dominant interests. Initially this autonomy was maintained through skillful manoeuvreing and crisis tactics, and later by means of the establishment of independent social bases of support and special tax legislation which provided the State with an important revenue base. The struggle between the State and the coffee producers was crucial in determining the efficacy of State programmes to modernise and diversify the old agro–exporting economy.

To begin, it will be helpful to see how the events of 1948 and the previous years established the preconditions for the anomolous (in Central American terms) course of political development that was to take place in Costa Rica in the years following the Civil War of 1948.

4.1 THE POLITICAL CONJUNCTURE OF THE LATE 1940s

In the preceding chapter, I have noted how the long–standing monopolisation of an essentially exclusionist 'national' politics by the coffee bourgeoisie had experienced a process of partial disintegration. This process was intimately connected, of course, with the crisis of the world capitalist economy to which this group was inextricably linked.

Over the longer term this was part of the 'downgrading' of those national bourgeois fractions most closely tied to the production and commercialisation of primary materials for this world market.

This disintegration was considerably advanced through this period by the groundswell of popular democratic demands emanating from the section of the agricultural proletariat that was organised and had found its political expression in the *Vanguardia Popular*, but also pressure for change articulated by elements of the urban and even rural petit bourgeoisie.[2] The polarisation of society that became increasingly exacerbated after 1945 required a solution that was in some sense decisive, but by 1948 it would seem reasonable to conclude that a solution within the confines of the existing political process was unlikely. I have already examined the basic elements that underlay the political conjuncture that had developed by 1948. The old system of domination could not contain the evermore forceful pressure of those social forces brought into existence by the export oriented coffee economy and the agro-industrial investment projects of foreign capital in the banana enclave. Moreover, the coffee oligarchy had reached a point in its historical life when, as a class, it had become detached from its traditional party and had not managed to re-establish a viable political vehicle by which it might continue to dominate the nation's political life.

On the other hand, the precarious alliance established by the government of Calderon was less and less capable of leading those social forces it purported to represent. It had progressively alienated much of its oligarchic support, and consistently ostracised the middle class through electoral and administrative irregularities without satisfying in any substantial way its aspirations. This left the regime susceptible to those types of political incidents that are capable, under favourable conditions, of provoking a 'crisis of authority', what Gramsci has termed the general crisis of the State.[3] The elections of 1948 proved to be the type of affair that would trigger such a crisis.

The particular form in which the liberal oligarchic State had been modified during the 1940s, the fact that the oligarchy had been detached from its traditional party, not only left this class in disarray at the political level for some time, but it had altered its relationship to the State as well. Eventually the oligarchic forces were to regroup behind Otilio Ulate and the *Union Nacional* party by 1948, but even then events were to prove that they were no longer necessarily in a position to dominate their temporary allies, the *Partido Social Demócrata* (PSD).

The existence of the PSD itself was testimony to the fact that those forces initially linked to the *Centro* and *Acción Demócrata* had achieved a sufficient degree of organisation to become a real force in the country's political life. Even so, it does seem unlikely that the PSD could have played a leading role should the anti-Calderon alliance have come to power through the 'normal' electoral route. Such a victory would have removed the *raison d'être* for the alliance itself and quickly brought to the fore the fundamental differences of the temporary allies and the superior resources at the disposal of the *Union Nacional*. Had the resolution to the crisis of 1948 taken this form, the social and economic aspirations represented by the PSD would undoubtedly have been largely thwarted, with the trajectory of national politics perhaps conforming more to that elsewhere in Central America.

By choosing to resolve the crisis by force of arms however, José Figueres and his forces accomplished two things, in the short term. Firstly, and most obviously, they prevented the *Calderonistas* from using the ambiguous outcomes of the elections to prolong their Government. Secondly, they took the initiative away from the new party of the traditional bourgeoisie – *Union Nacional* – and thereby forestalled, for a time at least, the return of the oligarchy to its former position of prominence. In the process they achieved a moral victory that, concretely, meant substantial popular support for their cause. This in turn considerably improved chances of survival of a political programme that was initiated by the PSD.

It is necessary to go one step further, however, and place these national struggles in their geo–political context. There is every reason to believe that at this time, a successful popular struggle in Costa Rica in which the local Communist Party figured very prominently would have been perceived by the US Government as counter to its strategic interests in the region. Even had American capital not been immediately threatened, the likelihood of armed intervention was far from remote, with Somoza's National Guard as the most likely vehicle of counter–revolution. The Castillo Armas affair in Guatemala some six years later was to demonstrate forcefully (and not for the last time in Central America) that the real question for a popular nationalist regime was not whether intervention would occur, but only how strong would the forces of counter-revolution be, and what popular support could the new regime mobilise to defend its gains. International considerations thus made the continuation of any regime in the region that did not fit the oligarchic mould (i.e. with a tradition of collaboration with US business interests) somewhat problematic, to say the least. This was all the more the case with a Government of identifiable Communist participation.

What was unique, then, to the Costa Rican experience was that the political conjuncture during the 1940s had led to a stalemated struggle between the forces of reaction and a substantial element of the popular classes – the former unable to re-establish its political dominance, the latter unable or unwilling (or both) to lead the other popular sectors towards a transformation of the old social order.[4] In this political context, a breach was opened for social elements with aspirations of promoting a more dynamic and diversified process of development, while not fundamentally challenging private property of the means of production as the basic organising principle of society. Moreover, these elements proved hostile to any attempts by the oligarchy to restore the political *status quo ante*. In this way the polarisation of society was circumvented, at least for a considerable period of time. A space was created for the State to mediate the process of agricultural modernisation and the renewed round of capital concentration within the country.

4.2 THE JUNTA OF 1948: THE QUESTION OF SURVIVAL IN THE SHORT TERM

Progressive nationalist movements in Central America, even those that have come to form governments, have for the most part been granted the same fate – annihilation. Until the Sandinista revolution in Nicaragua it was only in Costa Rica that an attempt to challenge the dominance of the landowning and commercial oligarchy has had any long term success, and even here this process has had its limitations. This section will examine why in this case the political challenge of the forces opposing the old structure of power proved to be viable in the immediate term.

To begin with, it must be noted that although the Junta led by Figueres came to power in Costa Rica by defeating its rivals through military action, even in the short term the continuance of the new regime was not secure, in large part because of the threat of external intervention of one form or another.[5] In this regard, one peculiarity of the political developments of the previous period appears, with hindsight, to have been especially fortuitious for the regime's short-term survival chances.

In the previous chapter it was noted how, in earlier years, a fundamental schism had developed between the different popular sectors – chiefly between the rural proletariat in the banana zones and the progessive urban and rural petit bourgeoisie, professional and intellectual groups and their respective political parties. In this important respect the Junta of 1948 differed in its political composition from the ill–fated Guatemalan regime of Jacobo Arbenz a few years later. This situation made it politically possible for the Junta to proclaim openly what was already inherent in the political philosophy of many of its members: that is, though its orientation was reformist, it was also definitely anti–Communist. Given the role of the *Vanguardia Popular* in the nations political life over the previous several years, the emergence of Cold War politics at the international level and the country's strategic position in geopolitical terms in the eyes of the United States, over the short term it was most important for the survival of the Junta that it could make this claim. With American warships off the Costa Rican coast and Somoza's National Guard having intervened from the north, there seems little doubt that a victory of a broad coalition of popular forces, including the *Vanguardia Popular*, would have very quickly faced a force much superior to that which such a popular government might have mustered.

In practical terms it made sense for the Junta to translate its anti-Communist position into a more concrete form. For not only was it unable to flagrantly disregard the fears of the conservative elements grouped around Ulate and the PUN, but the relatively well-organised cadres of the *Vanguardia Popular* constituted a force with the potential to limit the maneouvreability of the new regime. Indeed, in an interview many years later, Figueres made it clear that it was this party of the proletariat that was the chief obstacle to constituting a balance of forces favourable to himself and the Junta.

When we recovered popular sovereignty in 1948, and began the construction task, we did not feel, quite frankly, we had the capacity to carry on a free and open battle with international communism. The Communists had external support. We did not. They had the strength derived from fanatacism. We did not. We resolved to put them outside the law, as a political party. A sign of weakness, one would say – yes! – a sign of weakness. I admit it, when one is relatively weak before the force of the enemy, it is necessary to have the valour to recognise it.[6]

Such were the conditions that formed the backdrop to one of the darker episodes of the country's contemporary political history to which Figueres alludes – the incarceration of the leading members of the *Vanguardia Popular*, the repression of its members and the formal proclamation of this Party's illegality.[7] In essence, and in a most unequivocal fashion, Figueres and the Junta denied a substantial section of Costa Rican society the opportunity to struggle for political power, and for a very considerable period of time given that attempts in later years to constitute a workers party 'above ground' were also thwarted by the state.[8] By so doing, they probably did more to tilt the scales in their favour in the short term than with any other single act. Keeping in mind the limited degree of manoevreability granted to any progressive regime at this period by those powerful external forces favouring the regional *status quo*, the fact that the Junta was not compromised with the Communist left allowed it to establish the necessary ideological distance from the latter, and even to demonstrate this distance in hard political terms.[9]

These initial internal and external threats however, (and among the latter should be included the attempted *putsch* in December 1949 by rightists elements of the Caulderonista's, with the aid of Somoza)[10] were only a preliminary to a struggle that was to be much more prolonged. And although this second struggle was never to be manifested in the more dramatic form of an armed struggle, it was, I believe, central to the long term viability of the political project favoured by the Junta. In this struggle the chief antagonist was the landowning and commercial bourgeoisie (in particular the *cafetaleros*) and their political representatives. While it was first and foremost a struggle for political power and ideological domination, of necessity it concerned the distribution of the social surplus generated within Costa Rican society as well. Before I proceed with this, however, it is necessary to consider the specific character of the State that was to forge ahead in an independent direction, a direction that was often opposed to what the old established order felt its interests to be.

4.3 THE SPECIFICITY OF THE STATE AFTER 1948

Historical situations characterised by a state of static equilibrium between two major social forces contending for class power are noteworthy for opening a breach for the appearance of a charismatic leader – perhaps attached to a political movement, but usually without an organised linkage to the major social antagonists. Gramsci, one of the few modern political theorists to consider this phenomenon with some rigour, situates this kind of development primarily with the immaturity of the progressive forces in society. Basically, he writes, 'it means that no group, neither the conservatives nor the progressives, has the strength for victory, and that even the conservative group needs a master'.[11]

Of course, history has demonstrated that such an 'intervention' in a nation's political life may only serve to provide a 'breather', so to speak, thereby allowing the dominant class to overcome a momentary political deficiency, such as might be produced by the disintegration of the traditionally dominant party due to the in–fighting of competing class fractions.[12] To the extent that this solves the political crisis, the situation is not typically characterised by a fundamental breakdown in the social and economic organisation of society. On the other hand, this phenomenon may come to constitute a real qualitative break from the past. Of this type, Gramsci argues that it represents 'the historical passage from one type of State to another type – a passage in which the innovations were so numerous, and of such a nature, that they represented a complete revolution.'[13]

These two variants could be said to be located at either end of the spectrum that has been termed the phenomenon of Caesarism or Bonapartism, which received its classic treatment in Marx's *The 18th Brumaire of Louis Bonaparte*, the former variant representing an intervention having a particularly reactionary significance, the latter basically progressive in its historical content. However, as essentially a system of compromises and limitations , Bonapartism would never seem to signify a simple restoration, a return to the *status quo ante*, or a complete revolution in social terms.[14] Rather, the objective conditions which open the way for a regime of the Bonapartist type typically give a substantially greater margin of autonomy to the State, which comes to constitute itself in the place of private interests as the leading social force in the reorganisation of society (whatever form this reorganisation may take). However, these same conditions usually place definite restrictions on the State's scope of action as well.

A *sine qua non* of the State as analysed by Marx and later Gramsci, would seem to be the aggrandisement of the State, its growing autonomy from society, especially the traditionally dominant class, and to a greater or lesser extent, its usurpation of the role of the political party. The State takes on this last role to the extent that it, and not the latter, comes to be the major force in developing and solidifying a particular social class or classes.[15] How, then, might this broad interpretive framework be applied to our subject?

The character of the Costa Rican political crisis of 1948, and of the specific solution Figueres and his forces provided to the increasingly disastrous stalemate between the Government alliance and the interests backing Ulate at first view suggest the kind of political development indicated above. The new regime was neither essentially reactionary though, nor wholly progessive in the sense of acting as midwife to a substantial transformation of society. Rather, at first view, Figueres would seem to have led a movement that conforms to neither of these extremes, but to have been more similar in its historical role, for example, to that of the Dreyfus movement in France, which Gramsci notes as having shattered 'stifling and ossified State structures in the dominant camp as well, and having introduced into national life and social activity a different and more numerous personnel'.[16] Whether this political development in Costa Rica actually went beyond such a characterisation to have a more profound influence will take a more detailed examination of the period following the 1948 military campaign.

The intervention of Figueres in 1948 did put an end to that prolonged struggle between the ruling Calderonista alliance and the various class intersts that had come to be grouped around Otilio Ulate. It is also clear that while Figueres and the social democractic forces had allied with the latter, the keyword in this political marriage was convenience. No deep ideological bond existed. Had the role of the Junta of 1948 been essentially to provide a 'breather' for the competing political antagonists – a necessary political space to allow for one of the old parties to reorganise and reassert its hold on the nation's political scene – then this intervention would be an historical curiosity, but litle more. In itself it would have had no far reaching social or political significance.

As I have already argued, the political deficiency of the traditional dominant class in Costa Rica was not simply a transitory phenomenon, but was more deeply rooted in the socio–economic organisation of the coffee economy that was ultimately the source of the longstanding political dominance of this class. Therefore, any longer–term solution to the chronic political crisis of the oligarchy required, as a minimum, some structural modifications, if not an entire transformation of the old agro–exporting scheme. Whether anything short of a complete social transformation could solve the inherent contradictions of the old system is certainly a pertinent question at this point. Suffice it to say for now that the analysis to follow will indeed be concerned with this matter of the efficacy of a State strategy of controlled economic reform which does not seek to get rid of the agro–export economy, nor the class interest it supports, but only to make it serve the demands of other sectors in society. It is clear that the Junta of 1948 and subsequent regimes had a different and more profound significance than would have been the case if they had simply played the part of a 'caretaker' government. In this regard, though the duration of the Junta was short, its actions demonstrated that from then on the State would be expected to have a different, substantially more interventionist role in the future. It will be useful to consider the ideological underpinnings of this new 'interventionism', before examining more closely the specific activities of the Junta.

4.4 THE 'DEVELOPMENTALISM' OF THE SOCIAL DEMOCRATIC FORCES

It will be recalled from the previous chapter that a central place was given to social legislation in the programmatic position papers developed by the intellectuals who constituted the *Centro Para el Estudio de Problemas Nacionales* in the early 1940s. However, attention to this alone, without renewed economic development in Costa Rica, was viewed as essentially unrealistic. In fact, in an article in *Surco*, this organisation's journal in these early years, Carlos Monge Alfaro stressed that while the *Centro* supported the establishment of the Labour Code proposed by the Government of Calderon,

> To believe that Costa Rica can save itself with the promulgation of a labour code is absurd. The *Centro* has among its objectives that of creating a generation capable of giving the country a new historical sense, capable of perfecting its institutions. The *Centro* must support all those means which tend to strengthen the social situation of the workers, but also promote a scientific economic organisation that exploits the resources of the country and encourages the spirit of enterprise and industry amongst Costa Ricans.[17]

Rodrigo Facio, the best known and most consistent intellectual and ideological source of the country's social democratic current, was even more to the point.

In a country such as ours, social justice can only be achieved by the double path of social legislation that guarantees juridically to the less fortunate classes their right to life, and by economic organisation which guarantees, materially, in terms of an augmented and diversified production, that the lower classes will be able to effectively exercise that right.[18]

Without an 'ambitious program of national economic recuperation', Facio argued, social legislation would remain ineffectual or, worse – should its application fall into the hands of 'radical or extremist circles' – it would lead to the paralysing of economic development and new social problems.[19]

It is most important to note, however, that together with this stress on the need for a programme of national economic development, the programmatic statements of the *Centro's* leading intellectuals increasingly gave the State a leading role in this process. Carlos Monge's more general theoretical critique of the classical liberal or "passive" State in the pages of *Surco* was a tentative first move in this direction. Arguing that in bourgeois society the struggle between unequal social interests over the distribution of wealth, given an essentially non–interventionist State, has historically produced acute social disequilibrium, Monge makes a case for a more active State that would promote the welfare of all social interests in society. This early attempt to argue for a more active role for the State is not yet integral to a well articulated analysis of the specific situation of backward capitalist countries, however. On the contrary, Monge makes recourse to classical liberal political doctrines to lend legitimacy to his position.[20]

Facio's justification for an interventionist State, on the other hand, was more in tune with the progressive nationalist ideological currents coming to the fore elsewhere in Latin America, such as the *Aprista* movement in Peru, and would appear to have been more influential in the formulation of a practical political programme after 1948. In a later polemic (1946) directed at the redistributionist tax on wealth proposed by the Communist wing of the Government alliance, Facio argued that efforts to redistribute wealth were desirable, but only if they were channelled through a State oriented towards planned investment that would improve and expand 'productive enterprises'.[21] This linking of the redistribution of national wealth with economic development was not a new theme, of course. What now comes to the forefront, however, especially in an important article published in

1948,[22] is the argument that the specific economic conditions in which a country such as Costa Rica finds itself makes it imperative that the State becomes the central motor force – through various kinds of direct intervention in the economy – behind the programme of modernisation and development. Introducing at this time – *in embryo* – an analysis that was to be developed, extended and widely diffused by Latin American political economists in the following decades, Facio laid down the basic constraints that were seen to prevent local private capital in a backward country from fulfilling its role as the 'prime mover' of capitalist development.

To demonstrate the historical incapacity of private capital to channel accumulated savings (profits) into productive investments stimulating local development was important in order to discount the argument traditionally offered to schemes aimed at taxing the privately appropriated surplus in Costa Rica. Any programme that envisaged a central role for State intervention would have to confront the problem of how this intervention was to be financed. It was equally clear that the financing of this programme would have to come largely from the private sector itself, given the level of development of the society as a whole. Here, Facio attempted to portray legislation that would transfer wealth to the State, in particular a tax on private profits – as a positive measure. Indeed, he argued it was necessarily integral to the only possible strategy – short of a complete socialisation of the economy – available to backward nations seeking economic expansion.

In sum, the Costa Rican *Social Democratic* movement had integral to it, from the very beginning, a kind of 'developmentalism' that accompanied, or rather was seen to constitute the necessary prerequisite for, the kinds of social and political reforms favoured by a broad spectrum of the progressive social classes in the 1940s. It would be fair to say that this developmentalism even had a certain logical priority in it, thinking. It is not clear, however, that this conception of economic development merits the designation of 'transformism' which has become popular with some contemporary observers. Certainly there is little evidence to suggest that the leading ideologues of this movement viewed the country's economic malaise as without remedy as long as private property in the means of production was the fundamental organising principle of the economy. On the contrary, private enterprise, if subordinated to an active State representing the interests of all the social classes, was generally viewed as an integral aspect of a programme of national economic recovery. Thus 'transformism', to the extent that it denotes substantial structural changes, is a less appropriate characterisation of the social and economic project they had in mind.

The foregoing has touched only certain dimensions of the ideological discourse that came to find its political expression in the Social Democratic Party in the late 1940s. The objective has been to portray its most essential distinguishing features *vis-à-vis* the other ideological currents present in Costa Rican society at this time, with a view to understanding the underpinnings of the specific programme which the Junta later initiated, and which subsequent governments were to carry on. The linking of social reform with economic development that went beyond the traditional framework of the agro–exporting economy, and the conception of the State as a motor force of this project, not only clearly differentiated their position from the economic liberalism of the old landowning and commercial bourgeoisie, it also was distinct from the essentially redistributionist social reformism that emerged out of the fusion of Calderon's Social Christian doctrine and the political line of the *Vanguardia Popular* during this period. These aspects of their ideology are, I believe, central to an understanding of the politics practised by the Junta and *Partido Liberación Nacional* in subsequent years. Their practical policies were not *ad hoc* in their conception but rather corresponded to a well–articulated analysis of what was required to overcome the long–term stagnation of an economy dominated by the agro–exporting system of the oligarchy.

4.5 THE BIRTH OF THE INTERVENTIONIST STATE

As Charles Ameringer has noted in his perceptive historical study of these years, the Junta that founded the Second Republic brought together individuals which, although largely sharing the basic aspirations of the Social Democratic movement, differed markedly in their beliefs about how these should be achieved.[23] The inclusion of such 'men of action' as Fernando Valverde Vega and Edgar Cardona (who apparently had little respect for such ideals) and the responsibility they were given for matters pertaining to internal security, was testimony to the fact that the forces led by Figueres had come to power through violent circumvention of the democratic traditions that they had so often praised, and indeed that they would not lightly countenance any challenge to their newly-won power.

Moreover, if historically a Bonapartist situation has given rise to 'great men' destined to promote and orient national energies, albeit outside of and often with little respect for the established constitutional framework, then the place of José Figueres in the nation's political life was to provide some confirmation of the regime's true nature. There was no question that Figueres was the leader within the Junta – the bond that held it together and gave it its orientation.[24] As we shall see, in future months and years he was to be the central figure in mobilising a social base of support for the programmes his forces favoured, whenever the latter was placed in jeopardy. In the first years at least, this threat was to emerge largely from those elements favouring a return to the previous social order.

In the initial months of the Junta, Figueres demonstrated his importance by giving concrete expression to the fundamental tenets of the economic and political philosophy of the Social Democratic Party. One of the first and most consequential acts of the Junta was thus to decree the nationalisation of the banks and a 10 per cent tax on wealth.

The Junta's decree on bank nationalisation was only the first step towards strengthening State power, but it was a key one. Figueres publicly argued on behalf of the Junta that through the control of credit the banks decided the fate of every enterprise, thereby reducing each business to a 'tributary' and determining the 'economic progress' of the nation. This power, he said, did not belong in private hands.[25] Such a move at this time certainly suggests that the Junta had no illusions as to the minimal conditions needed to allow the State to begin to play the role in the economy they believed was necessary. The longstanding orientation of the banking institutions in Costa Rica to the needs of the previous agrarian order,[26] the close ties of commercial capital to the large coffee producers–processors, and the conservative investment policies that had traditionally characterised their operations, meant that in their existing form the banks were unlikely to serve the process of economic reorganisation that was envisaged.

In addition to giving the new State economic institutions more manoeuvrability, this move by the Junta probably had other objectives. A key one would have been to deflate the representatives of financial capital who had traditionally been a bulwark of reaction in national politics, and thereby smooth the way for further interventionist policies in the future.[27]

A nationalised banking system gave to the State, for the first time, a very important instrument without which its influence over a broad range of economic activities would have been greatly reduced. This action was a most important break with the past. Essentially it was a shift away from liberal oligarchic State structures and thus would appear to be a move against those class interests that had been the chief beneficiaries of the old political scheme. Nevertheless, the relatively limited opposition to the decree suggests that this act did not contravene interests that were particularly vital to the traditional bourgeoisie as a whole, even though it ended a privileged monopoly within the class. Some attempts to undermine the decree were indeed evident and a polemic emerged in the press painting a picture of widespread public distrust in the nationalised bank. The Junta responded, mobilising the able intellectual resources of a longstanding partisan and mentor in economic matters – Rodrigo Facio.[28] The importance of the bank nationalisation for laying the groundwork of a new economic and social order was soon to be demonstrated with the establishment in 1949 of what could be considered a cornerstone of the State sponsored infrastructural development: the Costa Rican Institute of Electricity (ICE). ICE was designed to develop and control the production and distribution of electrical energy throughout the country and spearheaded the State's move into areas that were previously the domain of private capital. Together with water programmes, it came to occupy almost a third of all public investments.[29] The connection between the existence of ample electrical energy at a reasonable cost and economic expansion being especially crucial, ICE was testimony to the Junta's concern with establishing the preconditions for private investment outside the traditional agro–export domain and their belief that only the State could adequately provide these. Further developments were to indicate the importance that continued to be given to this particular State role, as public investments in electricity and water programmes jumped from a scant 500000 in 1950 to over 88 million by 1965 and increased even more dramatically to 350 million in the ten years after. Meanwhile, the production of electricity expanded by a factor of ten over this period.

ICE was only a first, albeit crucial, step towards the amplification of the State's presence on the national economy, and was a necessary outgrowth of the attempt to concretise the Junta's well-defined conceptions as to what directions the Costa Rican economy should be oriented towards. As Rodrigo Facio noted,

What the scheme of autonomous organisations attempt is clear: to permit the administrative and technical expansion of the State in an epoch whose problems require its growing participation in social and economic life.[30]

One of the few other developments the Junta was able to put into motion were plans for the creation of a National Council for Production. This was conceived in order to rationalise and stablise the supplies of basic food stuffs in the national market. It was intended to counteract the speculation and resultant artificial scarcities integral to the organisation of the commercialisation of these commodities along capitalist lines.[31]

Before further developments of this type could be undertaken, however, a number of serious problems confronted Figueres and the Junta. The success in handling these was to determine whether or not their initial attempts at economic reorganisation would be continued and broadened, or terminated, either abruptly or through a process of prolonged strangulation. Indeed, the latter possibility seemed the more likely given the commitment the Junta had given to allow Ulate to constitute the Government by the end of 1949.

The first matter that jeopardised the foundations layed by the Junta then, was precisely the problem of Ulate's claim to the Presidency and a return to 'normal' electoral practices. Furthermore, given the presence of powerful enemies, Figueres could not expect to push further ahead in the future without first locating new social bases of support. Finally, there was a critical need to establish a revenue base for the interventionist project favoured by those forces grouped around Figueres. Ultimately, solutions had to be found before any substantial headway could be made in a State–sponsored reorganisation of the economy. The matter of a strategy aimed at ensuring the efficacy of a State interventionist project over the longer term is the subject of the next chapter. However the immediate problem was still that of securing the gains that had been made.

4.6 PROTECTING THE CONTINUITY OF THE INTERVEN-TIONIST PROJECT

Neither the nation's political traditions nor the particular circumstances surrounding Figuere's coming to power favoured a prolongation of the unchecked rule of the Junta of 1948. As we have seen, the restraints placed on the oligarchy's political power had historically tended to distinguish Costa Rica from the other

Central American countries where countervailing pressures were not articulated until much later. Electoral politics here, even when shot through with corruption and fraud, had a long history, while the exercise of dictatorial powers over extended periods had never been as integral to oligarchic rule as elsewhere in the isthmus. Particularly after 1940, political parties with a mass base had become increasingly important in articulating the interests of the popular classes there. These factors, together with the recent memory of the success of Ulate's Party at the polls, a success which, when contested, Figueres and his supporters had ostensibly taken up arms to defend, gave a definite resonance to the demands of Ulate and his party for a return to constitutional rule. 'Figueres was the hero and he had the guns', Ulate was to say, 'but we had the legitimacy.'[32] These conditions dictated the dissolution of a Junta ruling outside the Constitution, even more perhaps than any desire of the PSD forces to decrease the gap between its past philosophical pronouncements about the importance of individual liberties, their criticisms of the previous 'undemocratic' Calderonista alliance, and their own political practice while in power.

Having rather quickly alienated a large part of the propertied elements of the old Opposition alliance with its moves to regulate private capital and even restrict the latter's sphere of operation, having mistreated and exiled many of Calderon's supporters, not to mention many members of the *Vanguardia Popular*, the Junta had rapidly, to quote one observor, 'used up much of its political capital'.[33] The deterioration of the PSD's political position was even further aggravated by the success of Ulate's new National Union Party (PUN) in the 1948 elections for the Constituyente (Constituent Assembly).

Within this context, the crisis tactics employed by Figueres in this period was indicative of the vulnerability of the regime at a time when it was no longer armed and thus could not easily resort to threats to force its measures through by these means. Nor had it yet cultivated a social base with which to augment its political clout. Although such tactics were reasonably successful in the short term, there was little evidence to suggest that Figueres' power would long remain suspended in mid air, as it were, bereft of some strong element of support coming from a fairly numerous element of society. Indeed, the actions of Figueres' and the PSD forces in the subsequent period clearly indicated that this was also their perception of the situation, and the need to do something quickly about it.

The most pressing problem was to secure a slate of candidates for the 1949 election that would safeguard the Junta's programme[34] and keep it on course until such a time that it could be mounted on a firmer political base. The move by Ulate and the opposition to block Figueres' candidacy indicated their own astuteness in appreciating his importance as a motor force behind the programme they sought to undermine. At this point the Junta's options were few indeed. Nevertheless, Figueres showed an uncanny ability to perceive the true weakness of his opponents of that time, deciding that the boldest route was the most likely to succeed. The threat of immediate resignation of the Junta so that they could take their programme to the people and thereby defend it 'from above and below' proved sufficient to force Ulate, whose forces were far superior in the Constituyente, to renegotiate the question of the upcoming electoral slate.[35] Once again the bourgeois opposition had shown its fear of extra-parliamentary politics and their perception that their interests lay in the most rapid return to government under the Constitution, which not only enshrined the inviolable rights of private property, but also guaranteed the primacy of electoral politics over which they would have some control.

By the end of 1949, then, as Ulate took over the Presidency, Figueres and his forces had managed to minimize the Opposition's manoeuvreability to undercut the new directions the Junta had forged in the previous months. Although the Opposition was able to block the passage of a new Constitution drafted by the Junta, the latter was able to amend the old Constitution sufficiently to lay the necessary groundwork for the further development of their interventionist program. As Charles Ameringer writes,

> The Constitution established the principle of public regulation of private property and enterprise, and enpowered the state to direct and stimulate production and to ensure the widest distribution of wealth possible. It even provided for the autonomous institutions, the principal contribution of Rodrigo Facio, . . . According to Carlos Monge, one of the four Social Democrats in the Constituyente, through ammendments and hard work the *Constitution of 1949 was 'a PSD document'*.[36] (Author's emphasis.)

Moreover, through his show–down with Ulate, Figueres had ensured that a slate of candidates favourable to the Junta's position was to be put forward in the elections of that year. Thus, although Figueres had to aquiesce to Ulate's claim on the Presidency by the end of 1949, much had been done to secure the Junta's political orientation until such a time as he could return to office through legitimate means. As the newspaper *La Nacion* was to note in retrospect some years later,

> The cabinent [of Ulate] included noted representives of *Figuerismo* and the same was true in the case of the directors of the [national] bank. In this form, the revolutionary group maintained for themselves an essential direction in the management of the State; it intervened in the formulation of law and in their executive application and, finally, what was of greater importance, it imposed its ideological orientation onto the political economy of the whole system.[37]

The continuation of the *de facto* Social Democratic influence is important to understand, I believe, as we turn to events that unfolded during Ulate's time in office.

4.7 STATE AUTONOMY AND THE QUESTION OF A SOCIAL BASE

Having alientated much of the capitalist class, it was obvious that with the return of constitutional government Figueres and his allies would have to strengthen and deepen their base to ensure the further viability of their partially initiated programme. As we shall see, they themselves were aware of the problem. Before coming to this, however, the question of the relationship between the state and the dominant class needs further clarification.

In previous decades, particularly prior to the anomolous situation that developed in the 1940s with the Government alliance, the state rested on the oligarchy itself to a considerable extent. Though not as exclusionist as elsewhere in Central America, the political process did not entail the interplay of parties with an organic relationship to the different social groups and classes, however amorphous these were. Rather, different political figures typically having roots in the oligarchy itself and never fundamentally questioning the primacy of the agro–exporting scheme, occasionally sought to mobilise the largely agrarian population by means of platforms that incorporated some minor concessions for the popular classes.

As I have already argued, in the 1940s there developed an unstable situation in which the State became clearly more autonomous from the large coffee and commercial interests than at any previous time, as the *Partido Vanguardia Popular* emerged as a salient political force through its contingent support of the governing party. I have discussed previously why the relative autonomy so achieved was inherently precarious. If the State was no longer simply an executive committee for managing the affairs of the oligarchy by the 1940s, what could be said about the relation between the State and the traditionally dominant class in the following decade? In essence, I would argue that a process termed by one political theorist the 'autonomisation'[38] of the State, continued and indeed was strengthened after 1948, although it came to rest on a different relation of forces in society than in the previous decade. I shall expand upon this.

One of the lessons we may garner from Marx's *The 18th Brumaire of Louis Bonaparte*, is that even a regime which has forcefully overturned the Parliamentary traditions and actual procedures of bourgeois power and made itself seemingly independent of that power (as did that of Louis Bonaparte in the France of 1848), is not 'suspended in mid–air', to use Marx's metaphor. Although brought to power and fortified in the short term by the military, the survival of Bonaparte lay more in the hands of the support he received from the most numerous class in French society, the small–holding peasantry, and especially its more conservative members.[39] This is not to say that the regime of Bonaparte, having received the passive support of the rural smallholders, comes to be the vehicle by which their specific class interests were promoted over those of the rest of society. On the contrary, Bonaparte's historical role was to protect a social order that had become thoroughly bourgeois when the bourgeoisie showed itself manifestly incapable of parliamentary rule. In effect, the regime protected above all else the material power of this 'middle class', and indeed fostered its development.[40] The regime's stability, nevertheless, was predicated on support from a substantial sector of society.

Not long after handing over the Presidency to Ulate, Figueres began organising to fortify the Social Democratic presence in the affairs of the State even further, and to ensure for it some degree of longevity. A first important step in this direction was the creation of a political vehicle to gain Figueres the Presidency in the elections of 1953 and thereby strengthen further the Social Democratic influence in the General Assembly. The creation of the *Partido Liberacion Nacional* in 1951 had this goal as its primordial purpose. At its inception it did not function in the manner of a traditional parliamentary party; rather Figueres' dominance was indicated by the fact that while he was to be the Presidential candidate, the Party did not nominate him in convention. Moreover, the absence of forums for internal political discussions at any level, or of party congresses in which could be discussed fundamental policy issues,[41] were further indications of the nature of this political machine that dominated in the period when the relationship between the State and civil society was being restructured.

Thus, although the ideological roots of *Liberación Nacional* as they were set down in its 'Fundamental Charter' were basically those established years earlier, especially by those intellectuals grouped around the *Centro*, its *raison d'être* could not be separated from Figuere's political ambitions, immediate and long–term. Beyond the personal, these ambitions were basically those the Junta had attempted to put into concrete form during the period of its tenure, many of which had yet to be realised.

Having established the requisite political vehicle, Figueres sought to maximise his chances of success and acquired financial interest in the newspaper *La Republica*.[42] This shrewd move suggested that the *liberacionistas* fully appreciated the importance of the Press to liberal democratic political process and that to counter the influence of the traditional dominant groups they would also have to be able to break the former's monopoly at the ideological level.

The substantial majority won by Figueres in the 1953 elections showed where his social base to be, at least in these early years. Support for Figueres and the PLN was particularly strong amongst the rural population of the *Meseta Central*, and considerably weaker among the banana workers on both coasts.[43] In the latter areas, the rates of abstention in 1953 were approximately double the national average, with both the *Calderonista* party and that of the Communists banned at the time.[44] Ameringer suggests that the political personality of Figueres played no small part in bringing an important section of the rural population to the PLN cause. He notes,

> although [Figueres] tended to talk down to his audience, he had the common touch; without regard for time or schedule, he mingled freely in crowds, visited private homes and took *arroz y frijoles* with the people of the villages and towns. He was at his best among the rural folk of the Central Plateau, but seemed unable to reach

effectively the urban poor of San José and the banana workers of both coasts.[45]

This support from the campesinos, it seems, stayed with Figueres in later campaigns. Figueres' appeal among small property holders in the coffee growing areas was surely not the whole explanation for his success there, however.

It also must have been of some consequence that the PLN counted among its top ranks some very influential members of this rural community, large coffee growers and processors well–connected to the rural middle class elements so crucial im moulding political support.[46] In 1953, then, there is some reason to believe that the success of Figueres and the PLN rested substantially with rural smallholders of the *Meseta Central*. Further clarification of this matter, however, awaits more historical research on this period. What is clear is that the PLN moved to establish additional support bases elsewhere, and quite rapidly too. With an historical perspective, it is apparent that the domination of the *Partido Liberación Nacional* in the nation's political life virtually since its inception was closely associated with the social consequences of its own programme. Given its decidedly statist orientation, it is not surprising to find that public sector workers, as a proportion of all workers, increased by the end of the first terms of *Liberacion Nacional* rule (1958). In fact the increase was quite dramatic – from 6 per cent of the active population in 1950 to 10 per cent only eight years later.[47] The further proliferation of the so–called 'autonomous institutions' of the State were, of course, integral to this growth. The massive programme of public works[48] and the new State institutions spawned by the *Liberacion Nacional* governments, and the Junta before it, did not, to be sure, guarantee the loyalty of State workers to Figueres. But he was not about to leave it to chance that this considerable and growing segment of society should make a connection between their own employment status and the fact that PLN formed the Government. The history of the *aguinaldo* is most interesting in this respect.

The *aguinaldo* was a type of bonus equivalent to one month's salary, although in the original proposal it was to be equivalent to only ⅓ of a month's salary. In 1953 there was a considerable budgetary surplus, not surprisingly given the new taxes recently implemented and the record high prices for coffee in the world market. This surplus corresponded with Figueres' victory in the elections of that year. Two days after becoming President, Figueres proposed to redistribute part

Table 4.1   Distribution of the unionised workforce by occupational category: Costa Rica, circa 1970

Category	% of total employed population	% unionised of total population employed per cat.
1. Professionals and Technicians	8.4	17.6
2. Small agricultural producers	10.0	2.0
3. Employees	10.8	40.9
4. Transport	3.0	35.9
5. Agricultural workers	20.4	9.2
6. Industrial and Construction workers	17.7	5.1

Source: Roberto Salom E, 'Estudio Sobre las Organizaciones Politico-partidistas de la Clase Dominantes en Costa Rica: El Partido Liberacion Nacional' (San José: Instituto de Investigaciones Sociales, 1978, mimeo) p.23, Table 2.

of this surplus amongst Government employees, although initially only employees of the Executive office. Within a few weeks this was approved by the PLN dominated legislature and not long afterwards the right of these employees to an additional month's salary per year was incorporated into the statutes of the Civil Service. Before long other State workers, including teachers, workers in the Legislature and the Judiciary and eventually municipal employees as well petitioned to be included in this legislation. Their requests were for the most part all approved, and Figueres the next year took the initiative to appropriate funds for the *aguinaldo*. By 1956 when the *aguinaldo* had been extended to workers of all levels of the State apparatus, including some pensioned workers as well, the budget for this payment had increased some five times the original proposal to over 11 million colons, about 5 per cent of all government revenues for that year.[49]

What we are speaking of, then, was a general increase in the level of salaries for a segment of the population that was becoming ever–more important in social and ultimately political, terms. This latter point cannot have been lost on Figueres and the *liberacionistas*. This whole episode has been viewed by some[50] as a well intentioned proposal (i.e. an effort towards a more equitable distribution of social wealth) that subsequently got out of hand as the growing State machine acquired a political force that could not be controlled. However, the original proposal and its timing was surely no strictly spontaneous act, and neither could the Government have been ignorant or totally naive of its probable trajectory. In the end, the *aguinaldo* reminds one of a 'grand gesture' which was not so much in accordance with the longstanding philosophy of the Social Democratic forces as it was the politic thing to do in order to build up a social base for the *liberacionista* programme in years to come.

Schemes such as that of the *aguinaldo*, however useful they many have been politically, were at best a tenuous basis upon which to build a base for a 'movement' such as was being constituted by the PLN. Over the longer term, the inroads made in integrating the public sector workforce into labour organisations of *liberacionista* doctrinal orientation[51] were unquestionably a more significant factor in establishing the hegemony of *Liberación Nacional* over this expanding sector of the country's workforce. In fact, the decade of the 1950s was a time of considerable change and reorganisation of the unionised workforce involving a very substantial expansion of unionisation amongst 'service sector' workers.[52] Moreover, data on the occupational bases of the major labour confederations in Costa Rica shows the strength of the reformist Costa Rican Confederation of Democratic Workers (CCTD) to be strongest in that sector including state workers, while the strength of the other major labour federation, the one traditionally under Communist hegemony, is much stronger among the traditional working class and independent artisan population.[53]

As may be appreciated from Table 4.1, those occupational categories grouping primarily State workers show, proportionately, a dramatically higher rate of unionisation than the remainder. Indeed, this situation has prompted the comment from one observer of the country's labour scene that 'the obvious conclusion . . . is that unionisation in Costa Rica is, fundamentally, a unionisation of the middle class'.[54] Despite the element of exaggeration here, it is apparent that those categorised as 'employees', most of whom would be employees of the State, have been the subject of considerable organisational activity, and especially since *Liberatión Nacional* became the major force in national political life. Of course, it is not only that this sector has been organised, but as I have suggested, it is much more significant that it has historically been organised into a structure with a specifically *liberacionista* ideological orientation.

Notes

1. Karl Marx, *The Civil War in France* (Moscow: Progress Publishers, 1967), p.54.
2. With respect to the latter, Delgado writes, 'A middle class and a professional sector, with capitalist aspirations and expectations for the industrial development of the country stimulated in this period by the industrial imports of the developed countries, found in the economic system of the nation a barrier to its pretensions. From here the struggle to break the structures that were frustrating them.' *El Partido Liberación Nacional* (Heredia: Editorial de la Universidad Nacional, 1980), p.71
3. Antonio Gramsci, *Selections from the Prison Notebooks of Antonio Gramsci*, Hoare and Smith (eds) (New York: International Publishers, 1971) p.210.
4. The reader may find Antonio Gramsci's discussion of 'organic' crises instructive here. Ibid., pt 2. ch.2.
5. The United States was particularly concerned about the significance of an alteration of the *status quo* in the country. This was evidenced by the presence of American warships off the Costa Rican coast, the presence of troops of Somoza's National Guard on the northern border and the mobilisation of US forces in Panama. It is apparent, however, that the US Government had decided that the previous government was the greater of two evils, undoubtedly because of the participation of the Communists. As President Picado is reported to have written to Calderon and *Vanguardia Popular* leader, Manuel Mora, 'I can assure you that insuperable forces are absolutely determined to have us lose this contest' (cited in Ameringer, *Don Pépé*, p.63). For a discussion of the intervention threat at this time, see also Stone, *La Dinastía*, ch.10.
6. Delgado, *El Partido*, p .123.
7. According to Schifter, Article 98 of the new Constitution that was to be established made illegal whatever party that was considered 'antidemocratic' or contrary to the established order and was used to keep the Communist Party outside of the political system after 1949. (*La Fase Oculta*, p.141).
8. Vladimir de la Cruz notes that a new party of the left, the *Partido Progresista Independiente*, was banned during the 1950s, while new working class parties were illegalised in both the 1962, 1966 and 1969 elections. 'Costa Rica: 100 Años de Luchas Sociales, Reseña Historica' (San José: Lecturas Complementarias no. 2, Escuela de Historia y Geografica, Universidad de Costa Rica, 1978),pp.22–3.

9. There is some reason to believe that as part of the pact between Figueres and Manuel Mora (VP leader) prior to the surrender of *Vanguardista* forces to the former, Mora and other Communist leaders were to leave the country so that Figueres could portray an anti-Communist image – with the agreement that they would be allowed to return quietly at a later period (See Ameringer, *Don Pépé*, pp.116–117). This also allowed Figueres to take a softer line towards the US banana companies. In Guatemala a few years later a much tougher position *vis-à-vis* this foreign consortium was to be elaborated. As Aybar de Soto (1978:204) has noted, 'both the Arevalo and Arbenz administrations set a precedent which, if continued, would have had serious international repurcussions for the corporate holdings of Ufco. (United Fruit Company) . . . The long term implications and possible escalation of adverse labour relations throughout all foreign holdings of Ufco shook the foundation of its profit structure.' Indeed, the dangers inherent in such a hard line position were soon to become apparent, of course, and in a most forceful way with the US orchestrated armed intervention of the forces of Castillo Armas.

10. Ameringer, *Don Pépé*, p.76–83 passim.

11. See Gramsci's notes on 'Caesarism', in *Selections*, p.221. The classical example he uses in this context is that of Napoleon III's regime after 1848 in France, which was given its most famous treatment in Marx's *18th Brumaire of Louis Bonaparte*.

12. It has been suggested that the historical significance of the regime of Napoleon I, for example, was of this nature.

13. *Selections*, p.222.

14. Ibid., p.219.

15. The significance of a State taking on the role normally left to political parties is discussed, although only briefly, in Gramsci, (ibid., pp.227–8).

16. Ibid., p.223. The historical impact of the Dreyfus movement in France was thus limited more to having coalesced the energies of certain progressive groups around problems more clearly related to the superstructure of French society, and in particular the need to remove the obstacles that had, over the long history of the Third Republic, prevented the establishment of republicanism on a firm basis. In a sense, then, the movement helped complete the unfinished business of Napoleon III's lengthy regime, what the authors of one popular historical survey refer to as the matter of 'domesticating democratic republicanism' (Palmer and Colton, 1971:630).

17. *Surco*, (October, 1943, no.40), p.26.

18. Ibid., p.28.

19. Ibid.

20. Ibid., p.25. He notes, for instance, that 'according to liberal-individualist concepts, the State is the organ of expression of the will of society organized politically, which it represents. Therefore, the right or capacity to intervene in the life of its members, protecting them and legislating for their well–being does not contradict the liberal definition of the State.'

21. See his article, 'Saben los Señores Diputados Cual es la Politica Economica Que El País Necesita?' published in *La Nacion*, (17 December, 1946).
22. This appeared in the Mexican journal *El Trimestre Economico (January–May, 1948) reprinted in Obras de Rodrigo Facio*, (1972).
23. *Don Pépé*, p.68.
24. Ibid., p.69.
25. Speech by José Figueres, cited in Jorge Rovira M., *Estado y Politica Economica en Costa Rica, 1948–1970* (San José: Editorial Porvenir S.A., 1983) p.48.
26. Or at least since the First World War, when local banks took over the role of lenders to the large coffee growers, a role previously filled by English capital (Stone, 1975:118). As the newspaper *La Republica* (5 November, 1966) noted years later in a series of articles on the history of the country's banking system, 'the experience of private banks in Costa Rica shows that they were interested in operations of low risk and over the shortest terms possible. As a result, the provision of credit was at no time oriented towards the achievement of greater economic development.'
27. Rovira, *Estado y Politica*, p.49.
28. Facio responded to these criticisms in a series of articles published in the newspapers, *Diario de Costa Rica*, and *La Nacion*, between 18 and 25 August, 1949. These are reprinted in *Obras de Rodrigo Facio*.
29. This and the following data pertaining to ICE are to be found in Oscar Arias Sanchez, *Nuevos Rumbos para el Desarrollo Costarricense* (San José: Editorial Universitaria Centroamericana, 1979),p.116–7.
30. Carlos Araya Pochet, *Historia Economica de Costa Rica; 1950–1979* (San José: Editorial Fernandez-Arce, 1976), p.11.
31. 31 *La Prensa Libre*, 13 December 1949. This was to be achieved through price regulation, a system of minimum prices, and the construction of a network of storage facilities among other measures. These are discussed in some detail in Araya Pochet, ibid., pp.26–8.
32. See Ameringer, *Don Pépé*, p.66 and John P. Bell, *Crisis in Costa Rica* (Austin: University of Texas Press, 1971), p.156.
33. Bell, ibid.,p.158.
34. Ameringer,, *Don Pépé, p.88.*
35. Ibid., p.87 and *La Prensa Libre*, 26–30 October, 1949.
36. Ameringer, ibid., p.90. Also see Rovira, *Estado y Politica*, pp.60–2.
37. *La Nacion*, 6 May, 1955.
38. This term is used by Draper in his recent and substantial work analysing the development of the political thought of Marx and Engels (1978:314).
39. Marx, *18th Brumaire*, p.105–7.
40. As Marx (ibid.) noted of Louis Bonaparte, 'by protecting its [the bourgeoisie's] material power, he generates its political power anew'.
41. Ameringer, *Don Pépé*, p.103. The internal structure and practice of the PLN is discussed in Robert Salom 'Estudio sobre los organizaciones politico–partidistas de las clases dominantes en Costa Rica', 1978 (mimeo. San José).

76		*Coffee and Democracy in Modern Costa Rica*

42.		Ameringer, ibid.,p.100.
43.		Ibid., pp.104–5.
44.		Jacobo Schifter, *La Fase Oculta de la Guerra Civil en Costa Rica* (San José: Editorial Universitaria Centroamericano, 1979), p.104. Schifter's study also shows that PLN support continued to be weak in the banana zones in subsequent elections (1979:105, Table 30).
45.		*Don Pépé*, p.104.
46.		Samuel Stone, 'Costa Rica: Sobre la Clase Dirigente y la Sociedad Nacional', *Revista de Ceincias Sociales* no.11, 1976.
47.		Stone, *La Dinastia*, p.329.
48.		Government expenditures, other than those transfers to households and private non–profit institution (i.e. social security, etc.) increased after l953 at a much faster rate than it had in previous years (see UN, Yearbook of National Accounts, 1958:54).
49.		Stone, *La Dinastía*, p.330–4.
50.		Ibid., p.334.
51.		Basically, we are speaking about an orientation towards so–called 'free' unionism, meaning essentially the formal separation of unions from politics, although still open to the active promotion of labour's economic corporate interests within society by means of their respective labour organisations. See Ponciano Torales, *Reseña Historia del Sindicalismo en Costa Rica* (San José: International Labour Organization, l978), p.23.
52.		Ibid., p.10. State workers would have comprised the major component of this category that was 'organizable'.
53.		Ibid., p.21.
54.		Roberto Salom E., 'Estudio Sobre las Organizaciones Politico-partidistas de la Clase Dominantes en Costa Rica', (San José: Instituto de Investigaciones Sociales, 1978), p.23.

5 The State and the Coffee Oligarchy: An Historic Compromise

> Many people do not realise that we live in an antiquated society that is disappearing. A society divided between 'the ruling class' and 'the people', each experiencing a different stage of civilisation. This phenomenon is most acute in other countries of Latin America, but it is also present in Costa Rica. (J. Figueres, *Cartas a Un Cuidadano*, 1956)

INTRODUCTION

One of the first tasks the Junta of 1948 set for itself was that of securing a revenue base to support the much more active role they envisioned for the State. Together with the necessity of developing a viable element of popular support for their policies, this matter of having the State capture a larger part of the social surplus was a primordial concern in these early years. In this chapter I consider this last problem in greater detail. My focus is around the merging struggle between the large coffee producers and the State, primarily over the appropriation of the social surplus generated by coffee production – especially the State's claim over part of this surplus, the manner in which it was to be appropriated and the uses to which the State's share of it would be put. I see the immediate consequences of this struggle as being the redefinition of the traditional economic prerogatives of the oligarchy, and the subordination of their interests to the wider configuration of interests personified by the State in this period. The really lasting significance of this struggle, I would argue, was the possibility it gave the State to embark on a major project of economic modernisation and reorganisation. In this process, the State can be seen as coming to represent – to foster – the various class interests of this developing capitalist society, without, it need be added, attempting to do away with the conditions which were

77

fundamental in the reproduction of these classes. The large coffee interests continued as an important element of a redefined and reinforced capitalist class, but no longer the hegemonic element.

5.1 WHO SHALL HAVE THE SURPLUS? CONFRONTING THE CAFETALEROS

The Junta's first move to put the State on a firmer financial base involved a 10 per cent tax on wealth, decreed soon after the regime was constituted in 1948. Such a move had been discussed openly, of course, by the PSD, only a year earlier.[1] Figueres attempted to lend further legitimacy to the measure in the pages of the *Diario de Costa Rica*, citing the lamentable state of each of the Ministries of the Government after years of 'administrative looting' by the *Calderonistas*, and the destruction of the recent fighting as necessitating such a measure.[2] By some accounts, however, the decree was poorly conceived and executed. In Ameringer's words, 'the affluent did everything they could to evade the tax, including false declarations and an outright boycott, and they rallied to the side of the Founding Junta's enemies.'[3] Because of this, the decree did not prove as lucrative for the State as might have been expected, though it was not as ineffectual as Ameringer, for example, suggests.[4] It did, however, spread the burden over the capitalist class as a whole. It is interesting to note that when the State moved in a more fruitful direction to tax the wealth that had traditionally flowed into the hands of the coffee oligarchy, the latter's response was that a more 'just' measure to raise revenues would be a tax on wealth.[5]

The experience of the tax on wealth suggested that any measure, to be really effective, would have to be much less subject to circumvention than this kind of tax apparently was. It is perhaps not surprising, given the fair degree of longstanding regulation governing commercial transaction in coffee, and given the economic significance of this activity for the country, that future moves to generate a resource base for the state would be oriented in this direction. Some progess was made with the successful passage of a law that obliged national exporters to sell to the Central Bank foreign currency earned by their exports.[6] As coffee exports generated at the time of the passage of this law (1951) were well over half of the total dollars entering the Official Exchange Market,[7] it was the coffee interests in particular that were affected by taking away the right to sell their foreign exchange in the free market. Indeed, there was some attempt to argue against such a law by the *Camara de Cafetaleros*, the organisation of the large coffee producer processors,[8] in the national press, arguing that such a law was not only an infringement on the rights of private property, but that any profits made on such exchanges would help to stimulate the national coffee industry, in any case.[9] On the other hand, there were sound arguments to be made why such legislation was in the 'national interests', given the monetary situation in which the country found itself in these immediate post war years. Despite the existence of sporadic outcries, [10] a well–orchestrated opposition to the legislation failed to materialise. In reality, the real fight was shaping up over a different matter, where the stakes were potentially much higher.

5.2 THE GENESIS OF THE ADVALOREM TAX ON COFFEE

At the time the Junta came to power in 1948, State revenues gained from the production of coffee were minimal, in large part due to the emergency decrees of the Calderon Guardia Government that had freed producers from most taxes and duties in 1940.[11] The creation of the *Oficina del Café* in 1948 had included the establishment of minor taxes, intended to finance the operation of the new institution. Early in the Ulate administration, however, efforts were renewed to solve the State's fiscal difficulties and generate a financial base for development purposes through a substantial tax on coffee exports. This tax, originally proposed by a Minister in the Ulate Government, was destined from its inception to be a hotly contested political issue, one that eventually took on a national character. This whole episode, including modifications of the original proposal, has considerable historical significance and merits further scrutiny. In the original law, proposed in March 1950[12], upon each *fanega* of coffee received by the *beneficios* was to be imposed a tax of 2¼ per cent of its value, and 4½ per cent if its value during the first year that the law came into effect. As with previous taxes, this new tariff would not be absorbed by the *beneficiador*, at least not in his capacity as processor, but would be entirely passed on by them to those who actually produced the coffee. Of course, to the extent that the *beneficiadores* were themselves producers, (and they usually were) they were also affected. Indeed, this last point is important in understanding the character and intensity of the campaign unleashed in subsequent months against this measure.

The initial tax proposal opened the way for the large coffee interests, represented by the *Camara de Cafetaleros*, to make common cause with the thousands of small and medium coffee farmers in opposing the legislation, despite the antagonism that was imminent in the relationship between the *beneficiadors* and the majority of growers who were strictly producers. It is not surprising, then, that a notable effort was made by the ideologues of the oligarchy to place at the forefront the plight of the small coffee growers, the *cafetaleros de solar*, and thereby highlight the 'popular' nature of the opposition. Much of the propaganda of this type was to be found in the pages of the newspaper *La Nacion*, a longstanding friend of the coffee oligarchy. In its pages, the mythical image of the small coffee farmer, bastion of the nation's stability and democratic traditions, was put to the partisan cause on numerous occasions. The following plea was fairly typical.

> Those coffee growers must not disappear, even if death threatens them as a result of the tendency to overburden them with taxes. They must not disappear because this fortunate distribution of land in small plots has endowed our country with a consistency of order, a spirit of peace, a love of freedom and a solid foundation for democracy.[13]

It was not the first time of course that the *cafetaleros* had argued for special dispensation for the coffee industry on the basis of the need to protect the mass of small producers as the incarnation of the nation's peace and political stability – nor would it be the last. It was, however, surely the most effective campaign of this nature to be mounted, for the small and medium coffee growers were indeed up in arms over this legislation and were themselves pulling together farmers from all the various coffee producing regions of Costa Rica to oppose the State's intervention in this sphere. In the months after the first tax proposal was initiated, the Association of Small Producers, which had formed a few years earlier but had not been particularly visible, intensified its educational and organisational work amongst the coffee farmers. By the middle of 1951 the Association was able to pull together a rally of several thousand farmers from diverse areas of the Meseta

Central. Their message was clear. They, the small producers, and not only the great landowners, (as government proponents of the tax had claimed), were unanimous in their opposition to any attempt of this kind to augment the State's Treasury. The statements of the Association's leaders were unequivocal about two fundamental matters that affected the mass of smallholders: firstly, that it was not the large *cafetaleros* alone that opposed the tax, as Government spokesmen attempted to portray. On the contrary, the Association and the producers it represented were also adamantly opposed to the tax. However, and secondly, they were opposed to it for their own reasons, and demanded to be recognised as interests independent of the large producers. As one leader put it,

> We are not in league with the big ones, because they are able to defend their interests on the basis of their own force or generally to defend themselves, because in the long run they possess the tools that enable them to overcome all emergencies.[14]

The two themes that comprised this popular protest of that time were expressed unequivocally by a leader from Villa Colon, who noted,

> When forty thousand agriculturalists come to the capital city to demand respect for our rights and to ask for justice, they have to listen to us. When we demonstrate that they have committed a serious mistake, they have to rectify their error. That is why we have to work together and in perfect unity. We have to defend ourselves against the big coffee growers who have amassed their capitals with our sweat and the sweat of our ancestors. We have also to defend ourselves from the many taxes that suffocate us.[15]

The import of this popular protest was not lost on the large coffee interests who, through the *Camara de Cafetaleros*, went to considerable pains to publicise the protests of the Small Producers Association in order to lend credibility to the former's claim that there was truly a national opposition to the Government's new legislation.[16] Up until the time when the mobilisation of small coffee farmers caught the public eye the *cafetaleros* had been waging a continuous propaganda campaign in the nation's press, chiefly *La Nacion*, through spokesmen both representing and outside of the *Camara de Cafetaleros*.

The full page 'DECLARATION' which appeared in *La Nacion*[17] in early 1950 was fairly typical of their efforts, and here it is interesting to note that the role of the *Oficina del Café*, now formally a State entity, in lending – in the tradition of its predecessor, the *Instituto de Defensa Del Café* – its sponsorship to a public protest organised by the country's largest producers.

None the less, it was surely the mobilisation of the small and medium coffee growers, and the protests articulated through the *Asociación de Pequeños Productores* which gave the necessary legitimacy to the claims of the *cafetaleros* that such tax legislation, being prejudicial to the coffee industry as a whole, was not in the best national interest. Given the increasing autonomy of the State since 1948 relative to the agro-exporting scheme of the oligarchy, it appears that this question of legitimacy was becoming even more central to the exercise of political power than at any previous time.

The Government's position, which not surprisingly was usually to be found in the pages of the *Diario de Costa Rica*, was that the revenues were needed to underwrite various programmes aimed primarily at stimulating rural development and raising the low productivity of the agrarian sector.[18] As one observer remarked, the proposed tax was the touchstone of the Government's project to unleash an intense campaign around the construction of public works (rural infrastructure), the augmentation of agricultural production and the expansion of agricultural credit so that it would be available to all rural producers.[19] Moreover, it was frequently pointed out that with the current upsurge in coffee prices, this sector could well afford such a tax.[20]

In retrospect, this matter of the price of coffee during this period would appear to have been of no small importance in determining the final outcome of this struggle over the surplus generated with coffee, and with it the efficacy of the State's interventionist project in subsequent years. Could the State have resisted the combined pressure of the mass of small farmers and the powerful producer–processors in a less favourable economic conjuncture? It does not seem likely. The coffee industry, that is, primarily the large producer–processors, had for many years carried on propaganda which sought to identify, in the public mind, the health of this industry with the well–being of the nation. Given the backwardness of Costa Rica in other agricultural and particularly industrial areas, this argument had more than a grain of truth to it, of course, and had times been hard for the coffee growers and processors, this argument surely would have carried the day. In reality, since the end of the war prices had been moving steadily upwards, and indeed they rose from 44 cents/lb to 55 cents/lb between the 1949–50 and 1950–1 seasons alone.[21]

At one point, perhaps sensing the commitment of the Government to the tax legislation, spokesmen for the *cafetaleros* put forward the idea of funnelling the revenues so collected into a bank specifically oriented to the coffee interests. Figueres himself responded to this proposal in the national press, and in arguing his opposition to it he provided a valuable insight into the problems that the Junta had already faced in confronting the economic power of the oligarchy.[22] He argues that a precedent had previously been set to indicate what would happen if such a bank were to be established. He proceeds to outline how, with the nationalisation of the country's hydroelectric network and the creation of ICE, the State had offered stock in its electrical concern which had then largely fallen into the hands of the *cafetaleros*. Figueres argues that with the creation of a coffee bank with the proposed tax, once again the State would be inadvertently facilitating the further concentration of national wealth. In the end, there did not seem to be widespread support for such an institution, and the issue receded into the background.

For its part, the oligarchy was not entirely unified in its response. Certain elements were attempting to turn the tax legislation to their advantage by proposing the creation of a coffee bank, while the most reactionary wing of the oligarchy carried on an extremely vitriolic campaign which received the tacit support of the large coffee interests as a whole against the proposed law and against the Government itself.[23] In the end, the pressure provided by the organisation of the small producers was probably decisive in the final outcome of this affair, not in defeating the idea of a tax but in pushing the Government in the direction of a compromise solution. In retrospect, it would appear to have been an historic compromise at that.

At the root of the compromise legislation that was passed into law in early January 1952 was a change in the initial proposal from a tax on coffee exports to one whereby there was to be a redistribution of the revenue producers had been previously paying to *beneficiadores*, so that now a portion of this was to go to the State, a portion that was itself geared to the prevailing world price of coffee. In sum, the old law governing relations between producers and processors legislated in the 1930s had allowed the *beneficiador* to retain up to 16 per cent of the sale price of the coffee he received for his processing services. Although hypothetically the competition among processors

Table 5.1 Costa Rica: Government revenues from various sources, 1938-54 (millions of colons)

Receipts	1938	1939	1940	1941	1942	1943	1944	1945	1946	1947	1948	1949	1950	1951	1952	1953	1954
Direct taxes on income & wealth	1.3	1.4	1.4	1.6	2.0	2.3	2.6	2.3	3.3	6.5	10.2	31.1	31.3	38.9	40.7	41.2	40.5
Custom duties	20.5	23.4	20.4	22.6	14.8	21.1	21.4	24.4	27.3	43.1	41.4	46.1	54.7	60.3	82.8	104.1	139.3
Other indirect taxes	3.7	4.6	5.8	5.6	5.1	7.0	6.9	7.9	8.9	11.6	12.5	20.2	28.5	31.3	37.4	42.1	35.5
Other receipts	12.0	13.3	14.1	12.8	15.0	20.0	21.9	25.9	23.4	26.8	26.0	28.0	23.5	29.6	28.6	28.4	18.2
Total	37.5	42.7	41.7	42.6	36.9	50.4	52.8	60.5	62.9	88.0	90.1	125.4	138.0	160.1	189.5	215.8	233.5

Source: United Nations Statistical Yearbooks, (1951, 1955, 1958), 'Public Finance'.

for the growers' coffee would force him to limit his profits to less than the 16 per cent to attract clients, in practice the majority of *beneficiadores* charged the full amount permitted by law.[24] Under the final version of the tax legislation, the proportion of the sale price of coffee that the *beneficiador* could receive by law was reduced to 9 per cent and that proportion more or less equal to the amount by which his income had been reduced (5 per cent), was to go to the State as a tax.[25] With this change, the actual producers of coffee were liberated from paying the tax, whereas under the original proposal the producers were to be in fact the sole source of such State revenues. As one deputy remarked during a debate in the General Assembly, 'this law does not establish simply a tax, but rather limits the earnings of the *beneficiador*, as the Law of Economic Defense limits those of the merchants.'[26] As a final note, it should be mentioned that this legislation entailed two additional compromises in favour of the coffee interests, large and small. Firstly, should the price of coffee fall below $40/quintal (46 kg.) no tax was to be payed. Secondly, the legislation stipulated that no additional taxes could be imposed on the production, processing and export of coffee for a period of ten years after the date that this law came into effect.

5.3 SIGNIFICANCE OF THE ADVALOREM TAX

It is curious that none of the better known studies dealing with the social and political aspects of Costa Rica's coffee economy of these years accords this episode of the tax legislation the significance that it is due.[27] Certainly, it was not ignored by the main social forces within Costa Rican society at the time. To view the final outcome of this affair in strictly economic terms would be, I believe, to miss much of the real significance it ultimately had in more clearly political terms as well. Nevertheless, its economic importance for the State should not be denied. This can be appreciated if we examine the Costa Rican national budget during the years before and after 1948.

By considering total Government receipts for this time period, the marked growth in State revenues is apparent after 1948, that is, when the various new taxes and the legislation on foreign exchange came into effect. The previous decade had been, for the most part, characterised by slow or even negative growth of income (see Table 5.1).[28] An examination of national account data for Costa Rica for

Table 5.2   State revenues from the advalorem tax and all coffee taxes
1950–70

| | (thousands of colons) | |
Year	Advalorem tax	All coffee taxes
1950	1258.8	1757.9
1955	11135.6	12099.9
1960	12161.6	13513.3
1965	22053.7	25905.9
1970	52254.7	57407.3

Source: Justo Aguilar, Carlos Barboza and Jorge Leon, *Desarrollo Tecnologico del Cultivo del Café*. (Consejo Nacional de Investigaciones Cientificas y Tecnologicas, 1981) Table 6–3.

the period 1950–5, furthermore, indicates that it was tax revenues in particular that accounted for most of the increase in general Government revenues at this time.[29] Of these revenues, those generated by taxing the coffee activity were not that significant, given its weight in the national economy. A few years later this situation had changed very noticeably. As Table 5.2 indicates, the jump in tax revenues generated from coffee was largely due to the *advalorem* tax.

At base, then, these various decrees provided the State with additional revenue sources not already committed to existing programmes, which could be utilised to expand State activity in the economy. Shortly after the law was passed, in fact, the Government announced a major programme to develop rural infrastructure, including electrification, roads, sewage facilities, etc., to be financed in part by revenues provided by the new *advalorem* tax.[30] Moreover, this tax guaranteed that the State would have a substantial share in the income generated by higher coffee prices in the future, income that in the past had been almost entirely appropriated privately by producers and processors, in proportion to their economic power. In this regard, data provided here show just how significant this revenue would be in an economic conjuncture characterised by high coffee prices (see Table 5.2).

From the political point of view, this struggle over the surplus produced with coffee would seem to have established a definite break, in terms of the relations between the agrarian bourgeoisie and the State. Part of the surplus that had traditionally been appropriated by the dominant social group within the coffee sphere – the producer–processors – in fact the most powerful economic interests in the country, had been tapped, breaking the long established custom of milking the small and medium farmers for the great bulk of State revenues. The fact that this legislation was implemented despite the protracted and at times shrill campaign of the *Camara de Cafetaleros* and spokesmen for the oligarchy outside this organisation beginning with the original tax legislation of 1950, is testimony to the fact that a new balance of political forces was taking shape within Costa Rican society. It had been taking shape, of course, for some time, but this episode demonstrates that the new configuration of power had matured enough to make some inroads in limiting the economic prerogatives of the agrarian bourgeoisie within the framework of parliamentary government.

At this point it would be *apropos* to note that this new relationship of political forces was not a transitory phenomenon. It in fact took on a degree of permanence, according to the crystallisation of a new social structure, itself the product of specific developments analysed in previous sections. Indeed, this was demonstrated to be the case when a temporary crisis was provoked with a severe downturn in prices in the late 1950s. The large producer–processors, through a publicity campaign in *La Nacion*[31] and through direct representation to the Government via the *Camara de Cafetaleros*, rapidly organised to gain certain concessions.

Their principal demands entailed a return of their right to dispose of export earnings in the free market (i.e. effectively a monetary devaluation), and the suppression of the 5 per cent *advalorem* tax. In addition, they were seeking the guarantee of a minimum price for coffee.

The response of the Government was unequivocal, at least on the first two demands. The *Camara* was informed by the Minister of Agriculture that the economic consequences of a devaluation for the wider society, in particular the immediate rise in the cost of living, was unacceptable to the Government.[32] The loss of the revenues to the State provided by the *advalorem* was also rejected at this time, because of the serious crisis it would provoke for State finances.[33] It was argued that this tax would be removed as soon as the price dropped below \$40/quintal, in any case. Only with respect to the last point – a minimum price – was a concession made, and here the Minister informed the *Camara* that plans were already developed to provide producers with a minimum price, should the world market price continue to fall.

This turn of events around the price decline of the late 1950s can be seen as a litmus test for the claim that a new relation of political forces had indeed been established, and that it continued to define national politics long after the initial historic struggle over the tax legislature at the beginning of that decade. Yet, it is also necessary to retain a certain perspective on this earlier legislation. For one thing, the Government had to compromise to the extent that no further taxes could be levied for a period of ten years. Even more important, the State had not undermined the economic base of the oligarchy – this was never the intention of any of the tax proposals of this period. It would be a mistake to see in this legislation, or the previous decrees of the Junta, for that matter, an attempt at radical reform that would eliminate the landowning and commercial oligarchy that up until then had dominated the economic and political affairs of the nation. Such was not the case, although certain elements in the Social Democratic Party, not to mention the now proscribed Communist party, clearly favoured a more radical reform. The essence of this legislation, however, was of a different nature.

Its sigificance was probably best articulated by the editors of the *Diario de Costa Rica*, which had taken a pro–Government view throughout the intense campaign against the tax legislation and had waged its own campaign against the polemics of the big coffee interests in *La Nacion*. In an editorial written just after the new tax legislation was passed in the legislature (January,1952), and exceptional for its candour on this subject, it is argued that the campaign of the wealthy over this tax was not a product of their interest in the national economy and their concern with productivity, as they claimed, but rather the narrow interests of a specific economic class. The editorial goes on to offer these same influential interests the following advice.

Do not fall into the class struggle but rather commit yourselves to the search for an understanding between all classes, and thus strive for the prosperity and greatness of Costa Rica.

There is something we want to express with the utmost sincerity. We sincerely feel that, by adopting the stand we took, we have defended the interests of all coffee growers better than the growers themselves who have been blinded by the interests of the class they belong to.[34]

What the editors argue here to be the merits of their public position is most insightful, I think, in determining, in retrospect, the real significance of the State's role in this political conjuncture. It suggests that, had the *cafetaleros* been allowed to pursue their narrow, and what were essentially short–term economic interests, the outcome would not only have been prejudicial to other social classes in society, but also prejudicial to themselves. Beyond this, it suggests there is a need for a force (and this is usually of necessity the State) to break the political power traditionally exercised by the dominant class, in order that the longer–term interests of society, and of the dominant class in particular, can be best protected and even actively fostered.

Any crudely instrumentalist view of the relationship between the dominant class and the State in capitalist society would have difficulty accounting for the legislation we have examined here, and indeed a good deal of the political activity since the Junta of 1948 took power. It would be a mistake to look upon the various decrees issued or proposed since 1948, including the ill–fated tax on wealth and the coffee tax, as ploys intended to dupe the people into believing in a reform programme that was not meant to be seriously pursued by its proponents. History is certainly not devoid of its conspiracies, but this was not one of them.

On the other hand, despite the serious intentions of certain elements in Costa Rican society, most notably the Social Democratic forces, to limit the economic prerogatives of the oligarchy, and indeed get a hold of some of the surplus that these interests had historically controlled, the oligarchy moved quickly to protect its economic position, and with some success. In the end, the historic compromise that was arrived at in the early 1950s had the oligarchy losing control over certain economic domains, such as banking and the freedom to dispose of foreign exchange earning in the free market. Through tax legislation the large coffee concerns were forced to cede a portion of the economic surplus generated in this sphere of activity also. Nevertheless, as a class the old, largely agrarian–based bourgeoisie was hardly decimated economically. No serious attempt had been made to expropriate their economic base through an agrarian reform, for instance, despite serious inequities in land distribution and the concentration of coffee production.[35] The legislation creating the *Oficina del Café*, moreover, had ensured that the large growers and processors would control the direction of the State institution that most directly affected the operation of their enterprises.[36] They had blocked further tax levies for the next decade, and had managed to ensure that much of the Government revenues generated by these taxes would go to the development of infrastructure to service and develop the coffee economy. Finally, despite some limitation on the amount of profits they could extract from producers, that which they were allowed was guaranteed them above their production costs – an enviable position that small coffee growers did not enjoy.

Notes

1. See reference to Rodrigo Facio's article in footnote 21, Chapter 4.
2. Ameringer, *Don Pépé*, p.7.
3. Ibid.
4. This tax apparently raised some 7200000 colons per year for the State in the early 1950s (*La Prensa Libre*, 29 November 1952), a substantial sum from one tax measure at this time. It was roughly comparable to revenues gained from the later and more controversial *advalorem* tax on coffee.
5. This is mentioned in an editorial in the *Diario de Costa Rica*, (18 January 1952).
6. This served to augment State revenues, writes one observer, in the following way. 'The Central Bank of Costa Rica sells some 15 to 20 million of these dollars per year in the Free Exchange Market (Mercado Libre de Cambio) with which it obtains a profit of 1.03 per dollar, which is destined to buy State bonds which gradually pass, together with their interest, to engross the capitals of the National Commercial Banks'. Fernando Barrenechea C. *Una Organización para Empresarios del Café (San Jose: Escuela Superior de Administración Publica, 1956), p.17.*
7. Barrenechea, *Una Organizacion*, p.17
8. Barrenechea mentions that, in the early 1950s, 80 of the country's 125 *beneficiadores* and 70 large 'producers' constitued the membership of the *Camara de Cafetaleros* which was founded in 1948. *Una Organización*, p.10.
9. The PSD forces, for their part, were better prepared this time and succeeded in presenting their case to the public by means of all the major newspapers. Again it was Rodrigo Facio who marshalled the arguments in favour of exchange controls. In the first of a series of articles he presented the basic elements determining the country's monetary problems of that time. Given the severe internal inflation during and since the war, he noted, 'the country had circulating many more colons to buy much fewer dollars, relative to the situation prevailing in the time during and after the War. If the exchange rate had been free, it (the price of the dollar in colons) would have risen until an adjustment in the supply and demand of dollars was achieved. But

as the exchange rate of the dollar has been fixed by law, at one dollar to 5.62 colons from 1937–46 and one dollar to 5.67 colons from 1947 to the present, that is, practically at the same level, the result was that the country has had, more or less since 1944–5 many more colons to buy, at the same price, many fewer dollars. The consequence is well known: the restriction of the official international reserves of the country and the formation, in the official market as well, of a glut of requests for currency awaiting payment.' *Obras*, p.310.

10. See, for instance, the series of articles authored by a prominent coffee grower and *beneficiador*, Florentino Castro, in *La Nacion*, (2 and 8 March 1950).

11. See Law No.115 (6 July,1940). See also Law No.37, (25 March,1939). These are listed in Alvaro Jimenez *Castro, Leyes y Reglamentos Usuales Sobre Café* (San José: Oficina del Café, 78).

12. This was Law No.1141 of 2 March, 1950. This legislation and its implementation is discussed in some detail in *La Nacion* (3 October 1950).

13. See 'En Defensa de los "cafetaleros de solar"', *La Nacion*, (21 December 1951).

14. For a detailed description of the rally of small producers and reportage of the major speeches given see the following: 'Cinco Mil Caficultores de Distintas Partes del País Se Deciden a Luchar Contra el Nuevo Impuesto', *La Nacion* (24 July 1951).

15. Ibid.

16. See, for example, the article by the President of the *Camara de Cafetaleros* at this time, Jorge Borbon Castro, 'No Son los Grandes Intereses Cafetaleros las que Unicamente Repudian el Proyecto', *La Nacion*, (11 September 1951).

17. *La Nacion*, (15 January 1950).

18. See the article, 'El Poder Ejecutivo Necesita El Impuesto Advalorem Para Atender Todo el Servicio de los Bonos de Café', *Diario de Costa Rica*, (11 August 1950).

19. *La Nacion* (15 October 1951).

20. *Diario de Costa Rica* (11 August 1950).

21. This was particularly so after 1949, when prices rose dramatically until after the mid 1950s as demand outstripped supply. See Thomas Greer, *An Oligopoly: The World Coffee Economy and Stabilisation Schemes* (New York: Dunellen Publishing Co., 1971), p.379.

22. See his article, 'Sobre el Banco Cafetalero', in *La Nacion*, (16 October, 1951.)

23. Most notable in this respect were a series of articles published in *La Nacion* during 1951 authored by the large grower and *beneficiador*, Florentino Castro.

24. This is mentioned in the remarkable editorial dealing with the final version of the law of 1952, published in the *Diario de Costa Rica*, (18 January 1952). This situation is not too surprising given the centralisation of processing facilities in the country that had proceeded steadily for many years.

25. See Law No. 1141 in *La Gaceta*, Seccion Oficial, (año LXXIV, no.21, January, 1952). In addition to the 9 per cent, the *beneficiador* could also

make certain deductions in his favour having to do primarily with various expenses involved the processing activity (see article no.6).

26. *La Nacion* (21 December 1951).
27. Stone (1973), for example, mentions this tax in passing without discussion of the political turmoil it provoked, nor of the significance of having the incidence of the tax fall on the *beneficiadores*, rather than the *productores*, as had historically been the case with taxes on coffee.
28. The jump in revenues in the 1946–7 fiscal year is an exception to this. The reasons for this sudden rise are not readily apparent to this writer.
29. UN, Yearbook of National Account, (1950:54). It is the rise in 'indirect taxes' that was most noticable.
30. *La Prensa Libre* (15 and 18 January 1952).
31. See, for example, the articles by the *Camara's* legal counsel, Edgar Odio Gonzalez, in *La Nacion* (12 and 13 August 1958.
32. See 'Politica actual y futura del Gobierno en defensa de la industria del Café', *La Nacion* (18 December 1958).
33. By 1958 this tax generated 13 million colones annually, See 'Demanda de los Cafetaleras Provocaria Alza en Costa de la Vida y Reajuste de Salarios', *Diario de Costa Rica* (5 July 1958).
34. *Diario de Costa Rica* (18 January 1952).
35. Seligson compares land concentration in Costa Rica to that of the other Central American countries, such as Guatemala and El Salvador, both having a high degree of concentration. Using the Gini coefficient, the results for 1950 are as follows, respectively: .899; .868; and .832, making Costa Rica the country with the highest concentration of land. See also chapter 7 for a discussion on the problem of concentration of land and production in Costa Rica at this time. *The Peasants*, p.47–49.
36. According to the decree of the Junta of 1948, the *Oficina del Café* would be directed by a Junta of five members, composed of a representative of the producers, the *beneficiadores*, the roasters, the exporters and a member from the Ministry of the Economy (Jimenez Castro, *Leyes*, pp.25–6). There was no stipulation that a processor who was also a producer and exporter could not serve as a member of the Junta Directiva either. Indeed, the *Oficina's* directorate was never structured so that it would represent the mass of small producers in the country.

6 Coffee and the Costa Rican Model of Development

> The development of a country is a slow process, much like the growth of a tree . . . And, as things are like this, it is necessary to plant trees, and undertake long term projects, and to have patience. (J. Figueres, *Cartas a un Cuidadano*, 1956)

After 1950 or so as part of the new development model envisioned by Costa Rica's political leadership, the State became a powerful social force in creating the preconditions for the modernisation of the economy. This was nowhere more true than with the nation's coffee sector. And the State's ability to make coffee the motor of economic development would not only determine the resources that could be put into a needed diversification of the country's economic structure, it would also inevitably impinge on the longer–term success or failure of a programme of welfare capitalism and the liberal democratic political structures that were just being given shape in the early 1950s.

In approaching the elaboration of State programmes with respect to this industry, it is important to keep in mind certain developments touched upon earlier, developments of a more clearly ideological and political nature. In the first place, there was the creation of a circle of intellectuals with an outlook distinct from that of the oligarchy in terms of its orientation towards developmentalist and redistributionist policies achieved by means of an 'active' national state. Secondly, the successful merger of these intellectuals with a wider group of professionals, entrepreneurs, students, etc., favouring a change in the *status quo* which, under the forceful leadership of Figueres, was able to assert itself politically, over the organised proletariat of the banana plantations and the cities, and the disorganised traditional bourgeoisie. Finally, these social forces – which only later found their concrete political expression in the *Partido Liberación*

93

Nacional – were able to force an historical compromise with the large coffee and commercial interests, which gave to the State certain crucial fiscal instruments, and a share in the social surplus generated by coffee.

The modernisation of coffee production entaiiled dramatic advances in productivity per unit of land, occasioned by a transformation of the technological basis of production. This process was predicated on the prior social reorganisation of production and together these changes inaugurated what Marx referred to as the real subsumption of the labour process by capital[1] in the coffee sphere. This modernisation and rationalisation the coffee complex had, in turn, further consequences for the class structure in the countryside, particularly the strengthening of the producer-processor fraction of the coffee bourgeoisie. Before considering the changes in this sphere, it will be helpful to first examine the socio-economic structure, that existed just prior to this period of transformation.

6.1 THE COFFEE INDUSTRY CIRCA 1950: THE STRUCTURE OF LANDHOLDINGS

The belief that Costa Rica is a land of peasant farmers, at the core of which lies a numerous class of small and medium coffee producers is still strong today. As the author of an important recent study on coffee in Costa Rica argues, 'both the Registry of Property of 1867 and following years, and the Coffee Census of 1935 clearly show that the *Meseta Central* developed as a region where small and medium size *fincas* predominated, whose owners, in large part, were *campesinos*.'[2]

In speaking of the 'predominance' of this class of small holders, however, particular attention must be given to the meaning of this word. As we have seen in Chapter 2, the term can only really refer to a numerical predominance, since an analysis of the coffee complex as a whole shows that small coffee farmers have historically been subordinated to the coffee bourgeoisie, both socio–economically and politically.

A better perspective on the structure of landholding within the Costa Rican coffee economy can be gained through a comparison with neighbouring coffee producing countries. Fortunately, the existence of a comprehensive United Nations study in the 1950s of El Salvador and Colombia provides us with two instructive points of

Table 6.1   Area in coffee by size of farm: Costa Rica, Colombia, El
Salvador

Size	Costa Rica		Colombia		El Salvador	
	No.(%)	*area (%)*	*No.(%)*	*area (%)*	*No.(%)*	*area (%)*
Up to 10 ha.	58	27	94	62	88	22
10 to 100 ha.	37	46	5	33	11	48
Greater than 100 ha.	4	27	.06	4	.9	28

Source: Censo agropecuario de Costa Rica, 1950 and 1955. (Figures are
only approximate); *Coffee in Latin America: I Columbia and El Salvador,*
(New York: UN/ECLA, 1958) p.27 Table 18 and p.109 Table 1. (Data for
Colombia and El Salvador are for 1955–6 and 1958, respectively.)

comparison. This survey shows that, with respect to the distribution
of landholdings at this time, Costa Rica fell somewhere in between
the Colombian and El Salvadorean situations (see Table 6.1). The
structure of landholdings in Colombia more clearly deserved the
term 'peasant economy', for not only did small commodity producers
constitute the vast majority of growers, but they also controlled an
amount of coffee land more or less proportionate to their numbers.
Very large farms were not a significant feature of the coffee
sector, at least. El Salvador is at the other extreme, in this
respect. Small peasant producers predominated here too, at least
in numerical terms, and yet the amount of land they controlled is
disproportionately small. A small minority of farms of medium large
and large size controlled the great bulk of the land there.[3]
The situation of Costa Rica was somewhere between these
polar extremes, although tending more towards the El Salvadorean
situation. Small producers constituted a substantial majority, though
not as overwhelmingly so as in the other countries. Yet the amount
of land they controlled was disproportionately small, though not so
extreme as in El Salvador. At the other end of the landholding
spectrum, about 4 per cent of the farms had close to a third of all
land in coffee. Clearly, the main distinguishing feature about Costa
Rica in this respect was the fairly substantial number of 'medium'
size farmers, that is, those with over 10 hectares but less than 100
hectares of coffee land. A majority of these, in fact, were over 20

hectares in size.[4] The presence of this group in the countryside did reduce somewhat the extreme polarisation that we found in the agrarian structure of El Salvador, although it must be kept in mind that only landholdings where coffee was grown are being considered here. If one were to include all landholdings in Costa Rica in an analysis of its agrarian structure, a great deal more concentration would be evident – in fact even more so than other Central American countries, including El Salvador and Guatemala, according to one calculation.[5]

If it is evident that small peasant producers in Costa Rica did not predominate, either in terms of the land or the production they controlled, it is also true that these two factors are only partial indicators of the real structural position the majority of coffee producers have historically found themselves in. It does not tell anything about their relationship to other sectors of society, in particular to those controlling processing and credit that are practically as integral to the coffee industry as land itself. In the depression years before and during the Second World War, the concentration of these two factors had increased as the number of *beneficiadores* declined. Of the 220 *beneficios* that existed in 1935, only 125 remained by the early 1950s.[6] As this process developed, the area serviced by each *beneficio* expanded concomitantly, so that after the War a single *beneficio* served a far greater area than it had 50 or 60 years previous.[7] In addition, despite the creation of a nationalised banking system, the great bulk of the credit going to growers was still funnelled through the same powerful group that controlled the nation's coffee processing facilities – the *beneficiadores*.

6.2 THE ECONOMIC SITUATION OF THE COFFEE PRODUCERS

The conjuncture of high prices during the early 1950s served to mask for a while the longstanding stagnation of the nation's agriculture, and particularly the most dynamic component – coffee production. While the momentary surge in growers' incomes for a time diverted attention away from the impending agrarian dilemma, it was clear that serious problems lay ahead. At a conference organised around

Table 6.2   Costa Rica: coffee exports, selected years, 1900–52

Year	Quintals Exported
1900	293 000
1910	312 000
1925	333 000
1935	464 000
1940	406 000
1943–44	412 000
1944–45	515 000
1945–46	283 000
1946–47	395 000
1947–48	506 000
1948–49	359 000
1949–50	433 000
1950–51	362 000
1951–52	385 000

Source: Barrenechea *Una Organizatión para Empresarios del Café*, (San José Escuela Superior de Administración Publica, 1956) p.3; M. Seligson *Agrarian Capitalism and the Transformation of Peasant Society: Coffee in Costa Rica*, (Council of International Studies, SUNY at Buffalo, 1975), Table 2.

the coffee industry in Latin America, one agronomist summed up the situation of the nation's coffee economy in the following manner.

> Coffee production in Costa Rica is in a state of complete exploitation. There is no technology. The agriculturalists are not concerned with conservation. They cultivate coffee like a mine, taking out and never returning anything to the land.[8]

Barrenechea's study provides a good indication of the state of the industry at this time. After the 1930s when the first comprehensive coffee census was taken, the total area planted in coffee had remained at about 69 000 *manzanas* until 1950.[9] Meanwhile, as Table 6.2 makes clear, total production had declined over this period, with the exportable harvest in 1950 considerably less than it had been 10 years earlier. Indeed no well-defined trend towards expansion of the nation's coffee production had been evident since the turn of the century. Productivity per unit of land in coffee had thus actually fallen over these years to an average yield of less than 6 *fanegas* per *manzana*, with a third of the plantings long past their prime producing age.[10] Yields in Costa Rica were among the lowest in Latin America, so low in fact that by 1950 many of the *beneficios* in the country utilised only half of their capacity.[11] Moreover, agronomists at the time were convinced that Costa Rica had appropriate ecological conditions to produce a minimum of 20 *fanegas* per manzana, and that average yields of 60 *fanegas* or more were not uncommon in other areas of the world particularly suited to coffee, such as Hawaii.[12] Production began to increase after 1952, approaching 600 000 quintals by the mid 1950s,[13] but this initial expansion took place within the logic of the traditional system of cultivation. In other words, growers responded to higher prices by extending the area under production, not by intensifying existing cultivation. The cost of labour was an especially central aspect of production costs, comprising about 60 per cent or more of total costs, and was on average two to three times as expensive as other producing countries.[14] Hourly wages for coffee workers had more than doubled since the mid 1940s though inflation would have seriously reduced any real increase in incomes to labour.[15] Nevertheless, this would have represented a real cost to growers whose profits were dependent on coffee prices determined externally, prices which increased little until the 1950s. For the large growers it was clear then, given a stagnating or even declining productivity and the rising costs of production inputs, that the further extension of the area under cultivation was not going to provide a longer term solution to a problem that was rooted in the structure of production itself.

These were some key dimensions of the national coffee industry in the early 1950s, both structural and economic. The crisis of this crucial sphere of the economy, though attenuated by the coffee boom of the early part of the decade, was longstanding and had both social and economic dimensions. The former entailed the plight of the thousands of small coffee farmers, who not only had much less productive farms,[16] but typically did not have sufficient land to meet their subsistence needs without working off their farms. This crisis also involved, inevitably, the landless and semi-proletarianised labour force that worked on the capitalist coffee haciendas, where living standards had been seriously eroded since the 1930s.

The economic crisis, on the other hand, was one of low and declining productivity and affected all producers, although naturally capitalist and peasant producers would be affected in different ways according to their differing cost structures. At this point I wish to examine the development of State sponsored programmes to confront this dilemma, and consider the forces influencing the specific directions that were taken.

6.3 CONFRONTING THE AGRARIAN PROBLEM: A POLICY FOR THE COFFEE PRODUCERS

Confronted with this social crisis in the countryside, together with the return of economic problems as coffee prices declined after 1956, the response of the *Liberación Nacional* dominated government went fundamentally in one direction: the increase of production by improving the productivity of the nation's coffee lands. The provision of special assistance to those producers less able to finance the necessary modernisation was in the end subordinated to this policy objective, although some formal attempts were made to broaden the overall impact. How this actually affected the different types of producers involved in the coffee economy will be dealt with below.

The direction of this State development policy first becomes apparent in the programmatic statements of the Government's leading spokesmen, and particularly with Figueres himself. During his first terms as President, he kept the problem of the low productivity of coffee in Costa Rica in the public eye, going so far as to argue that any economic progress for the nation was dependent upon increasing productivity of the coffee lands.[17] Figueres managed to avoid the issue of land reform in these early years, entirely favouring the productionist solution to the agrarian problem.[18] By this, however, the PLN and Figueres were not being inconsistent with their earlier thinking on agrarian matters. Despite their frequent focus on the problems of the coffee economy, even the most articulate and systematic critique of coffee monoculture – that of Rodrigo Facio, in which the high degree of concentration of means of production is expressly noted – did not go so far as to call for changes in the structure of land tenure, let alone offer any more radical solutions to the social and economic dilemmas posed by the private appropriation of coffee lands. Neither the original twelve point programme of the Social Democractic Party in the 1940's or the Fundamental Charter of *Liberacion Nacional* offered any more commitment to structural reforms in agriculture.[19]

The writings and statements of key figures in the *liberacionista* group, moreover, contain little or no analysis of the internal structure of coffee production. At most they focus on either the deleterious effects produced by the dependence on one basic crop for much of the national wealth, or on the economic performance of the coffee economy as a whole, ignoring the fact that different classes with conflicting interests constituted this sphere of activity. To the extent that the inequalities between producers were recognised, solutions never went beyond the proposal for special assistance to disadvantaged sectors. The roots of the inequalities that are to be found in the way the system of production, commercialisation and financing of coffee was organised were rarely confronted.

That *Liberacion Nacional* in its political practice should pay little attention to such structural problems as the concentration of land and resources, and the impoverishment of the rural population, must be viewed in another light as well. Key figures at the centre of this movement, and most notably Figueres himself, were less than at arms length with respect to the economic activities over which the future agrarian policies were to have a profound influence. In 1953, the same year he assumed the Presidency, Figueres became part owner with his brother of one of the largest coffee haciendas in Costa Rica, located in the Turrialba region. His farm was later to become a microcosm for the technological advances he and other *liberacionistas* envisioned for the nation's agriculture, and the Figueres' themselves can be seen as the pioneer modernising landowners in contemporary Costa Rica.[20]

If Figueres was himself a most significant representative of modernising agrarian capital, the same could be said of others at the centre of *Liberación Nacional*. Francisco Orlich, among the most influential of *liberacionistas* (a member of the Junta of 1948 and the successful PLN presidential candidate in 1962), was the largest coffee exporter and a major *beneficiador*, with extensive landholdings in the San Ramon area.[21] And despite the fact that *Liberación Nacional* contained a considerable left faction that occasionally constituted an important internal force, it was the former men and their circle, and not the latter, who largely molded PLN policies and determined their practical application through such institutions as the National Banking System, the Ministry of Agriculture and the Coffee Office.

6.4 MODERNISING PRODUCTION: CREDIT FOR THE 'REPOPULATION' OF PLANTATIONS

A cornerstone in the model of agrarian development that was being elaborated was the replanting of the coffee plantations, the *cafetales*, with new hybrid varieties capable of much higher yields given the appropriate conditions.[22] In 1950 almost 90 per cent of the country's coffee farms had been planted with the variety *Café Arabigo,* which provided an excellent quality coffee but at the expense of low yields per plant.[23] As mentioned, a third of the country's plantings were long past their prime productive age. With the gradual replanting of these old and unproductive *cafetales,* the foundations were to be laid for the transformation of coffee production.

The introduction of the new high yielding coffee varieties in fact produced a major technical transformation in the way coffee is produced. Not only is the system of shading provided by overhanging trees abandoned in favour of a minimum or no shade at all, but the arrangement of the plantings is considerably affected, so that the density of trees per unit of land can be increased from 200 to 500 per cent.[24] In addition, pruning methods changed and the applications of herbicides, fungicides and especially substantial applications of fertilisers became integral to the successful cultivation of the new varieties. During the 1950s the old plantings of *Café Arabigo* began to be replaced by such local hybrids as *Hibrido Tico* and *Villa Sarchi.* By the 1960s even more productive varieties, such as *Caturra* were introduced from Brazil. Towards the end of the decade almost half of the coffee plantings in the country were of the new varieties.

By 1950 or so the National Bank was already allocating funds for the replanting of coffee. At this time, experiments were being carried out by the Ministry of Agriculture, in conjunction with a number of the nation's major coffee growers,[25] to find the most suitable combination of new varieties and technological inputs for the different ecological zones. In 1954 the Banco Anglo Costarricense began a programme of 'repopulation' of ten thousand *manzanas* of coffee land over a period of 5 years, about one fifth of all land in coffee, at a total cost of 25 million colons (or 2,500 colons per *manzana*).[26] This longer–term credit that was to be provided to producers had particularly favourable terms, so that recipients were under no obligation to repay the principal and interest until the fourth year after the initial payment, by which time the replanted coffee would have begun to provide substantial and increasing yields. Repayment, moreover, was scheduled over a period of four years, so that eight years would lapse before the grower had to cover the loan completely.

It must be pointed out that this programme was not to be available to all farmers having *cafetales* of low productivity The small, so–called 'marginal' farmers, those with less than two *manzanas* of land in coffee, were eliminated from the beginning as it was not considered feasible to include them in the program. Assuming that on average with the traditional methods of cultivation one *manzana* of coffee land was planted with 1000 trees, it is apparent from the data provided in Facio's classic study that farmers with less than two thousand trees (i.e., those with less than two *manzanas* of coffee land) were in fact the great bulk of the country's coffee growers – approximately 75 per cent in 1940.[27] This 'detail' is somehow overlooked in one of the most important economic histories of coffee in Costa Rica to date.[28]

6.5 PROMOTION OF FERTILISERS: THE SECOND CORNERSTONE OF MODERNISATION

The primacy of expanding the regular use of fertilisers to achieve a solution to the economic crisis affecting coffee production has been noted in a major study conducted by the Coffee Office.

> If one analyses carefully the characteristics of the different systems of coffee cultivation, we find that the basic factor in achieving the desired reduction in costs through the increase of productivity lies in a system of intensive fertilisation. . . . Fertiliser is the basic factor and indispensable starting point for the realisation of any program for the improvement of the plantings, and by itself it is of real value for increasing production per unit of area.[29]

Beginning in 1950 the State set aside revenues to finance the importation of additional quantities of fertilisers.[30] Subsequently, other resources were made available for the utilisation of capital goods, agro–chemicals and fertilisers by coffee growers, by the Ministry of Agriculture and Industry, the Coffee Office and the National Bank. Particularly noteworthy were new programmes providing credit over the medium term, as up until then credit to producers had been normally on a yearly basis to finance the standard costs of production and harvesting.[31]

Further measures were taken at this time, as well, to spur the introduction of fertilisers in coffee cultivation. The law of Economic Defense (no. 1208) of 1950 had already placed a limit on the profits local merchants could make on the commercialisation of fertilisers, while a law freeing imported fertilisers from all duties was passed in 1954.[32] Furthermore, the Department of Agriculture was by this time operating a plant in Patarra producing the nutrient calcium carbonate, and providing this at cost to farmers.[33]

In 1953, the first year of Figueres' term of office, the Government introduced its plan of financial aid to growers, principally in the form of special credits and technical assistance, to spur the use of chemical fertilisers on a much wider scale.[34] Like the credit programmes discussed previously, loans were provided over a period of several years, without amortisation over the first couple of years until production began to increase. An unfortunate condition, at least as far as the thousands of small marginal producers were concerned, was the fact that such credit was only make available to cover three quarters of the cost of the fertiliser. As Hall suggests, 'this probably discouraged many *campesinos*, since it was difficult for them to take from their own funds the remaining 25 per cent to acquire an element of production that, during the first three years, would not translate into a significant increase in the productivity of their coffee.'[35]

Coincident with the world price downturn of the late 1950s the State unveiled a plan that would have dramatically accelerated the incorporation of chemical fertilisers in the *cafetales* and completed the transformation from extensive to intensive cultivation in a much broader range of coffee *fincas*. At base, the *Plan de Abonamiento Intensivo* sought to (i) reach the very numerous small producers who did not apply fertilisers regularly, by making the purchase of fertilisers on an annual basis obligatory for all farmers and, (ii) through specific controls avoid the chronic problem of having credits intended to finance productive inputs for coffee from being diverted to other spheres that may have been more lucrative in the short term. The *Plan* was notably ambitious in its scope, in that not only did it intend to make fertiliser use obligatory, but it proposed to make this realisable by means of specific measures which would dramatically reduce the price of fertiliser (in large part imported at this time), by some 30 percent or more. It was felt that Costa Rica was the only coffee producing nation that could successfully carry out such a scheme, because it was only here where the State had the key institutional mechanisms to implement it and make it effective.[36]

This programme faced a contradiction, however, which ultimately prevented its planned implementation. While it was a response to a downturn in the world price, and sought to provide a solution to the crisis of producers by assisting the latter to raise productivity, the growers were characteristically much less likely to invest in such productive inputs when their incomes declined. While the obligatory nature of the *Plan* might have helped to resolve this matter, its goal to augment production did not offer much of a solution to the conjuncture of low prices and the crisis of overproduction of coffee that lay at its roots.

6.6 THE ROLE OF ANNUAL CREDITS TO COFFEE PRODUCERS

The yearly financing of coffee production, from cultivation through harvesting and the commercialisation of the crop, was not specific to the post-1950 period and the establishment of a nationalised banking system. Nevertheless, in the years after the creation of the latter in 1950, the amount of annual credits going to coffee producers in particular, expanded rather dramatically, as I show below. The attitude of the State towards the coffee economy is not only suggested by the volume of credits directed towards the latter, but also by the rates of interest producers were charged, since, as the price of capital, the interest rate in effect helps determine the relative costs of capital and labour. Where the price of capital is made artificially low the substitution of capital for labour power is 'naturally' favoured. Both factors should thus be examined. In Costa Rica this type of financing has proceeded in three stages each year. The first, the *etapa de asistencia*, is aimed at helping producers cover costs incurred with the actual process of cultivation. These credits become available in the month of February. The second stage, the *etapa de recolección*, beginning in the month of July, is intended to finance the extra costs incurred by producers during the harvest period, especially the need to hire on substantial numbers of extra labourers for a short period of time. The third stage of credits, the *etapa de mercadeo*, is destined solely to processors to ensure that they have sufficient resources to realise the provisional liquidations of the harvest with their client producers.

The role of British capital in providing such credits to Costa Rican coffee farmers until well into the present century was especially prominent. The dislocations of the Second World War essentially forced local capitalists to take over this role, which was taken over again by the National Bank and considerably expanded. The amount of credit that was channelled by the National Banking System for each productive cycle of coffee has been expanding rapidly since the mid 1950s and continued to do so, unlike the other types of credits discussed above which have been restricted in more recent years. By the early 1970s the volume of loan capital going to coffee producers was over five times that of the early 1950s, having increased from 51.2 million colons in 1950–1 to 271.6 million colons in the 1970–1 harvest year.[37] What this meant was that not only did the supply of credit keep up with production, which itself was expanding at a steady rate, but that these annual credits expanded at an even faster rate.

Producers thus had an increasing amount of credit available for each *fanega* of coffee they produced in the decades after 1950. Data provided by the Central Bank, for example, demonstrate that while the average amount that each *fanega* of coffee was financed in the early 1950s was around 137 colons, by the early 1960s this sum had increased to around 162 colons per *fanega*, or slightly over 20 per cent. By the last half of the 1970s the amount of credit going to each *fanega* of coffee had increased over 50 per cent from the early 1950s.[38]

The fact that the amount of credit supplied annually for each *fanega* of coffee was increasing is especially significant when it is realised that these types of credit were, in terms of their volume, by far the most important credits going to producers.[39] Not only were these credits offered to producers on favourable terms, but they were granted more or less automatically, through a long established institutional set–up in which the *beneficiador* remained central in terms of local distribution. What this meant is that coffee farmers would have available to them loan capital on favourable terms over and above their normal production requirements to apply to the improvement of their *cafetales* by means of increased fertilisation and the incorporation of other technological inputs, replanting, etc. This would be the case especially during periods of high coffee prices.[40]

In general then, it would appear that these annual credits, particularly those allocated to the *etapa de asistencia*, have played a most central part in expanding the use of those circulating elements of productive consumption (herbicides, pesticides, and especially fertilisers)[41] and certain elements of fixed capital such as irrigation systems, that are chiefly responsible for the increase in the yield per unit of land, and the reduction of costs per unit of land as well.[42] State policies concerning the coffee economy have thus favoured an 'expansionist' approach, but one which is strongly biased towards intensification as the road to an increase in national output. Indeed, after the mid 1960s credits 'for investments', such as in land to expand area in production or in installations, were cut back dramatically,[43] in accordance with Costa Rica's commitment to limit its production under the terms of the International Coffee Convention.

6.7 CREATING THE TECHNICAL CONDITIONS FOR MODERNISATION

The role of the State in the development, testing and diffusion of agricultural technologies has been especially noteworthy with respect to coffee, at least for the years after 1950. Since the first experiments with new varieties carried out on the farms of some of the country's most important *cafetaleros*, State involvement in the development of new planting techniques and technological inputs has been a central aspect of overall strategy aimed at the intensification of coffee farms.

State initiatives of this nature took place under the 'umbrella' of the Coffee Office in cooperation with the Ministry of Agriculture and Livestock, and especially through the Centre for Investigations in Coffee (CICAFE), which has a number of research stations in different ecological zones of the *Meseta Central*. Activities include: (1) the cultivation of new hybrid varieties to further gains in yields per plant, increase resistance to disease (especially coffee rust) and development of trees of a stature that is most easily accessible to harvesters, in order to reduce labour costs; (2) experimentation with fertiliser application; (3) production of seeds of high yielding varieties for distribution to producers and; (4) the testing of new planting and pruning arrangements. In the experimental coffee processing facilities of CICAFE, and in its laboratories, testing of selected seed varieties, new hormones affecting the maturation of the fruit and enzymes that determine the period of fermentation during processing have been undertaken.[44]

Certainly an important part of the reason for these experiments, as with some of those in the area of cultivation, is the imperative of reducing particularly labour–intensive tasks. Harvesting is one aspect of the productive process where trees of low stature are more easily worked by women and children, an important consideration as able bodied men become more expensive and scarce. Another labour intensive activity is the final processing of the coffee bean to remove the mucilage covering it after the pulp of the coffee cherry is removed. New technologies to replace the old system of tank fermentation are being developed and should become more widespread in *beneficios* in the future. In addition to this research, considerable agricultural extension work takes place throughout the year, with hundreds of visits being made to assist in the diffusion of technologies associated with more intensive production methods.[45]

6.8 THE CO-OPERATIVE MOVEMENT AND COFFEE PRODUCERS

The concept of cooperatives in the spheres of finance, production, commercialisation and consumption has a long history in Costa Rica, though a viable and expanding co-operative movement in various sectors of the economy is a more recent phenomenon. In the 1940s the intellectuals of the *Centro* were interested in the promotion of co-operatives, and this interest eventually emerged in the policies of *liberacionista* governments as well. Co-operatives are of varying importance in the national economy, depending upon which sphere of economic activity one is talking about. There is no doubt, however, that their impact has been substantial in the coffee economy. Clearly, the co-operative movement has had some success in penetrating the spheres of capitalist accumulation formerly the domain of the oligarchy; in particular processing and the provision of certain types of agricultural credit. For this reason alone it merits consideration here.

Although there existed during the 1950s a Department of Co-operatives as part of the National Bank, it was only in the 1960s that more serious attempts were made to institutionalise co-operatives and expand their influence in the economy. With respect to coffee, one author notes that the development of co-operatives was given real impetus in the period of 'tense' relations between producers and processors during the price slump of the late 1950s and early 1960s. The more marginal coffee farmers outside the Central Valley were hardest pressed and were the ones to take the initiative.[46] These co-operatives were oriented to providing processing, commercialisation and credit services to their members, with the establishment or purchase of *beneficios* to process members' coffee being the most visible and costly co-operative investments. This development was given a considerable boost with the establishment of the Federation of Co-operatives of Coffee Growers (FEDECOOP), in 1962 at the initiative of the Department of Co-operatives.[47] This organisation was oriented to solving major problems of commercialising the coffee of its members and providing technical assistance, problems which had plagued early co-operatives. By the late 1960s in fact, FEDECOOP managed the commercialisation of some 70 per cent of its member's coffee through its agents established in various international markets. In this way co-operative members were able to circumvent the profit made by the heavily monopolised exporting business.[48]

Co-operatives were given further encouragement by the State with the Law of Co-operative Associations.[49] This law also provided a regulatory framework within which co-operatives were confined to work. Co-operative enterprises were granted a number of concessions under this law, among these were included exoneration from payment of the land tax for 10 years, exoneration from the payment of customs duties on tools, materials, machinery, fertilisers, agro–chemicals and other necessary imported goods, and preferential rates on electrical power consumed. Finally, the fact that the Banco Nacional de Costa Rica had several of its own *beneficios* available to create an embryonic co-operative sector was initially a further impetus.[50]

The establishment of an over–arching organisation such as FEDECOOP to take care of crucial spheres like commercialisation, and with the establishment by law of important concessions to co-operatives, would appear to have made them particularly attractive to small and medium growers. Undoubtedly, part of this attractiveness was due to the depressed prices through the late 1960s and the necessity for producers to reduce their costs whenever possible. In this political and economic context the expansion of co-operative enterprises has been dramatic, at least after 1960. The few co-operative processing plants existing in 1960 had increased to 31 by 1979. These included several *beneficios* as large or larger than most owned by private capital, with the most modern electronic and mechanical equipment presently available.[51] Though only slightly less than three thousand *fanegas* of coffee was processed in co-op *beneficios* in 1957–8 (a small part of the approximately 177000 *fanegas* produced that year) this had expanded five–fold by 1963–4, and more than tripled again to over 53000 *fanegas* by 1970.[52] By this latter date co-operatives were thus processing a very substantial proportion of the country's coffee harvest, about one third by 1975, and the trend was for this to increase.

Figure 6.1   Costa Rica: Area in coffee and total production 1942–78

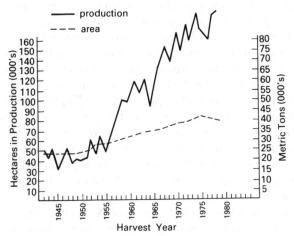

Sources: Oficina del Café. *Plan de Abonamiento Intensivo,* (San Jose: 1959); Oficina del Café, *Informe Sobre la Actividad Cafetalera de Costa Rica.* (San José, 1979.)

6.9 EVIDENCE OF PRODUCTIVITY CHANGES IN COFFEE CULTIVATION

The Social Democratic ideological current in Costa Rica has long been critical of the old agro-exporting scheme of the oligarchy, and of the inequities that derived from the concentration of resources in the coffee economy, in particular. Despite copious rhetoric over the years by *liberacionista* governments on the importance of the small agriculturalist, especially as a bulwark of the local variant of liberal democratic processes, at no time were serious efforts made to strengthen this group of producers through reform of the landholding structure, i.e. a redistribution of a vital and highly concentrated commodity – the land. In fact, as noted above, the essence of the Costa Rican model of agrarian development lay elsewhere. At this point it is necessary to examine more closely the nature of the modifications produced by a State oriented towards the modernisation of this key economic activity. This State, it need be reiterated, corresponded to a different balance of forces than that typical of the oligarchic State elsewhere in Central America, and yet it continued to be located in a context in which the material interests of the traditionally dominant class remain essentially intact.

Probably the most graphic indication that there has been a change in the way coffee is cultivated comes from a comparison of gross production figures and area in coffee land over several decades. Figure 6.1 shows that while coffee lands did expand from the late 1940s onwards, in the years after 1950 the relationship between the expansion in area and the increase in production altered dramatically. If we take the 1950 and the 1973 agricultural censuses as benchmarks, we see that the area in coffee production expanded about 60 per cent to around 80 thousand hectares. The expansion in production on the other hand, was disproportionately greater, at approximately 300 per cent, rising from an average of roughly 440000 quintals annually, to over 1.76 million quintals by the latter date. Thus, the shift to a more intensive form of cultivation is demonstrated by this historically unprecedented increase in the productivity of coffee land. Figures provided by the Ministry of Agriculture show that the average yield of coffee per hectare rose from about 8 *fanegas* to in excess of 20 *fanegas* per hectare by the early 1970s, an increase of about 170 per cent in two decades.[53] By the late 1970s, in fact, Costa Rica had virtually the highest productivity per hectare of any other coffee producing country in the world.[54] An increase of productivity of this magnitude is a testament to the efficacy of initiatives, especially those of the State, to transform this key agricultural activity from a very backward technological base, even relative to its underdeveloped neighbour producers, to a point where by the late 1970s Costa Rican coffee cultivation was considered to be at the very forefront of all coffee producing countries in terms of technological innovation.[55] What, then, were the various components figuring into this aggregate productivity change, and how were they distributed among the different classes of cultivators? It is to such questions that I turn in the next chapter.

Notes

1.   See pages ch.2, p.27.
2.   Hall, *El Café*, p.88.
3.   The relatively small number of these and the considerable amount of land controlled indicates that these farms are on average closer to the upper limit of the category than the lower.
4.   Sandner, Gerhard Agrarkolenisation in Costa Rica, (Kiel, 1961), Table 18, p.167.

5.   At least this is what is indicated by the Gini index of concentration for these countries at this time. See Seligson, *Peasants*, figures 1 to 5.
6.   Barrenechea, *Una Organización*, p.21.
7.   Seligson had calculated that there was one *beneficio* for every 12.7 square kilometres in 1887, while by 1973 there was one for every 2252 square kilometres. Ibid., p.24.
8.   *La Nacion*, (20 July 1952).
9.   Barrenechea, *Una Organización*, p.2.
10. Oficina del Café, *Plan de Abonamiento Intensivo* (San José, 1959), p.7 and *Programa para la Rehabilitación de Cafetales* (San José, 1954), p.6.
11. Hall, *El Café*, p.159.
12. Ministerio de Agricultura e Industrias, 'El Abonamiento del Cafeto', *Boletin Devulgativo*, no. 18, (San José, 1953), p.5.
13. Barrenechea, *Una Organización*, p.4.
14. Ministerio de Agricultura e Industrias, 'El Abonamiento' p.2.
15. Details on the legal minimum hourly wages that prevailed is found in Justo Aguilar F., Carlos Barboza V. and Jorge Leon S. *Desarrollo Tecnologico del Cultivo del Café* (Consejo Nacional de Investigaciones Cientificas y Tecnologicas, San José, 1981), p.3–39, Table 3–10. They also provide figures indicating that the actual wages paid did not vary too much from the legal minimum, during these years, though by the 1970s actual wages lagged somewhat behind the legal minimum.
     In 1950 local agricultural experts had noted that despite the rise in wages, coffee workers were able to cover substantially less of their necessities with their salaries than in the mid 1930s. See A.T. Blanco and J. Morales, 'Los Salarios en Café no Cobren el 38 por ciento de las Necesidades de los Trabajadores', (Instituto Interamericano de Ciencias Agricolas, San José, 1950).
16. Average productivity on farms under 10 ha. was 5.3 *fanegas/manzana*, whereas on the large farms (over 100 ha.) it was 7.9 *fanegas/mz.*, or about 50 per cent more (calculated from the Censo Agropecuario, (1950), p.58.
17. *La Republica* (24 April 1956).
18. Ameringer, *Don Pépé*, p.205.
19. The former are recounted in Manuel Rojas Bolanos, 'Clase y Lucha de Clases en Costa Rica: 1940–48' unpublished Ph.D. thesis (Universidad Nacional Autonoma de Mexico, 1977), pp.148–49. The latter is detailed in Delgado, *El Partido*, part II.
20. The innovations made with respect to the organisation of their estate, and the 'productionist' ideology of the new owners, is discussed in Antonio Arce's 'Rational Introduction of Technology on a Costa Rican Coffee Hacienda', unpublished Ph.D. thesis (Michigan State University, 1959), pp.92–96.
21. See Stone, *La Dinastía*.
22. The old coffee variety would produce only 12 or 13 *fanegas/manzana* with the application of fertilisers, while the hybrid varieties would yield 20 to 26 *fanegas/manzana* in the same area. See Hall, *El Café*, pp.160–1.

23. Interview with Mr Rodrigo Cleves, Chief of the Centre of Investigations in Coffee, June, 1979.
24. See Justo Aguilar F. *et al.* 'Desarrollo Tecnologico', pp.2/14 – 2/17.
25. See Ministerio de Agricultura e Industrias, 'El Abonamiento'.
26. Banco Anglo Costarricense, *Programa para la Rehabilitación de Cafetales*, (San José, 1954), p.6.
27. Facio, *Obras*, pp.102–3.
28. I refer to Hall's study which does go into some detail about other aspects of the programme. See *El Café*.
29. Oficina del Café, 'Plan de Abonamiento Intensivo', (San José, 1959), p.10.
30. *La Prensa Libre*, (12 September 1950).
31. Banco Anglo Costarricense, 'Programa para la Rehabilitación', p.2.
32. See Banco Central, 'Reduce Impuesto de Importacion de Abonos Arancel de Aduanas, Ley no. 1738 de 31 de Marzo de 1954', *Memoria Anual* (San José, 1959), pp.319–20.
33. Hall, *El Café*, p.161.
34. This plan was introduced by Figueres in 1953, and is reported in *La Nacion* (21 November 1953).
35. Hall, *El Café*, p.161.
36. Oficina del Café, 'Plan de Abonamiento', p.33.
37. William Hayden Q., *Relación Entre el Credito Ortogado al Café y la Expansion en su Producción*, Banco Central, series no. 5 (San José 1970), p.19.
38. Calculated from data found in Oficina del Café, *Informe Sobre la Politica de Credito a la Actividad Cafetalera Durante 1979*, Appendix A (San José, 1979), Table 1.
39. Hayden Q., *Relación Entre el Credito*, p.16.
40. This is discussed in Banco Central, *Politica Crediticia en Relación con la Actividad Cafetalera*, (San José, 1972), p.5 and *passim*.
41. This is noted, for example in Banco Central, *Programa Nacional de Credito para Abonamiento de Cafetales* (San José, 1976), p.3. The impression that part of such credits would be destined to such ends was also supported by interviews with personnel in the Ministry of Agriculture and Livestock (April 1980) and by the study carried out by Aguilar *et al.*, 'Desarrollo Tecnologico', pp.6/46.
42. Hayden Q. *Relación*, p.17 also makes this point. Herbicides, especially, have produced a reduction in unit costs.
43. Ibid., p.7.
44. These remarks are based on interviews with personnel of CICAFE, and the Oficina del Café's *Informe Sobre la Actividad Cafetalera de Costa Rica* (San José, 1979).
45. See, for example, Oficina del Café, *Informe de Labores, 1976*, (San José, 1977), p.48.
46. See José Cazanga S. 'Las Cooperativas de Caficultores de Costa Rica en el Proceso de Desarrollo del Capitalismo en el Café' thesis for the Licenciatura (Universidad de Costa Rica, 1982), p.147.
47. See 'FEDECOOP: Qué es la Federación de Cooperativos?' in *Cooperativos de Cafecultores Desarrollo de Costa Rica*, Centro de

Estudios de America Latina (San José, 1970), pp.2–3. In addition
to the provision of technical services, the statutes of FEDECOOP
state, among other things, that its function is to (1) acquire
for commercialisation or industrialisation within the national and
international market all the coffee of its members, including articles
related to the production, harvesting, packaging, transport, storage
and exporting of coffee, and (2) to acquire or fabricate for its affiliates
all the materials, implements, machinery and accessories needed by its
members, including the provision of credit for their purchase.

48.   See Rafael Cartay A., 'La Comercialización de Café en Costa
      Rica a traves de Co-operativos', Masters of Science thesis (Instituto
      Interamericana de Ciencias Agricolas, 1969), p.54.
49.   Ley de Asociaciones Cooperativos, no. 4179, *La Gaceta* (22 August
      1968).
50.   Cazanga, 'Las Cooperativas', p.149.
51.   This evaluation is based on data provided by the Oficina del Café,
      Department of Liquidations and Inspections, and the author's own
      fieldwork in June, 1979.
52.   D. Zuniga, 'El Café: Su Imperativa Economica, Politica y Social
      en Costa Rica', thesis for the Licenciatura (Universidad de Costa
      Rica, 1971), p.88
53.   This is reported in Oficina del Café, *Informe Sobre la Actividad
      Cafetalera de Costa Rica* (San José, 1976), p.9, table 1.
54.   See FAO *Production Yearbook*, vol. 33, (Rome, 1980), pp.178–9. Only
      Sri Lanka and Democratic Yemen had higher productivity in 1979, but
      the production of these countries was inconsequential.
55.   For example, C.A. Krug and R.A. de Poerck, authors of the
      World Coffee Survey, (FAO, Rome, 1968), p.226 remark that 'Costa
      Rica is an outstanding example of the effect of improved technology
      on production.' See also the article 'Costa Rica tiene una de los mas
      Avanzadas Tecnologicias para Producir Café' *La Prensa Libre* (8
      February 1975).

7 Changing Class Structure in the Coffee Sector: 1950–78

The Junta of 1948, and subsequent regimes, set about the task of reorienting Costa Rican society away from the traditional economic dependencies and longstanding political arrangements that had been established by and in the interests of the dominant coffee growing families. In Chapter 5 we have seen that certain limits on this process were set during the struggle with the oligarchy over legislation affecting both economic and political dimensions of their domain. The large coffee interests were not eliminated as a class by far reaching agrarian reform legislation, for example. Rather, their political prerogatives were circumscribed by the State, their potential profits reduced in size. Given these apparently significant changes, was it now possible to ensure that other sectors of the coffee economy would benefit from efforts to modernise production? Did the continuing existence of a large landowning class in this key economic sector effectively block attempts to modernise the economy? Moreover, did the new economic model being charted by an interventionist State during the 1950s further erode power of this traditionally dominant class, or did the compromises conceded in the struggle with this group in the early years after 1948 lay the groundwork for their future resurgence as a major political force? There are no simple answers to these questions, but in this and the following sections I begin to approach these matters with an assessment of the economic and social impact of programs to restructure the coffee economy.

7.1 EVIDENCE OF STRUCTURAL CHANGES IN COFFEE CULTIVATION

The first question to consider is the impact of State intervention among the non-capitalist small producer sector, that is, the semi-proletarian and family farms. But before looking into the question of

114

the distribution of benefits among different classes in the countryside, it will be useful to define more precisely the class structure of the coffee sector. According to the schema I will use here, coffee farmers with up to 4 hectares of land are considered as semi–proletarian, or 'sub-family' farms. These farms would not generate enough income from coffee to provide subsistence for the producer and his family.[1] Coffee producers with between 4 and 20 hectares of land are classified as 'family' farms, that is, they would provide sufficient income to provide subsistence for a family. Sub-family and family farms together constituted about 73 per cent of all coffee farms in 1950, with 40 per cent of all land in coffee and 43 per cent of total production.

Coffee farms with 20 hectares and more of land will be classed as 'capitalist' farms – large and small.[2] These were about 27 per cent of all coffee holdings in 1950 and they had 60 per cent of land in coffee and almost 67 per cent of total production.

As mentioned in the preceding chapter, the introduction of new higher yielding varieties of coffee trees through the replanting of the *cafetales* was in effect a foundation for intensive cultivation, as it stimulated more productive planting patterns and required or promoted the use of further technological inputs on a continuous basis. Both the census of 1963 and that of 1973 report the area of new hybrid plantings in coffee farms of different size categories. This data indicates that even by 1963, considerable progress had been made in the repopulation of the country's coffee farms. Of the roughly 80 thousand hectares in coffee land in 1963, more than one third (27000 hectares) were planted in the new hybrid varieties.[3]

As might be expected, given the terms of the credit programmes financing replantation (see chapter 6), the distribution of replanted land is skewed towards the larger farms. Of the census farms greater than .69 hectares,[4] the semi–proletarian holdings had a scant 11.6 per cent of the replanted land, though they were 38 per cent of all farms. The larger 'family' holdings, 36 per cent of all farms growing coffee, fared considerably better with 28 per cent of the replanted land. Finally, the 26 per cent of the farms that could be considered as capitalist units have 60 per cent of the land in hybrid plantings in 1963. Recalling the proportion of coffee land controlled by each category of farm, it can be seen that the amount of replanted land in each category was roughly proportional to the amount of land found in each. Thus, with regard to the replanting of old coffee trees with the high yielding varieties, the old inequalities of resource allocation were being perpetuated.

Table 7.1   Chemical fertiliser use on coffee farms by category of
landholding, 1963

Category	No. (ha.)	%
.69 to 3.9 ha.	3715	10.1
4 to 19.9	9797	26.5
20 to 99.9	12002	32.5
100 +	11413	31.0

Source: Censo agropecuario, (1963), p.176, Table 137.

If State initiated programmes designed to spur the replanting of
cafetales did not redress existing inequalities, data from the 1973 census
suggests that in the absence of such programmes, such inequalities
would be exacerbated.[5] After 1963, the capitalist farms had proportionately more land in new plantings than did family and subfamily
units, relative to the coffee land controlled by each category.

The incorporation of chemical fertilisers on a regular basis is
at the heart of the intensification of coffee cultivation and has
historically been an integral component of State programmes aimed
at the improvement of the coffee economy. The use of fertilisers by
coffee producers has, not surprisingly, given the rise in production
cited above, shown a dramatic increase since the early 1950s. Only
20 per cent or so of the land in coffee was fertilised regularly in 1953,
according to a study by the Coffee Office.[6] By 1960 this had doubled.
The census of 1973 indicates that the area fertilised had continued to
expand during the 1960s, though not at such a fast rate – to 55 per cent
of all land in coffee.

Concerning the distribution of fertiliser used among census farms,
comparable census data with respect to chemical fertiliser use is limited to information on the area treated with chemical fertiliser within
each size category.[7] For the period ending in 1963, the distribution
of fertilised land is disproportionate to the land controlled within
each of the categories distinguished above, though not markedly so.
Semi–proletarian units, with 14 per cent of the land in 1963 had 10
per cent of coffee land treated with fertiliser (see Table 7.1). The
slightly larger family size farms with 30 per cent of coffee land had
27 per cent of the fertilised land. On the other hand, capitalist units
up to 100 hectares had an amount of fertilised land (32.5 per cent)
more or less proportionate to the coffee land found in this category,

although larger capitalist units with 25 per cent of the land in coffee had a disproportionate 31 per cent of land treated with chemical fertilisers. The only salient change in this pattern indicated for the 1973 census is an improvement in the position of the small producers, especially the family size farms. The improvement in the position of these two categories may have been due to the preferential credit policies established by the State in the mid-1960s for producers with less than 20 *manzanas* of land, credits that were expressly intended for the intensification of production.

With the somewhat less 'divisible' technologies such as agro-chemicals (herbicides, fungicides and insecticides) the inequalities in the distribution of these inputs is considerably more marked.[8] Semi-proletarian farms have only 4 per cent of all land treated with chemicals, family units have 19 per cent, while capitalist farms have a disproportionate 77 per cent. It is also interesting to note that this data indicates the use of fungicides and insecticides is more widespread relative to herbicides in the non–capitalist units, while this relationship is reversed for the capitalist farms. This reflects the different internal cost structures of various kinds of producers. Where wage labour is a major cost of production, as with the capitalist farms, the greater is the use of herbicides to replace the very labour intensive weeding operations.[9]

In lieu of more adequate comprehensive surveys, we will have to rely on the type of evidence presented above to gauge the implications of State programmes for the different classes of coffee producers in Costa Rica. The analysis presented here does receive some support, however, from a more recent study that solicited the opinions of a sample of local agronomists and functionaries who deal with coffee growers on a regular basis, on matters dealing with aspects of coffee cultivation. Notably, this survey sought to discover how informed observers view the distribution of various technologies among different categories of producers.[10] It is the opinion of the informants, for example, that 'small producers' are generally much less likely to use the most key agricultural inputs – high yielding varieties, chemical fertilisers and agro–chemicals – and employ modern planting techniques, than medium and large growers. Especially noteworthy is the consensus that about one third of the 'small producers', even by the late 1970s still do not employ fertilisers at all. The vast majority of the larger farms, what I have called family and capitalist farms, are thought to employ these key inputs, on the other hand.

Figure 7.1   Distribution of coffee farms by number, 1950–73

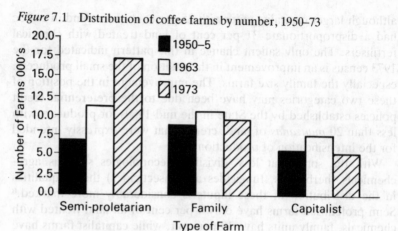

Source: Appendix, Table A.1.

Evidence so far considered, together with the survey of informed sources, indicates various inequalities – some more serious than others – regarding the distribution of agricultural inputs and the adoption of new planting techniques among the different classes of coffee farmers in the Costa Rican countryside. It still remains to assess the impact of these disparities in resource allocation.

It is apparent from Figure 7.1 that one of the most salient changes in the landholding structure of the coffee sphere since 1950

Figure 7.2   Distribution of coffee farms by area, 1950–73

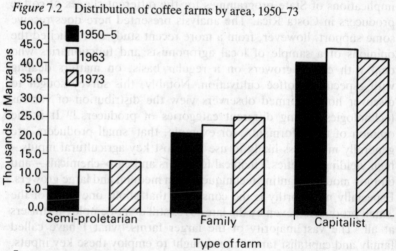

Source: Appendix, Table A.2.

Figure 7.3   Productivity of coffee farms by farm size, 1950–73

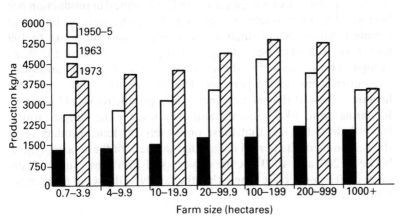

Source: Appendix, Table A.3.

has been the growth of what I have called semi-proletarian holdings, an increase of some 145 per cent up to 1973 (from approximately 7000 to 17000 farms).[11] No other category witnessed such a change, although some initial expansion and subsequent contraction in farm numbers in the other categories was typical of this period. By 1973 over half of all coffee farms were less than 4 hectares in size and over 70 per cent had less than 10 hectares. Although the total land area in coffee controlled by farms under 4 hectares increased along with the number of these farms (see Figure 7.2), it did not expand sufficiently to avoid a further fragmentation of them. Thus while the average area in coffee over the 1950–73 period increased for all other categories, the average area for farms under 4 hectares (the majority of coffee producers) declined somewhat to .85 hectares.

In absolute terms family size farms remained more or less numerically stable, while the number of capitalist farms declined, although not markedly. The expansion in average area planted in coffee per farm was most dramatic for the largest capitalist units, those over 1000 hectares, which on average doubled the area they had in coffee at this time. Of course, these farms typically had considerable land not previously planted in coffee, and sufficient resources to finance a major expansion of their *cafetales*.

Trends in productivity on coffee farms are indicated in Figure 7.3, and they provide a further insight into the consequences of the State programmes I have reviewed above. Several tendencies are apparent. In the first place, all categories of farms experienced very marked productivity increases up to 1973, measured in production per hectare. The most dramatic increases, however, were to be found among family size and small to medium capitalist units (up to 199 hectares), with increases averaging 190 per cent or more for these groups. The increase for the mass of semi–proletarian farms was substantially less, at 166 per cent. The largest farms, those over 200 hectares, showed the smallest increase in productivity (144 per cent for farms up to 1000 hectares, and even less for the largest farms). Nevertheless, the fact that these units were far more productive at the beginning of the period meant that the bulk of these farms (those between 200 and 1000 hectares) were still producing substantially more coffee per hectare than either the family or the semi–proletarian farms, by 1973.

7.2 SUMMARY

At the end of the two decades of post–war expansion then, the situation with respect to the nation's coffee economy was as follows. The State conceptualised and promoted programmes for the intensification of coffee cultivation had brought Costa Rican producers from what was – by the standards of Third World commercial agriculture at the time – a very backward state, to a position at the forefront of coffee producing nations in terms of the technology employed and productivity per hectare.[12] The most favoured groups of farmers, judging in terms of productivity changes in this period, took place with family and small capitalist farms. With respect to the former category, it is likely that the intensification of production had lead to structural changes, in particular the hiring of a substantial element of wage labour as part of a process of differentiation of these farms. Recent studies indicate that on family farms under 20 hectares in size, particularly the larger ones, the element of wage labour is often considerably more significant than family labour, and that the proportion of wage labour to family labour increases with an increase in the technological level of the farm.[13]

Not only were semi–proletarian farms becoming more fragmented over these years, but they have experienced declining relative productivity as well.[14] While semi–proletarian coffee growers were just as productive as family farms under 10 hectares and only slightly less productive per hectare than the bulk of capitalist farms (those under 200 hectares) in 1950, by 1973 a distinct productivity gap had developed to the detriment of the smallest producers.[15] Though the consequences of fragmentation and declining relative productivity are not well known, one of the few studies explicitly focusing on the situation of the small coffee farmers in an historical way indicates that, at least in the area studied, the economic position of the semi-proletarian farmers had indeed deteriorated in recent years. By the 1970s the salary they gained as wage workers on a nearby large coffee estate had become their principal source of income, more important than the revenue gained from their own plots.[16]

Is the fate of these small producers likely to be that indicated by Palacios for a large part of this class in Colombia: their progressive transformation into temporary day labourers?[17] This is likely to depend on geographic and economic factors, in the short and medium term. In the marginal coffee zones, away from the pressure of the medium and large farms and rural employment opportunities, these producers could expect to be relatively stable, especially when coffee cultivation is part of a more mixed rural economy. In the highly specialised Meseta Central, however, a progression of the proletarianisation process that has already occurred seems more probable, despite some successes of these farms in intensifying their cultivations. This may be all the more likely as the deterioration of price levels from their record highs in the mid 1970s continues.

In considering the net impact of these tendencies, it may be useful to note that coffee farms over 200 hectares in 1950 were only 4 per cent of all farms and yet produced an average of 45000 kg. of coffee each, and 37 per cent of the nation's coffee as a group. On the other hand, one third of all farms that were semi-proletarian units, produced an average of 1300 kg. each, or 3 per cent of the average production of the large capitalist farms. The rest of the producers fell somewhere in between. By the early 1970s, large capitalist farms were producing an average of 110000 kg. of coffee each. Semi–proletarian units were still only producing on average about 3 per cent of this, but now over half of all coffee growers were in this position. Viewed in this way, it is clear that the post Second World War period has seen a polarisation in class terms among the country's coffee producers, despite the fact that an important segment of family size farms maintained themselves, in terms of their abso-lute numbers, and their relative productivity *vis–à–vis* the larger farms.

7.3 THE CAPITALIST COFFEE FARMS: EVIDENCE OF STRUCTURAL CHANGE

The evidence presented above suggests that capitalist farms have indeed participated in the modernisation of the coffee economy, although the real dynamism in this sector has been among the smaller capitalist operations. Clearly, the patriarchal social relations that historically characterised the capitalist estates (see Chapter 1), have not proved to be an overwhelming impediment to the modernisation of this important sector of producers. In this section we will see that this is so in large part because the estates have undergone some important changes in their internal structure. These structural changes have and will have wider social consequences, as will be seen once we have delved into the nature of the transformations that have taken place.

Though most existing studies dealing with the contemporary period have restricted their focus to the quantitative dimensions of productivity change in this sphere, there is some evidence of *qualitative* changes in the social organisation of the capitalist estates. The study by Stone,[18] one of the best informed observers on the situation of the large coffee producers, is noteworthy in this respect. Though somewhat impressionistic on this score and lacking in empirical data, the study does give a picture of more recent qualitative changes in fundamental social relationships on the estates.

Excluding those well–placed landowners near expanding urban areas who became more oriented to speculative rents gained from rising land values, Stone notes an important reorganising of the labour process on the estates that he studied, a change that occurred both on those estates that had intensified production and those still holding to traditional cultivation methods. This is the marked tendency of estate owners in recent years to cut down on the number of permanent *peones* attached to the estate in favour of short term contract labour.[19] As an illustration, Stone notes one estate that had reduced its work-force from 170 to 40 *peones* in a few years. This kind of observation is supported by another study, which notes the central role of herbicides on the large farms in reducing requirements for permanent labour. Cases are reported where 'the chemical control of weeds in coffee cultivation reduced the permanent labour force 50 to 60 percent and provoked an increase in the utilisation of a seasonal labour force during the harvest, thereby increasing sub–employment.[20] Estates with a high volume of production are more likely to incorporate innovations into the traditional social organisation of the farm, according to Stone, such as profit sharing schemes for the administrative personnel. While the rationalisation of production and the incorporation of such incentive schemes benefit administrative personnel, Stone sees these changes as largely negative for the new majority of workers hired on a contractual basis. With reference to them he remarks,

> At present, due to the measures adopted by the *patron* to confront the increase of costs of production, the majority of the *peones* find themselves without a house and without a job, except during the harvest period. Moreover, they cannot hope to easily find employment in other activities outside the sphere of coffee. If before the *peon* depended on the *patrón*, who offered him no possibility of economic or social mobility, today though he no longer depends on him, his situation is more serious: the *patrón* now feels no legal or moral obligations to the *peon*, and the latter must count solely on the good nature of the *patron*.[21]

From the point of view of the landowner, the new system of contract labour has the advantage of relieving the former of social obligations to make various kinds of social security payments established by *liberacionista* governments since 1953, as well as enabling him to increase the proportion of the younger and more productive workers he employs.[22] Moreover, this must be viewed together with the increasing tendency to have technical personnel mediating between *patrón* and *peon*, and the fact that the children of the old coffee workers are better educated and less parochial in terms of their experience than their parents. This all is seen by Stone as having diminished considerably the patriarchal nature of social relations internal to the estate in the last few decades.

The somewhat older study by Antonio Manuel Arce,[23] an in–depth case study of a large coffee estate at two different points in time, is a useful complement to Stone's work, especially in terms of the detailed empirical data it provides. Arce's work spans the period when the State shifted from extensive to intensive agricultural practices and so is particularly useful for illustrating the types of structural changes in the labour process implied with this development.

Prior to the adoption of new agricultural practices the estate had utilised the *colono* system on two thirds of its land. Though not widespread in Costa Rican coffee estates, it was well adapted to areas where ecological conditions make for a prolonged harvest season, as it provided the required labour force for the multiple harvesting that was necessary.[24] With this system the *colono* contracts to care for and harvest a coffee plot (*colonia*) from three to ten acres for a fixed payment. As the *colono* provides the labour of his family as well, the estate secures its labour supply when it is needed, and at a minimum cost. Most *colonos*, in addition, had a garden plot and some pasture for the animals they owned. The rest of the estate land was worked by permanent labourers (*peones*) who were numerically about equal to the *colono* group on the estate.

The adoption of new cultivation practices on the estate in the 1950s after a change in ownership brought with it more than technical changes. The traditional social organisation of the *finca*, especially having a large portion of the estate labour force work its land in a semi–independent fashion, was viewed as inimical to the intensification of production. One of the new owners expressed this problem as follows:

> To have the maximum production will be our main concern. In order to have more production we must make the coffee plant produce, making use of fertilisers and applying other agricultural practices. To do this we must get rid of the *colonias*. With this system it is impossible to make changes because some persons will adopt the practice, others will do it in their own way, and still others might not want to make changes.[25]

The intensification of cultivation on the estate studied by Arce was thus accompanied by key changes in the structure of its organisation, as the *colono* system was eliminated and along with it certain longstanding rights of the estate labour force, such as access to pasture lands to graze the livestock they owned. Under the new agricultural system then, virtually all land previously given over to the use of permanent estate labour was now utilised by the estate, while *peon* families were restricted to owning only chickens, for the most part. The estate came to be worked in its entirety by *peones* who were essentially dependent upon a wage for their subsistence and were directly under the supervision of estate management, without the previous rights of access they had enjoyed.

What would appear to be the chief peculiarity of this estate is the continued presence of a sizeable permanent wage labour force, albeit strictly wage labourers since the mid 1950s. This was in good part a product of the local ecological conditions in the Atlantic zone in which the estate was located, which produces a very uneven ripening of the coffee fruit.[26] With the labour requirements thus spaced out more evenly over the year, it has made it more feasible to maintain a permanent labour force proportionately larger than elsewhere in Costa Rica. Moreover, the lower population density of the region in which the farm is situated undoubtedly impinges on the estate's ability to easily hire short–term contract labour.[27] Nevertheless, the modernisation of the estate has entailed some constriction of this permanent work force. Arce's data indicates that a small reduction in the number of labour–force families took place in the 1950s, while this author's own information based on interviews with administration personnel of the same estate some twenty years later indicated that further reductions in permanent labour had been made.[28] This is despite the fact that since 1959 the land in coffee has increased from 386 to 571 hectares. The widespread use of such labour-displacing inputs as herbicides on the estate was certainly instrumental in this reduction.

From my discussion of the dynamics of estate agriculture as a system of production (see Chapter 2, section 2.2 and note 35), it will be recalled that the change in social relations on the estate was integral to a shift from the formal to the real subsumption of the labour process by capital. Furthermore, this process accompanied, or rather constituted the social basis upon which estate owners could institute agricultural practices and annual productive investments associated with an increase of production through the *intensification*, rather than expansion, of cultivation.

It is evident from Arce's data that in his case study, this was precisely the kind of development that got underway on this estate during the 1950s. Production under the old agricultural scheme averaged 6778 *fanegas* annually; by the end of the 1950s an average of 9,250 *fanegas* were being produced with a minimal increase in land under cultivation. Thus, production per unit of land had increased from 12 to 17.5 *fanegas* per *manzana* between 1950 and 1959. And by the late 1970s the estate's *cafetales* were producing 24 *fanegas* per *manzana* of land in coffee.[29]

That these post–war changes in the social organisation of the coffee estates have had important repercussions with respect to the agricultural proletariat involved in coffee there can be no doubt. Whether through the relatively abrupt swing from permanent labour to contracted workers that Stone has described, or the slower process detailed by Arce in areas where estates still have peculiar labour supply problems, the patriarchal relations that had imbued estate farming in previous times and which had been inimical to the development of even those organisations that might be oriented solely to the protection of the economic-corporate interests of this population, were slowly giving way as *peones* became wage workers, pure and simple. This situation is clearest, undoubtedly, in the case of the growing population of *adicionales*, the workers hired for a short-term on the basis of a verbal contract. Not only are they exempt from social security and economic benefits of the remaining permanent labourers, but neither do they have even the relative security of the traditional coffee *peon*.[30] Besides this, it is clear that the chief beneficiaries of the periods of high prices in recent years have been agrarian capitalists, and not the rural labour force. Data provided by Aguilar [31] show that while the legal minimum hourly wage for coffee workers in real terms (adjusted to 1966 *colons*) rose marginally from the early 1950s to the late 1960s, it has not improved substantially since. In fact, there has been a real decline in the legal minimum hourly wage since 1970, despite record high prices to producers during this decade. The situation in the mid 1970s was most telling in this respect. In 1974 for instance, coffee for export was selling at slightly less than 10 *colons* per kilogram. Prices skyrocketed over the next few years to a high of 37 *colons* per kilogram during 1976–7, thereafter declining slowly. Thus, between 1973 and 1976 the value of the coffee harvest jumped from 955 million to 2584 million *colons*,[32] inaugurating a period of the '*vacas gordas*', to use the felicitous phrase of one local journal. Legal minimum hourly wages for *peones* in coffee cultivation were 2.15 *colons* per hour in 1973, and rose to 4 *colons* by 1977. Meanwhile, the consumer price index during these years was rising at a rate of 20 to 30 per cent per annum.[33] In other words, during this bonanza of high prices, incomes to agricultural labour, utilising officially established minimum wages which were not infrequently ignored in practice,[34] essentially failed to even keep up with the rise in consumer prices during these years.

Given this particular combination of factors, especially the deterioration of the economic position of the agricultural proletariat in coffee accompanying structural changes in the production process, it is not surprising that this group has begun to respond in more typically class terms. The sporadic strike activity, accompanied by the appearance of rural trade unions in the rural coffee zones by the 1970s is indicative of an awakening to changed material circumstances.

Nevertheless, some small scale studies suggest that the old patriarchal world view is very tenacious among both permanent labourers and the semi-proletariat working in coffee, and they note as well that until as late as 1976 there were no unions that included only coffee workers. By this later date the now legalized *Partido Vanguardia Popular* (formerly the Communist Party of Costa Rica) had noted at its 12th Congress that, with respect to the national labour movement, 'one of the factors of weakness of the working class is the low level of organisation of the proletariat of the coffee and sugar plantations. This sector is organising very slowly.'[35]

7.4 CHANGES IN THE AGRO-INDUSTRIAL SPHERE

In Cardoso's study of the early beginnings of coffee cultivation in Costa Rica, there was mention of the three bases or spheres for the accumulation of the coffee bourgeoisie: land, processing and commercialisation. With respect to landholdings, we have seen how capitalist producers, large and small, have fortified their positions in the decades after 1950, as part of a State impelled project that placed the intensification of coffee production at the centre of a strategy of agricultural development.

The processing plants or *beneficios* were traditionally another major sphere for the investments of productive capital for at least the economic nucleus of the coffee bourgeoisie. Since mid–century, moreover, new pressures have been brought to bear on this group that would presumably have an impact on their viability. The outcome of the struggle over tax legislation and the growth of a system of co-operative *beneficios* are only the most important pressures in the contemporary period. I shall consider a few others also.

One of the most obvious indications that important forces have affected the agro–industrial sphere of the coffee complex is the concentration and centralisation of production. By the former I mean the concentration of means of production, including labour, at the command of a single capitalist, what Marx[36] referred to as reproduction on an extended scale. By the latter we mean 'the concentration of capital already formed, destruction of their individual independence, expropriation of capitalist by capitalist, transformation of many small into few large capitals', which occurs through a simple change in the distribution of capitals already existing. The concentration of means of production, at least in terms of processing facilities, was already fairly marked by 1888. At that time processing technology by the so-called 'wet method' was sufficiently costly so that of the 7490 coffee farms, there were only some 256 *beneficios*, with some processors owning more than one plant even by that time.[37] For the next half century or so coffee processing technology was standardised and changed little. Thus, despite the effects of the World Depression on local producers, by 1940 there were still some 221 *beneficios* operating in the country.[38] As we have seen, during the years prior to 1950 the economic crisis of the industry had forced processors to operate far below the capacity of their plants. In fact, the period during and after the Second World War would appear to have been especially critical for the survival of many processors, as their numbers were reduced to 125 by the mid-950s, according to Barrenechea.[39] After 1950, new opportunities were to present themselves to *beneficiadores*, but it is clear that only some of them would be in a position to take advantage of them.

Since 1950 the amount of coffee available for processing has expanded like at no other time. During this same period, however, the number of processing facilities contracted at a rapid rate, particularly after 1960. Of the 125 privately owned firms in 1955, only

Table 7.2   Control of coffee harvest by size of firm: 1965–6 and 1978–9[*]

	1965–6			1978–9		
Firm size	No. of firms	Coffee processed	(%)	No. of firms	Coffee processed	(%)
Less than 5000 fanegas	52	123999	(10)	14	42494	(3)
5000 to 9999	17	123093	(10)	11	76726	(5)
10000 to 29999	22	342594	(29)	27	483747	(33)
30000 to 49999	11	462185	(39)	4	143974	(10)
50000 to 69999	2	129750	(11)	3	177112	(8)
70000 +	—	—	(0)	6	552847	(37)
Total	104	1181621	(100)	65	1476900	(100)

[*] Co-operatives and Government processing facilities excluded.
Source: Oficina del Café, Departamento de Liquidaciones e Inspectores, 'Total de Café Declarado por los Beneficiadores' (1966 and 1979).

108 existed in 1965, and 65 in 1978.[40] The process of the centralisation of processing facilities in Costa Rica had thus reduced the number of *beneficios* by 43 per cent since this earlier date.

If we examine the structure of this sphere of production, it is evident that by 1965 there was a very marked differentiation among *beneficio* operators within the country. Of the total of 108 firms in 1965, 52 of these processed less than 5000 *fanegas* of coffee (see Table 7.2). At the other end of the scale 11 firms processed more than 30000 *fanegas*, and three had more than 400000. Over the next decade or so it is apparent that it was the smaller undercapitalised processors that bore the brunt of the economic changes forced upon this industry. An examination of data collected on *beneficios* by the Coffee Office shows that of the 52 smallest firms (those processing less than 5000 *fanegas*) operating in 1965, only 17 were still operating in 1978. The decline in this group of firms, then, accounts for almost 70 per cent of the number of firms that either went out of business or were merged with other firms during this 18-year period.

While the centralisation of capitals in the coffee processing sphere since 1965 meant the death–knell for the greater part of the smallest processors, it was quite another story for the more substantial *beneficiadores*. Between 1965 and 1978 the country's largest processors had expanded the volume of coffee they controlled like at no other time. The 13 largest firms, for example, expanded their control of the harvest from 49 per cent to 55 per cent. The top 6 firms performed

Figure 7.4   Control of Harvest by size of firm, 1965–66 & 1978–79

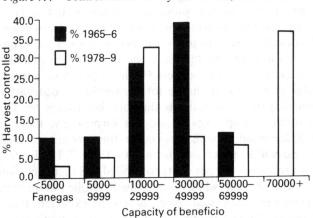

Source: Table 7.2.

Table 7.3 Number of processing firms by the amount of capital controlled per year, 1975–6

Capital Controlled	No. of Firms	%
Less than 1 million colons	15	21
1 to less than 3 million colons	31	44
3 to less than 6 million colons	14	20
6 to less than 9 million colons	4	6
More than 9 million colons	7	10
Total	71	100*

* Does not add to 100% due to rounding.
Source: Garita and Leon, 'Diferenciación al Interior del Bloque Cafetalero' (San José: Universidad de Costa Rica, 1977) p. 78.

even better, increasing their share of the harvest controlled by private processors from 22 per cent in 1965 to over 37 per cent in 1978 (see Figure 7.4).[41] This concentration of production in fewer and much larger firms over this period is forcefully illustrated by an examination of the differentiation of the 20 largest *beneficiadores*. Though in 1965 there was a certain amount of differentiation among the top 20 largest firms, the largest processors still only processed slightly over twice the amount of coffee as the smallest, within this top twenty. By 1978, however, the largest firms were processing more than eight times that of the smallest among the top twenty *beneficiadores*.

The economic power of the processing group is not only a result of the fact that they provide the essential processing service, of course. Historically, and still today the *beneficiador* is the usual channel through which credits for the *etapa de asistencia* and the *etapa de recolección* flow to producers.[42] The 2 per cent interest the *beneficiador* is allowed to charge for his service as distributor of credit emanating from the Bank is thus another source for the accumulation of this group. Again, and not surprisingly, there is also a clear differentiation with respect to the amount of loan capital controlled within processing firms. As Table 7.3 indicates, the majority of processors (65 per cent) controlled less than 3 million *colons* worth of loan capital, while seven firms controlled more than nine million *colons* of credit each. And, as is to be expected, those firms controlling the largest volume of credit were precisely those *beneficiadores* who were the largest processors of coffee.[43]

What, then, has been the force, or combination of forces, behind this impressive centralisation of capitals in the agro–industrial sphere of the coffee economy, and the rapid concentration of production in a few of the largest firms? In considering this question, it would be useful to return to historical evidence, I believe, for different forces have been at work at different points over the past several decades.

With respect to the rapid decline in *beneficios* between the end of the Great Depression and the mid 1950s, I have already noted before that processors could not be expected to have escaped the general malaise that characterised the national coffee economy after 1930, and towards the end of the Depression in particular. In addition to this, the introduction of motorised transport, together with the changing structure of the external market during the war years,[44] forced a development that appeared to have considerable impact on the structure of this industry. This was the system of *recibidores* initiated at the beginning of the Second World War. Barrenechea describes the situation as follows.

> The *recibidores* were small receptacles of wood to receive the coffee fruit; they were located in zones far from *beneficios* to which they belonged, that is, in regions in which there already existed *beneficios* to accommodate local production. The immediate consequence was that all the *beneficiadores* copied this system, creating an absurd competition, while each *beneficio* processed a quantity of coffee that would have been the same as that produced in its zone if the system of *recibidores* had been eliminated.[45]

Another consequence of this system was to give an advantage to the larger and better financed processors, since growers now had some choice as to whom they delivered and could be attracted by the more lucrative advances the larger firms could offer.[46]

If the pressures of the industry's longstanding structural crisis, and the advent of the *recibidor* system accounted for the initial centralisation of this industry in contemporary times, other forces have been more salient in recent years. These were also more closely linked to State policies affecting the coffee industry. Certainly one of the central forces affecting Costa Rican processors in the last two decades has been the increasing cost of labour over this period. Not only have wages increased since the late 1950s, and especially those of the 'qualified labourers', but as the State in these years expanded the scope of social security legislation, the *aguinaldo* and severance pay beyond certain sectors of urban workers, processors' profits began to be affected.[47] Exacerbating matters was the fact that such legislation came to affect processors coincident with the low market price for coffee throughout much of the 1960s, a time of world overproduction and increased competition from new producing countries, principally in Africa.

The possibilities for *beneficiadores* to counteract the effect of rising labour costs on profits was also important because of the fact that the wet phase of the processing at least, takes place during a very limited time period, making it all the more unprofitable to keep a permanent labour force throughout the rest of the year.[48] The incentive to shift more to seasonal labourers, to the extent this was possible, thus became stronger with such legislation. For the most part, however, the processors' ability to attack this situation was linked closely with the possibility of mobilising capital so that certain of the most labour intensive tasks could be replaced by mechanical and electronic equipment. Mechanical dryers and mechanical and electronic sorting equipment have been perhaps the most important innovations in reducing labour costs for the processing firms. One medium size firm studied by the author, for example, had reduced its permanent labour force from 100 to around 30 to 40 with the introduction of such technology in the last 15 years. Another small *beneficio* that was part of a larger agro–business operation had reduced the number of persons employed in the sorting process from between 20 to 30 labourers to only 2 with the benefit of new sorting equipment.[49]

The high costs involved in such an automation were not easily borne by the large number of the smallest processing operations, those under 5000 *fanegas*, particularly if they were not part of a larger corporate structure.[50] This factor would seem to be the most important in restructuring this sphere of production in the last two decades.[51] As can be seen from Table 7.2, those firms that have survived are on average of much greater capacity than was usual even by the early 1960s.[52]

Another factor that certainly figured in the centralisation and concentration of *beneficios* has been the rapid expansion of co-operative processing plants throughout the coffee zones of Costa Rica. Again, we are speaking of a development that has had a differential impact on private *beneficiadores*. Co-operative *beneficios*, which it will be recalled expanded in number most dramatically after 1960, vary considerably in size and degree of modernisation. On average they are considerably larger than private *beneficios* (52776 *fanegas*/plant

Table 7.4   Coffee processed in private and co-opertive beneficios (in fanegas, selected years)

Year	Private beneficios	(%)	Co-operatives	(%)
1965–66	1080594	(88.4%)	141274	(11.5)
1967–68	1391712	(88.6)	214274	(13.3)
1969–70	1437624	(81.1)	333945	(18.8)
1971–72	1346039	(70.6)	558104	(29.3)
1973–74	1380618	(67.5)	664495	(32.5)
1975–76	1121713	(65.9)	578465	(34.1)

Source: Torres Rivas, *Elementos para la Caracterización de la Estructura Agraria de Costa Rica* (San José: Instituto de Investigaciones Sociales, Universidad de Costa Rica, no. 33, 1978) p. 43, Table 5.

versus 22721 *fanegas*/plant in 1978). However, the country's largest operations are still private concerns.

Many co-operative operations, especially some of the largest, are of fairly recent origin and thus had the advantage of beginning with the most up to date equipment available. In addition to often being modern and hence efficient operations, co-operatives do not face the same pressures to generate profits as is the case with the capitalist operations. These considerations have allowed co-operatives to offer farmers very attractive prices,[53] a fact that even private operators are forced to admit. With the organisation of FEDECOOP and the possibility of co-ops marketing their own coffee, prices to producers were even more favourable, so that co-ops have had good success in attracting the small and medium size farmers, in particular. As can be see from Table 7.4, by the mid 1970s one third of the harvest was in the hands of cooperatives. Table 7.4 also illustrates another important fact. Despite the dramatic growth of the co-op sector, the absolute amount of coffee processed by the private sector has not declined significantly. At the same time, of course, many fewer private firms are around to process the same amount of coffee. In large part, then, at the level of the processing sphere as a whole, the unprecedented expansion of the annual coffee harvest since the early 1950s allowed for co-op *beneficios* to be accommodated without taking away a substantial part of the business previously the domain of private capital. This may in part explain why as yet there has not been greater concern articulated by private processors and their representative organisations. Of course, at the level of the individual firm, especially a small one, the establishment of a co-op plant nearby may well have provided competition fatal to the former. This is because the expansion of co-op *beneficios* has meant something different for the small and the large processors. The small, undercapitalised and less efficient *beneficios* have considerably higher unit costs than the newer, larger and more modern co-operative plants and hence cannot hope to offer growers the same attractive prices as the latter.[54] Thus, for small processors, the establishment of a co-operative sector of processors throughout the country has likely hastened their demise.

Larger processing firms with the capital to finance automation, on the other hand, would not have had the same difficulties coping with this new development. For such firms, it would seem that at most, the appearance of modern co-operative *beneficios* only acted as a further stimulus to their own capitalisation, and their ability to modernise their operations enabled them to offer their clients the most favourable prices. Indeed, a representative of one of the very largest processing operations noted that 'una convivencia sana' had existed between private and co-operative *beneficios* in Costa Rica, and that the latter had helped bring about 'a needed rationalisation of production in the processing industry'.[55] Of course, for this large firm, such a stimulus basically meant the need to get big faster. For many small firms the situation fostered by State promoted co-operatives only meant their demise would come sooner rather than later.

There were other factors that figured in the restructuring of the agro–industrial sphere of coffee production, factors related to the economies of scale that accrue to large firms. Larger operations, for instance, were more likely to have sufficient facilities to warehouse much of their own coffee, which is an advantage in that it allows these firms to wait until market prices are most favourable before getting rid of their coffee. Economies of scale also obtained in the area of administrative costs. State intervention in this activity, since the 1950s especially, has involved the increasing regulation of all aspects of the industry. And while all processors have thus been faced with administration costs that go along with such regulation, these costs do not increase in proportion to the amount of coffee processed, placing the smaller firms at a relative disadvantage.

It is thus the imperative to modernise, and the financial basis this requires, in combination with certain economies of scale, that appear to be the leading factors enforcing a restructuring of this activity in which a numerous group of small *beneficios* servicing a limited number of nearby clients have much more restricted possibilities of surviving. However, agricultural credits originating from the National Banking System have been utilised by processors to modernise and enlarge plants, and thereby have promoted the centralisation of capital in this sphere. This was occurring even in the early post-war years, as Barrenechea indicates. He notes that by the mid 1950s, it was estimated that one third of the 30 million *colons* of outstanding debts to the coffee system in fact pertained to processors who had utilised the loan capital, ostensibly destined to producers to cover the production and harvest costs, to introduce improvements in these operations.[56] Certainly, an abundance of credit had flowed into the coffee economy since the early 1950s, and experts on credit matters have long known that a not insignificant amount of this capital was directed into other areas than those for which it was originally intended.[57] Processors who constituted an all important conduit for the credit destined for coffee growers, were obviously in a favoured position to take advantage of any superfluous credit that headed their way, and apparently did.[58] Here again, the larger processors would 'naturally' benefit the most since it was they who handled the greatest volume of credit.

7.5 FROM LANDOWNING CAPITALISTS TO INDUSTRIALISTS?

One more issue is the emergence of an evermore developed division of labour between different fractions of capital, be it agricultural, industrial, financial or commercial, that is usually considered as one of the central dynamics of the process of capitalist development. Here this involves the separation of the two distinct operations historically taken care of by the large capitalist coffee producer – cultivation and processing. This specialisation suggests that the final logic of the development of capitalist estate agriculture is the gradual transformation of agrarian capitalists into industrial capitalists, pure and simple, though still closely linked with agriculture through their role in transforming agricultural commodities. Such a development could be most interesting in economic and political terms. In the economic sense, because such a transformation could indicate the final elimination of a powerful fraction of the national bourgeoisie, which because of its connection to the land and its ability to appropriate rent has, in some contexts, posed a barrier to the further modernisation of agriculture that is seen as integral to successful capitalist development. In the political sense it could signify the demise of a traditionally powerful bourgeois fraction whose connection to production organised on a relatively backward social basis has typically made it a staunch foe of the extension of the basic civil, social and political rights that constitute a mainstay of liberal democratic political stability.

The contemporary evolution of this particular agro-industrial sphere in the Costa Rican economy does not stand as an exception to this rule, or so what evidence this author has discovered would suggest. It is not, however, a process without its contradictions and limitations, and there is some reason to believe that the functions of processing and cultivation, traditionally united in the person of the large *cafetalero*, have in many cases not yet been separated into two distinct spheres controlled by what in effect would be different fractions of capital, whether rooted in the old coffee bourgeoisie or not. In any case, I do not pretend to offer conclusive evidence one way or another, but only attempt to shed a little more light on an issue that has received some discussion in the literature.

The notion that a separation was taking place between the traditional function of the *cafetalero*, – cultivation and processing – has been considered in a work by Garita and Leon.[59] They also provide some evidence of the development of a nucleus of very large and interlocked firms at the top of the processing 'hierarchy'. Torres Rivas has presented perhaps the best articulated argument with respect to this process of separation. He writes,

> The process of specialisation which the development of the pro-
> ductive forces brings, separates in many cases (the most important
> at least), the productive activities strictly speaking – those that
> are realised by planters/harvesters – from those functions strictly
> agro–industrial. Since the latter is the privileged sphere for
> accumulation . . . the *beneficiador* is thus the most representative
> figure of the agrarian bourgeoisie, a capitalist that is divorced from
> his condition as landowner and converted into agro–industrial
> entrepreneur, unencumbered by the risks of agriculture. . . . The
> dynamic of the concentration/centralisation of capital in the coffee
> activity only confirms the general tendencies of the movement of
> capitalism, be it agrarian or industrial.[60]

The evidence to date supporting the above argument is hardly complete, it should be mentioned. On the surface there is evidence to suggest that this separation of functions has taken place, and especially with respect to the most important firms, as Torres Rivas suggests. Data from the Coffee Office, for instance, show that the proportion of coffee registered as 'bought' from other producers has been growing, relative to the quantity of coffee processed belonging to the *beneficios*.[61] In 1965–6 over 11 per cent of coffee processed by the *beneficios* was registered as belonging to them. By 1978 this had fallen to 5 per cent. In addition, of the six largest processing firms, only one is listed as having processed any of its own coffee by the 1978–9 harvest. There has certainly been the development of a tendency to the formal separation of the cultivation and processing spheres, whereby increasingly private firms are established which engage in processing alone. However, this fact by itself is not sufficient proof that a real separation of functions is becoming the norm, if we consider that the appropriate unit is not the firm, but individuals or groups of individuals linked primarily through kinship ties.

At the level of individuals and families, there is some evidence to indicate that this separation is somewhat less than complete in anything more than the formal sense referred to. Interesting in this respect is the comment of a representative of a very large processor, who noted that for 'accounting purposes' many families now wish to keep the agricultural and processing parts of their concern apart in separate companies. Thus a separation of functions may in many cases be more of a formality, designed to reduce administrative costs, or reduce the impact of tax legislation, while the same family in fact still controls both operations. Within the limited sample of *beneficiadores* interviewed by the author, for example, two firms which were not registered by the Coffee Office as processing their own coffee still did, in fact, cultivate a substantial quantity of coffee. In another case of an old established coffee estate–owning family, it was well known that one branch of the family had specialised in the processing end of production, and the other managed the *cafetales* the family had traditionally owned.

Finally, some additional evidence on this matter was obtained by the author through a check of the Registry of Property in San José. This procedure also indicated a further difficulty inherent in ascertaining the real social nature of the category of *beneficiador* in contemporary times. Since the largest processing firms also tend to be the most modern, they would be most representative of a trend towards the specialisation of capitals in specific spheres of production. As information was available concerning names of owners among the top eight largest firms it was decided to limit the investigation to this group. A search was made for landholdings listed under the name of the firm and under names of those individuals that are associated with these firms, according to the earlier study by Garita and Leon.[62] This search revealed that of the firms and closely associated names, only three had what could be considered as insubstantial landholdings, that is, holdings of a few hectares. And of these, one family firm was known to have sizeable holdings of coffee lands, though no records of this could be located. The remaining five firms were all found to have more considerable landholdings, very considerable in a couple of cases. Landholdings ranged from 51 hectares to in excess of 1000 hectares, in two cases. It is possible, of course, that additional landholdings pertain to closely related family of the individuals associated with these firms, so that this estimate of landholdings of large *beneficiadores* must be viewed as a conservative figure if we are to take the family and not the individual as a more adequate unit of analysis.

Unfortunately, it was not possible to verify land use on these property holdings, therefore no conclusive answer can be given to the more specific question of whether agricultural and industrial activities have become separated, at least with respect to these firms. This evidence does indicate that even amongst the largest and most modern firms 'landholding' continues to be a favoured sphere of investment within the processing activity itself. Whether this indicates a continuation of the participation of *beneficiadores* in productive agricultural activities, or whether land has become simply a sphere for speculative investment for this group is an important issue that future research in this area might pursue. In two cases, however, sizeable properties were in or near major urban centres, suggesting that the latter type of investment activity is of some importance with this group.

7.6 SUMMARY

In considering the global social impact of State programmes to modernise coffee production, we were led first of all to examine the small producer sector, that is, the semi–proletarian and family farms. Here, a dramatic increase in the number of semi–proletarian holdings was evident in recent times, but this appeared to be due to the fragmentation of these farms. Family farm numbers, on the other hand, have been fairly stable. These farms have definitely benefited from the State programmes directed towards coffee, more so than the semi-proletarian units where a decline in productivity has occurred. However, there was noted a tendency for family farms to undergo a process of differentiation, so that the larger family units increasingly took on the internal characteristics of small capitalist farms.

Capitalist farms, on the other hand, were seen to have appropriated a disproportionate share of the new technologies associated with the modernisation of coffee. However, among the capitalist coffee farms, which have declined slightly in numerical terms, it is the smaller farms that appear to have incorporated new technologies most rapidly and experienced the greatest productivity increases. Overall, the progressive fragmentation of the mass of semi–proletarian holdings, the differentiation of family farms, and the growing productivity gap between large and small coffee farms generally, all point to a polarisation of the rural social structure in the coffee sector.

The available evidence also indicated that changes in the internal structure of the capitalist farms have been promoted by the exigencies of new cultivation techniques. A shift from traditional permanent workers to increasing reliance on seasonal contract labour has considerably modified the nature of social relations on these large farms. The old patriarchal system of authority on the estates has been largely destroyed and the labour force increasingly transformed into a modern rural proletariat integrated into the capitalist productive process on a seasonal basis.

Finally, the contemporary forces reshaping the powerful producer–processor fraction of the capitalist coffee sector were assessed. Such factors as competition from co-operative processing operations, labour legislation effectively raising the cost of labour, and the possibility of using State credits to modernise processing facilities all contributed to the concentration and centralisation of production. The evidence would suggest that a clear differentiation of this group has occurred, together with the fortification of a small number of powerful processors. By the late 1970s only 6 *beneficios* processed 37 per cent of the nation's coffee, excluding that which went to cooperative processors.

Furthermore, it was noted that one authority had argued that the general tendencies towards the concentration/centralisation of capital in the coffee sphere in Costa Rica only confirms the general tendencies of the movement of capitalism – the divorce of the large agrarian capitalist from his condition as landowner and his conversion into an industrial entrepreneur, pure and simple. If the data we have examined above do suggest a tendency in this direction, it would also indicate that this process is not complete, even for the largest and most dynamic elements of this group. Definite ties to the land, often masked for administrative reasons, appear still to be the norm. Whether the persistence of landownership within the most powerful elements of the coffee bourgeoisie has the same significance it once did, given the transformation of social relations in agriculture in recent decades, is an open question awaiting further research. The prevailing model of economic development in Costa Rica during the two decades after 1950 was clearly not one that only favoured the interests of the large agro–export sector, a pattern that has indeed been more commonplace in neighbouring Central American countries. Nevertheless, conditions were established whereby the most dynamic elements of the coffee bourgeoisie could expand and prosper, and in fact did. In the process, the whole system of coffee production and processing has been transformed.

If the old coffee bourgeoisie was to emerge strengthened, albeit in a reconstituted form, it was no longer to be as prominant an element of the national capitalist class. The diversification policies of PLI regimes since the early 1950s have stimulated other influential sectors of the agrarian bourgeoisie, as well as industrial capital. In the next chapter I explore briefly some dimensions of this effort to diversify the national economy.

Notes

1. I base my classification essentially on the income gained per hectare of coffee land, in 1960, taking 18 *fanegas* as the national average yield per hectare at that time, and 216 colons as the prevailing liquidation price for a *fanega* of green coffee. This yields a gross income of approximately 3900 colons or $650/ha. (at the prevailing exchange rate of 6 colons to the dollar). Given that the average rural labourer and his family had an income of 4818 colons ($727) in 1961 in Costa Rica (see ECLA. *Tenencia de la Tierra y Desarrollo Rural en Centroamerica* (EDUCA, San José, 1973), Table C-11), it is clear that a coffee grower with 1 ha. of land would not even be able to live at the level of a landless worker. Since coffee farms below 4 ha. had on the average slightly less than 1 ha. of land, I have classified this group as 'sub–family'. Coffee farms

in the 4 to 20ha. category had on average 2.3 ha. of land planted in coffee, which at prevailing yields and prices would provide a gross income of 8942 colons, before costs. This corresponds roughly to the ECLA estimate of average income for 'family' size farms in Costa Rica (7101 colons). I refer to these as 'family' farms here.

A recent economic study by Gamboa Marin of coffee producers in Costa Rica does lend support to a categorisaton by structural features of the unit such as I have presented. (See 'Analisis Economico de la Producción del Café en Costa Rica: Cosecha 1976–77', San José: Oficina del Café, 1977). In this study of coffee producers, family labour clearly predominates in farms less than 5 ha. while wage labour becomes more important in units up to 10 ha., though generally it does not exceed family labour inputs. Units larger than 10 ha. tend to have proportionately more wage labour than family labour, however, although wage labour appears to be proportionately more important the more technically advanced the farm is. Given the generally lower technical level of small farms in 1960, I would suggest that at that time family labour was still predominant in farms up to 20 ha. In more recent years 'family' farms might have to be restricted to farms less than 10 ha. or so.

2. Farms between 20 and 100 has., the next census category, average about 4 ha. of land planted in coffee. As units get to be this size, the amount of wage labour required becomes substantial in a cultivation as labour intensive as coffee. This size holding would have provided an income of about 15552 colons or $3000, again what ECLA found to be the average for 'multi–family medium' type farms, that is, farms that can support more than one family. I refer to this fairly substantial group as 'small capitalist' farms. Coffee farms larger than 100 ha. I refer to as 'large capitalist' units, because of the nature of labour requirements of a unit of this size necessitates a considerable labour force, including the hiring of an administrative staff for the larger holdings.

It need be added that a categorisation based on income is possibly an insufficient criteria for distinguishing farms on the basis of certain structural features, especially given the possibility of increasing production very markedly in certain types of agriculture without increasing the component of non-family labour concomitantly due to labour saving machinery. Coffee cultivation is not easily mechanised, however and therefore an expansion in production does generally imply an increase in non–family labour.

It must also be noted that as the technological conditions of production change, the specific structural features of individual farms will come to depend more upon the adoption or non–adoption of these technologies, because these influence the labour requirements for different aspects of the productive process, and the income generated from a given unit of land.

3. *Censo Agropecuario*, (San José, 1963,), Table 97. See, also, J. Aguilar *et al*. 'Desarrollo Tecnologico'.

4. Data on area for coffee farms is only available for farms larger than 1

manzana(.69 ha.) for 1963.

5.   *Censo Agropecuario*, (San José, 1973), Table 77. Oficina del Café 'Plan de Abonamiento', p.7.

6.   See the study by the Oficina del Café, *Plan de Abonamiento*, p.7.

7.   Even this data is not without its problems, due to the fact that the most recent census lumps together coffee and sugar cane farms with regards to this variable. I have attempted to disaggregate this data and while the results cannot be taken to be precise, they should be sufficient to indicate basic trends.

8.   *Censo Agropecuario* (San José, 1963), Table 137.

9.   One recent study by the Coffee Office, for example, shows that the regular application of herbicides reduces labour costs in 1 ha. for weeding operations from 502 *colons* (with little or no herbicides) to 108 *colons*. Weeding operations consumed more labour than any other activity under the traditional system of cultivation. See Oficina de Planificación Sectorial gropecuario, *Programa de Mejoramiento de la Producción de Costa Rica*, (San José, 1979), Annex 7 and 8.

10.   Eduardo Andrade E., *Recursos de los Paises Para Transferencia de Tecnología en Café* (Instituto Interamericano de Ciencias Agricolas, San José, 1979).

11.   Undoubtedly, some of the increase was due to the expansion of marginal coffee zones, in such outlying regions as Coto Brus, San Carlos and Sarapiqui during the periods of more favourable coffee prices.

12.   As an example, Krug and De Poerck note that while productivity of Costa Rican coffee farms in 1950 was on average considerably below that of coffee land in El Salvador by 1960 Costa Rican coffee land was more productive than the latter, and almost twice as productive as Guatemalan producers. *World Coffee Survey*, p. 193, 202, and 226.

13.   See Gamboa, 'Analysis Economico', in particular the table showing kinds of labour used for each strata of farm. For the relationship between type of labour used and technology, see tables 63, 69 and 75. Referring to the situation in the mid 1970s, another study also confirms that it is possible for a farmer and his family to attend to a coffee finca up to 10 ha., but that a larger farm requires additional permanent and seasonal labour. See Nora Garita B. and Maria del Rosario Leon Q., 'Diferenciación al Interior del Bloque Cafetalero', Thesis for the Licienciatura (Universidad de Costa Rica, San José, 1977), p.85.

14.   By 1973 the subfamily fincas were 12 per cent less productive than family farms and 36 per cent less productive than all but the largest capitalist units.

15.   The exception to this are the very largest farms, the few over 1000 hectares.

16.   See Margarita Bolaños A. and Nancy Cartin L., 'Obstaculos Ideologicas al Desarrollo de Organizaciones Reinvindicativas de Clase en el Proletariado y Semi–Proletariado del Café', thesis for the Licienciatura (Universidad de Costa Rica, San José, 1979), p.206.

17.   Palacios, *Coffee in Colombia*, p.246.

18.   Stone, *La Dinastía*.

19. Ibid., ch. 4.
20. Cited in Edelberto Torres Rivas, *Elementos Para la Caracterización de la Estructura Agraria de Costa Rica* (Instituto de Investagaciones Sociales, San José, 1978), p.50.
21. Stone, *La Dinastia*, p.144.
22. Torres Rivas, *Elementos*.
23. Antonio Arce, 'Rational Introduction of Technology on a Costa Rican Coffee Hacienda: Sociological Implications', unpublished Ph.D. thesis (Michigan State University, 1959).
24. Ibid., p.74.
25. Cited in ibid., p.95.
26. The uneven ripening of Atlantic grown coffee relative to those of the *Meseta Central* is discussed by R. Cleves in *Rendimientos de Beneficiado de Café: 1977–8* (San José, 1978).
27. This was indicated to this author during an interview with the administrator of this same estate in April, 1980.
28. The administrator informed this author that between the early 1970s and 1980 the permanent labour force had declined from 450 to 320 permanent field hands. During the harvest, on the other hand, the estate labour force swelled to about 1000 persons, so contract labour is clearly a very important aspect of this estate's operation during a certain part of the year. Other than for harvesting, however, temporary labourers were generally not utilised.
29. This is based on the author's own fieldwork (1980) and the work by Arce, 'Rational Introduction', p.77, 104. The estate had expanded its land in coffee by the late 1970s to 828 *manzanas* but production had increased more than proportionately, to an average 20000 *fanegas* annually.
30. Bolaños and Cartin, 'Obstaculos Ideologicas', p.102.
31. J. Aguilar *et al.*, *Desarrollo–Tecnologico*, Table 3.10.
32. Oficina del Café, *Informe Sobre la Actividad Cafetalera de Costa Rica*, (San José, 1979), p.35.
33. *El Agricultor Costarricense*, no. 7 (1977).
34. This, for example, was the situation on the estate studied by Bolaños and Cartin, 'Obstaculos Ideologicas'.
35. Ibid., p.109. The following unions of agricultural workers have been established in recent years: Sindicato de Trabajadores Agricolas de Coopevictoria; Sindicato de Trabajadores Agricolas y Plantaciones de Cartago; Union de Trabajadores Agricolas de la Provincia de Alajuela; and the Sindicato de Trabajadores Agricolas Unidas de Alajuela. See ibid., pp.110–11 and de la Cruz, 'Costa Rica: 100 Años de Luchas Sociales', pp.41–4.
36. Karl Marx, *Capital*, vol. 1, (Moscow, 1967), pp.586–7.
37. Cardoso, 'The Formation of the Coffee Estate', p.36.
38. *R.I.D.C.*, (1940), pp. 338–43.
39. Barrenechea, *Una Organización*, p.21.
40. This and the following information is elaborated from data provided by the Coffee Office, Department of Liquidations and Inspections, unless otherwise indicated.

41.   These six largest processing firms were Beneficiadora Cachí (2 *beneficios*); Beneficiadora La Meseta Ltda.; Beneficio el General S.A.; Beneficio La Ribera S.A.; Cafetalera Industrial La Meseta Ltda.; and Peters S.A. (3 *beneficios*).

42.   Of all credits that went to producers from the National Banking System for these two stages in 1975, 75619556 colons went through *beneficiadors* and only 2,032,400 *colons* went directly from the Bank to growers, according to Garita and Leon, 'Diferenciación', p.71.

43.   Ibid., p.78.

44.   With the closing of the European markets during the Second World War, local processors were no longer able to ship select coffee under their own brand names. Rather, when the US became the major buyer of Latin American coffees through agreement with its allies, a single price was set for the coffee of each country. No longer was there a disincentive to mix different grade coffee from other areas, since the American market had traditionally absorbed low grade coffee, and such factors as taste and the appearance of the bean were much less important. (See Seligson, Agrarian–Capitalism, p.27.) Thus, from the private point of view of the *beneficiador*, it now made sense to compete for coffee outside his traditional receiving zone, and mechanised transport and better roads allowed him to do just that.

45.   Barrenechea, *Una Organización*, p.22.

46.   Seligson, *Agrarian Capitalism*, p.26.

47.   Stone, *La Dinastía*, pp.136–7.

48.   The remarks which follow are based in part on a series of in-depth interviews conducted by the author with *beneficiadores* or their representatives in April, 1980, and visits to various processing plants in June 1979 and April 1980. The firms involved represented a wide range of situations. A representative of one of the country's five largest processors was interviewed while other interviews included a medium size and a small firm. The sample included firms with modern facilities, as well as one with a very old *beneficio* with few recent technological innovations. Finally, within the sample there was a diversity of geographic locations, including a firm on the edge of metropolitan San José, and another outside of the *Meseta Central*, and some distance from any major urban centre.

49.   There are obstacles to this labour displacement strategy, at least for some firms. The current labour shortage during the harvest has necessitated the use of 'lower quality' labour. Consequently, the coffee received by the *beneficios* often has many more impurities, requiring the retention of more sorters to act as a check on the automatic equipment.

50.   Interviews with managers of processing firms, 1980.

51.   The author was informed by one manager that the price of a mechanical dryer in 1980 would vary between 150000 to 200000 *colons* ($17000–$23000), for a machine to be used for about 15 days of the year. The largest *beneficios* might have 10 or more of these.

52.   The increase in plant capacity is indicated by the fact that the average amount of coffee processed per plant was 11361 *fanegas*

in 1965; in 1978 this had doubled to an average of 22721 *fanegas* per plant.

53. Gerardo Viquez and Leonidas Lopez, 'Informe de Costa Rica', in *Café y Cooperativismo en America Latina*, no. 40 (CEDAL, San José, 1971), p.4.
54. This information was offered by a representative of a firm owning one small *beneficio* to the east of San José.
55. Interview, 1980.
56. Barrenechea, *Una Organización, p.24.*
57. See Aguilar *et al.*, *Desarrollo Tecnologico*, p.6–40.
58. This is noted in a lengthy communication between the sub–director of the Coffee Office and the manager of the Central Bank, reported in *La Nacion* (19 April 1964). The author's own interview with *beneficiadores* confirmed the impression that, despite the absence of special credit programmes for processors, credit had been available to finance the modernisation of their facilities.
59. 'Diferenciación al Interior', (1977).
60. Torres Rivas, *Elementos, pp.44–5.*
61. Department of Liquidations and Inspections, various years.
62. 'Diferenciación al Interior' (1977).

8 Diversification beyond the Agro-export Model

Costa Rica has experienced notable economic development in non-traditional spheres since the Second World War – even though coffee has not been entirely displaced as a central component of the national economy. The external environment played an important role in determining the limits of what development took place, of course. Noteworthy in this regard was the formation of the Central American Common Market which gave a definite boost to intra-regional trade and thereby stimulated some industrial development, at least until the troubled times beginning in the late 1970s. The nation's economic expansion must also be situated within the context of the long period of post-war prosperity for Western capitalism which began to falter seriously in the early 1970s, and most definitely by the end of this decade.

In an important sense, it is changes outside the traditional agro-export system that seem to point up the *limits* of the developmental model sponsored by *Liberación Nacional*, particularly with respect to the redistributionist aspect of their political project. In summarising the features of this economic diversification, I will look at non-traditional agricultural development before turning to new industrial activities.

8.1 AGRICULTURAL DIVERSIFICATION

In Costa Rica since the early part of the 1950s, the modernisation of coffee production – both its agricultural and agro-industrial aspects – has been part of a wider project of agricultural development in which the State has played a salient role. In the coffee sector it is apparent that small and medium size farms have participated in the contemporary modernisation of this activity, as productivity data make clear. However, two thirds of Costa Rica's farms lie outside the coffee sector,[1] the majority small and medium enterprises engaged in the cultivation of traditional basic foodstuffs. Here, productivity for

146

such widespread crops as corn and beans has shown little increase since 1950. Where significant productivity gains have been made, as with rice, it is only the largest producers that have substantially boosted their yields, indicating it was they who appropriated most of the substantial State agricultural credits going to these activities.[2]

The very sizable amounts of State credits going to non-coffee producers in the countryside helped stimulate a type of development involving a tendency towards concentration of production in large units that has been considerably more pronounced than in the case of coffee. Meat production, for example, which was highly concentrated in 'medium' and 'large' farms by 1963 (67.4 per cent) was even more so by 1973 (72.5 per cent).[3] Even basic grains cultivation, traditionally more a preserve of the sub-family and family size units, has become more and more the field of capitalist farms. Thus, 'large' farms increased their proportion of national production of basic grains from 22.3 per cent to 49.4 per cent in the ten year period after 1963.[4]

This situation was itself nothing more than a reflection of the high degree of concentration of resources that characterised the national agrarian economy as a whole by the 1970s. The concentration of land was, not surprisingly, a central element of this situation. Of the total number of farms in the country (81562 in 1973), the 44338 with under 10 hectares had only 4 per cent of all land in farms. At the other end of the spectrum, less than 1 per cent of the farms (795) controlled 36 per cent of all land in farms.[5] In this vital respect, then, Costa Rican agriculture exhibited the extreme inequalities that are well-known to be typical of its Central American neighbour countries.

Behind this accelerated development and concommitant resource concentration in agriculture outside of the coffee economy, has been State support for the diversification of the monoculture that was so typical before the 1950s. This is evident in State credit policies, above all, with a declining proportion of credits going to coffee producers in recent years.[6] This expansion of non-traditional spheres of capitalist production, such as with the expansion of beef cattle ranching, rice, sorghum and cotton farming, has tended to create and fortify new modern fractions of the local agrarian bourgeoisie, although in the case of a few products, such as in the dairy industry, family size farms have managed to maintain a significant proportion of national production.[7]

8.2 NEW INDUSTRIAL ACTIVITIES

The emergence of new entrepreneurial groups in the countryside has really only been one aspect, however, of the expansion of capital in previously underdeveloped areas of the local economy, and industrial activities in particular. This expansion took place during the period when *Liberación Nacional* emerged and consolidated its hegemonic position in national political life (having always had control of the Legislature and/or the Executive from the early 1950s until the 1970s). In its main lines this development largely accorded with early *liberacionista* thinking. Their orientation had, of course, always viewed 'development' in terms of diversification and stimulation of the national economy, by means of an active State creating the necessary conditions for the expansion of private capital.

The first phase of industrial expansion has largely involved agricultural processing and transformation activities. In this sphere there have been more State measures to foster the involvement of local capital, as I note below. On the other hand, it appears that a much heavier dependence on foreign capital has characterised the subsequent industrialisation phase. Such industries as petro-chemicals, auto assembly, and tyre manufacturing are notable examples of industries established in this next stage, generally necessitating considerable investment in costly technology that is usually supplied by foreign multinational firms.

The most decisive State measure to achieve these ends was the Law of Industrial Production and Development (no. 2426), passed in 1959. This legislation had a long gestation period and had been in the making since shortly after Figueres and *Liberación Nacional* founded the Government in 1953. The objectives of this decree are bluntly stated in its first two articles and are worth citing in full:

Article 1 – The present law has as its fundamental objective to constitute, by means of the development of industries to be specified, the diversification and strengthening of the economic activities of the country, endeavoring to channel national savings and to attract investment originating in the exterior in order to create new sources of better renumerated employment as an essential measure in obtaining the general welfare of the people.
Article 2 – The State will seek to maintain a free industrial development avoiding the concentration of industrial capital functioning monopolistically.[8]

The law itself entailed both protectionist measures involving heavy duties on a specified range of imported commodities (see article 12), and provisions especially designed to promote the establishment of new industries. These latter included, notably, the making available of credits and generous exemptions from various custom duties, the land tax, the tax on profits (for earnings reinvested in improvements) and all export duties for enterprises falling within the terms of the law (article 19), for a maximum period of ten years.

Within this favourable economic environment, industrial capital flourished, at least relative to previous times, and Costa Rica experienced one of the highest annual rates of industrial growth in Latin America. The gross domestic product of manufacturing industries tripled between 1961 and 1971 alone, and as a proportion of the national GDP it rose from 13.4 per cent in 1950 to 19 per cent in 1973.[9]

Agriculture related industries have been a very major part of industrial activities in contemporary Costa Rica, and despite the growth of other industrial branches, the former still produced 48 per cent of the value of all industrial production as late as 1974.[10] Moreover, these agricultural transformation industries, at least those with a high percentage (90 per cent or more) of local primary materials received special treatment under the Law of Industrial Protection and Development, in that the State would guarantee all credits such enterprises needed to obtain in order to finance their establishment (article 29).[11]

The food industry alone has experienced rapid growth during this period and a change in its structure. The value added in this sub-branch of industry had in fact grown from 98 million to 279 million *colons* in the 1953–63 period.[12] Moreover, many new activities have grown up where once one activity, coffee processing, contributed the bulk of production. Between 1957 and 1974 the contribution of coffee processing had declined from 53 per cent to 27 per cent of the total value produced by this branch of the economy, despite the fact that the volume of coffee actually processed has grown without precedent,[13] indicating a rapid expansion of non-coffee industries in this key industrial branch. It is also interesting to note that, with the exception of beef products and sugar, the majority of this production goes to the home market.[14] Furthermore, despite the dramatic inroads made by foreign multinationals in the non-traditional spheres of production throughout the rest of Central America, in Costa Rica this key branch of industry has clearly been a sphere for the expansion of national capital. The law protecting industry had explicitly encouraged this, in fact, as the special provisions allowing for agricultural transformation industries were restricted to enterprises owned or controlled by nationals (see article 29, section a.). By the early 1970s about 60 per cent of the capital in this branch was owned locally, even excluding the coffee processing industry from this estimation.[15]

It need be mentioned, finally, that this industrial expansion has been clearly linked with the development of the nation's agriculture, which I have discussed previously, and has not simply entailed the further elaboration and/or packaging of primary materials imported from abroad. Thus, more than 72 per cent of primary inputs utilised in this branch are of local origin, and this figure excludes the coffee industry, where the primary material is naturally 100 per cent of local origin.[16]

The modernisation of the coffee economy itself should be viewed in light of the effect this development would inevitably produce given the *liberacionista* policies favouring the establishment of indigenous industrial enterprises related to agriculture. Not the least important results produced by the intensification of coffee cultivation has been the sustained and growing demand for considerable quantities of agro-inputs it created, with fertiliser consumption being the most important. The consumption of chemical fertilisers in coffee and sugar cane cultivation has been a major component of the home market, and between 1963 and 1973 this consumption increased by about one third. This demand was sufficient to justify the establishment of an extensive chemical complex, for example, producing fertilisers and other agro-chemicals for the local and regional markets.[17]

The modernisation of the agro-industrial sphere of the coffee economy has also created other possibilities for local manufacturing. Machinery that in the old days was of largely English manufacture has in many respects been replaced by improved technology of local origin. This is true for such major recent investments in this sphere as mechanical driers, and even the electronic sorters are now beginning to be produced locally.[18]

Overall, the relationship between the agrarian sphere and industrial capital, referring now more narrowly to the economic relationship, continues to be important, even central, to the contemporary phase of industrialisation. Protectionist measures and State incentives gave a big push to the first phase of import-substituting industrialisation by the early 1960s, with industries processing agricultural products being the leading edge of this phase. I have already suggested some of the ways this expansion of commercial agriculture was creating a home market for industrial capital with the examples of fertiliser and other agro-chemical products. Other commodities might be mentioned as well. Undoubtedly this agrarian transformation has not only stimulated the demand for production goods, but for wage goods as well with the progressive expansion of the landless, wage-dependent rural labour force.[19] On the other hand, commercial agricultural production, and by this I mean large capitalist producers and some family and small capitalist farmers, were benefiting from the expansionary State credit programmes of this period.

Finally, it is interesting to compare the character of this contemporary industrial expansion, with the stated policy objectives of *Liberación Nacional* dominated governments. Clearly there has been some of the sought-after diversification and strengthening of what was previously a very small narrow industrial structure, although the bulk of production remains confined to the traditional agriculture-related industrial areas. With respect to two other objectives that were to be, ostensibly, primary guidelines for the State's industrialisation plan – the desire to avoid economic concentration and the provision of employment opportunities – the results have been less salutory.

Regarding industrial concentration and the tendency to monopolisation, it would seem that State policies have done anything but hinder such a process. To note a few examples, meatpacking and processing were dominated by three firms with 90 per cent of the value of production, milling was dominated by one plant with 40 per cent of the value of all milled products, one plant generated 66 per cent of the value of all milk products; one plant produced 72 per cent of the value of all vegetable and animal oil production and two plants accounted for 65 per cent of the value of all fruit canning and processing. Of the entire agro-industrial branch (which produces 36 per cent of the 'value added' of all industry), 19 firms produce almost 40 per cent of the gross product value, if one excludes coffee processing.[20] I have already considered the marked centralisation of capital that has characterised this latter sphere.

One could only expect that in other branches of industry that are especially capital intensive (such as the metal and chemical industries), that the tendency to monopoly will be even more severe than with agro-industrial firms. As one indication of the degree of centralisation and concentration of the industrial sphere as a whole, it is significant that of the 1361 'industrial enterprises' enumerated by the census of 1973, the 15 largest enterprises had 20

Table 8.1   Costa Rica: small, medium and large industrial firms by occupied
workforce and value added: 1958, 1964 and 1975

Size*	1958		1964		1975	
	Occupied workforce	*Value added*	*Occupied workforce*	*Value added*	*Occupied workforce*	*Value added*
Small	58	34	56	32	20	10
Medium	24	27	22	24	20	17
Large	18	39	22	44	60	73
Total	100	100	100	100	100	100

*Small: less than 19 employees; Medium: 20 to 69 employees; Large: 70 and
more employees.
Source: Liliana Herrera and Raimundo Santos, *Del Artesano al Obrero
Fabril* (San José; Editorial Provenir S.A., 1979) p.44, Table 3.

per cent of all industrial workers – the equivalent proportion to
the 1037 smallest enterprises. Table 8.1 shows in rather dramatic
fashion the rapid acceleration in the concentration of production
in the largest firms that took place in the decade after the State
moved to protect and promote industry. And as one study that
has viewed the question of concentration internationally has noted,
the level of industrial concentration in Costa Rica is considerably
greater than in Mexico, a substantially more industrialised country, and much more so than is the case for the United States,
for example.[21]

Finally, with regards to the goal of expanding employment
there is some evidence to suggest that the creation of employment
opportunities has lagged substantially behind the rate of expansion
of industrial output. For the 1963–8 period, a time of considerable
industrial growth, gross industrial output increased about 27 per
cent. The number of 'employees' in industry, however, grew at
a much slower rate, about 15 per cent for these years.[22] Given
that relatively large, modern and hence capital intensive firms have
spear-headed industrial growth since the early 1960s, and indeed have
managed to monopolise many important industrial sub-branches, the
slow growth of industrial employment relative to increase in output
must be seen as the logical outcome of an industrialisation process
taking this form.

If there is anything to differentiate this development model from
that of the ultra-conservative oligarchic regimes of neighbouring

Central American societies, at least in more economic terms, it would seem to be that in Costa Rica the State has played a more forceful role in attempting to compensate for the rapid concentration of wealth and resources that is so characteristic of late capitalist development in backward social formations. This has been attempted through the extension of already existing social programmes and the development of new redistributionist measures in very recent times.[23] Meanwhile, conservative wage policies have meant that with the inflation of the 1970s, there was a considerable deterioration of minimum wages in real terms.[24] This policy of stimulating the engines of private capital accumulation and afterwards having the State siphon off some of the resulting surplus is, it should be noted, only the practical consequence of the implementation of a political philosophy first articulated by the intellectuals of the *Centro* as far back as the early 1940s.

Notes

1. *Censo-agropecuario* (1963 and 1973), p.3.
2. For data on production per hectare for the most important crops produced in Costa Rica, see Sergio Reuben Soto, *Capitalismo y Crisis Economica en Costa Rica*, San José, Editorial Porvenir S.A. (1982), p.212, Table 8.
3. *Censo agropecuario*, (1963 and 1973).
4. *Ibid.*
5. *Censo agropecuario*, (1973). A further indication of the existing concentration are the results of a recent study which found that 67 per cent of the value of all agricultural production was produced by medium large and large farms, by 1973. Oficina de Planificacion Sectorial Agropecuario, *Programa de Mejoramiento de la Producción de Café de Costa Rica*, San José (1979).
6. The proportion of all agricultural credits going to coffee producers declined from 58.7 per cent to 35.6 per cent between 1973–4 and 1975–6 alone, according to data provided by Garita and Leon, 'Diferenciación al Interior', p.39. This is a relative, and not an absolute decline, it should be stressed.
7. *Censo agropecuario* (1973).
8. *La Gaceta*, no. 203 (9 September 1959).
9. Calculated from United Nations *The Growth of World Industry 1938–61* New York (1963), p.70 and José Salazar *et al.* 'Costa Rica: Una Politica Agraria Innovadora', *Estudios Sociales Centroamericanos, no. 20 (1978), p.50.*
10. Juan Carlos Del Bello, 'El Sector Agroindustrial en Costa Rica' *Estudios Sociales Centroamericanos*, no.22 (1979), p.58, Table 3.

154   *Coffee and Democracy in Modern Costa Rica*

11.   Subject to certain conditions concerning the nationality of the capital involved. This is discussed below.
12.   United Nations, *The Growth of World Industry*.
13.   Del Bello, 'El Sector Agroindustrial', p.60, Table 5.
14.   In fact, 73.7 per cent of the production of this branch is consumed locally according to data found in Del Bello, ibid., p.61, Table 6.
15.   Ibid., p.62, Table 8.
16.   Ibid., p.61, Table 7.
17.   Consumption of chemical fertiliser was computed from the agricultural censuses of 1963 and 1973, using the average number of kilograms consumed per hectare in 1973 as a guide for 1963 for which data on the quantity of fertiliser used are unavailable. This would likely give a somewhat inflated figure for consumption per hectare for 1963, so that the percentage increase in consumption is most likely greater than I have suggested.

       The fertiliser complex of Fertica S.A. is located in Puntarenas. For a list of the concessions granted this company by the State, refer to Fertica S. A., *Informe Anual* (1977). The export of fertilisers was the most valuable chemical product exported by 1974. See Dirección General de Estadisticas, *Anuario Estadistico de Costa Rica*, San José (1974), Table 157.
18.   Information provided to the author by representatives of *beneficio* firms in 1980.
19.   According to the 1963 and 1973 population censuses, the number of 'remunerated' workers in agriculture grew from 101958 to 122600 in this brief period (1973 data includes forestry and fishing, but the number of individuals involved is very small).
20.   Del Bello, 'El Sector Agroindustrial'.
21.   Ricardo Dias Santos, *Datos Basicos de Costa Rica*, Instituto de Investigaciones Sociales, no. 14 (1976), p.27, Table 21.
22.   Calculated from data found in U.N. *Growth of World Industry, 1972* (1974).
23.   By the early 1970s the State was expanding resources allocated to social services, which entailed such items as expanding disabliity and old age pensions to those sectors not covered by the social security system, and the Family Allowance Program, designed to raise rural living standards through expansion of rural infrastructure. Economic Commission on Latin America, *Economic Survey of Latin America*, Santiago (1976), p.152.
24.   Ibid.

9 Landlord Capitalism, Development and Democracy

> The fate of German democracy depends largely on the solution of the agricultural problem in that country. If no radical solution for this problem can be found, then the policy of democratic peace here advocated becomes impossible of maintenance. . . The first and foremost necessity for agricultural reconstruction . . . is the elimination of the Junkers, who have been the authors or coauthors of all the acts of aggression perpetrated by Germany in the last seventy or eighty years.(A. Gerschenkron, *Bread and Democracy in Germany*, 1943)

At this point it is appropriate to take stock of the materials presented so far, and to return to the main themes broached in the Introduction. This will involve, first of all, a reconsideration of estate agriculture as a 'model' or 'path' of rural development that is especially prevalent in the underdeveloped countries, and a discussion of the insights that may be offered by the Costa Rican experience.

The second task will be to reassess the roots of Costa Rica's political 'exceptionalism'. This chapter will attempt to distil some of the material from previous chapters in order to provide a final analysis of the roots of this 'exceptionalism', its relationship to the specific features of landlord capitalism in Costa Rica, and the lessons this historical experience may have for developments elsewhere in the region.

9.1 THE PROBLEM OF LANDLORD CAPITALISM

Recent historical scholarship has made clear that a significant aspect of the emergence and expansion of the world capitalist economy in the nineteenth century was the creation of commercial agricultural estates outside of those countries undergoing the Industrial Revolution. In Eastern Europe, parts of North Africa, and in Central and

South America, the organisation of wheat, cotton, coffee and beef production on large estates for the industrialising European countries marked an important historical break from earlier economic patterns. It was not that large landowners engaged in commercial production was new, for this had occurred in earlier times in many different places. Rather, from 1850 or so onwards, what occurred in these economically backward regions was a veritable transformation in the social relations of production, together with an expansion of the scale upon which agriculture was organised, and a rationalisation of the production process.[1] This development, in turn, provided impetus to the large–scale construction of economic infrastructure – roads, railways, electrification, port facilities – which transformed these regions in the last century. A further outcome of this event was the consolidation of an agrarian–based class which in a number of societies became the dominant force in national politics for an entire era. In a few countries it remains so.

The study of this modern form of agrarian structure is not well advanced, but in terms of offering analytical insights into the phenomenon of estate agriculture no studies are more important than the crucial work by Max Weber on the classical estate–owning class – the Prussian Junkers. Both his more general essay 'Capitalism and Rural Society in Germany', but especially his detailed studies of the East Elbian political economy that formed part of his work for the *Verein fur Sozialpolitik*[2] provide us with the most significant case study of the internal dynamics of a rural economy dominated by estate production.

A few recent studies have already suggested the geographic *scope* of this kind of agrarian change in the last century. Richards, for example, has shown the fundamental similarities in the internal structure of nineteenth century modernising estates in such disparate regions as Prussia, Egypt and Chile, while attempting to examine the phenomenon of estate agriculture in more analytical terms as well.[3] Cristobal Kay's earlier study documents the important organisational features shared by precapitalist manorial economy in Eastern Europe and Central Chile just prior to the consolidation of modern estates there.[4]

Much of the discussion of the different paths or models of agrarian change – certainly in the Latin American context, has typically built on the classical Marxist literature in an attempt to conceptualise agrarian change. It is in this regard that Lenin's analysis of 'paths' of agrarian development becomes relevant, and especially his discussion of the Prussian or landlord path of capitalist development. In this regard, Lenin was to place the agrarian question at the centre of the discussion of the transition to capitalism. It was he who considered in the first serious way the implications of having large landed property as the basis of retrograde form of capitalist development in the countryside. From his specific vantage point – a backward social formation in the throes of a rapid transformation of its economic base – Lenin was in a favoured position to examine the struggle of two main historical possibilities, or 'paths', of development and to understand the implications of each kind of development for the future of political struggles and economic change in Russia.

> Those two paths of objectively possible bourgeois development we would call the Prussian path and the American path, respectively. In the first case feudal landlord economy slowly evolves into bourgeois, Junker landlord economy, which condemns the peasants to decades of most harrowing expropriation and bondage, while at the same time a small minority of *Grossbauern* (big peasants) arises. In the second case there is no landlord economy, or else it is broken up by revolution, which confiscates and splits up the feudal estates. In that case the peasant predominates, becomes the sole agent of agriculture, and evolves into a capitalist farmer.[5]

It is clear that neither road represents a going back to the old order: rather they were seen as two distinct lines heading towards a developed capitalist agriculture, both necessitating a structural reorganisation in the countryside. It is Lenin's discussion of the landlord path of agrarian change though, which appears most relevant to the historical experience of many Third World countries. His discussion is significant because he was the first to indicate the specificity of a landlord type of development. Moreover, he provides insights into the impact of landlord capitalism in the countryside, not only for the character of development there but, by implication, for the way this would tend to structure the whole economy. Unfortunately, Lenin did not return to develop further this promising discussion.

This state of affairs explains much about the treatment of this model of agrarian transition in the literature on Latin American development, for instance. Mention of the 'Prussian path' to characterise a pattern of agrarian economy dates at least from Roger Bartra's work on Mexico where it was used to typify agrarian organisation before the revolution of 1910.[6] The concept is also used extensively in Agustin Cueva's well known synthesis on Latin American development, where it is also referred to as the 'reactionary' or 'oligarchic' path of agrarian development. Cueva used the concept to help explain the notably backward and unequal development of the productive forces in Latin America, and the notorious presence of a diversity of social relations of production in the countryside even in recent times.[7] None the less, even Cueva does not attempt to analyse the concept of the 'Prussian path' in its own right, in order to further draw out the insights and problems it contains. Subsequently, use of the concept has generally been more uncritical, even contradictory. Some authors use it to characterise agrarian change in a wide range of Central and South American contexts, while other have rejected it as a suitable concept for a backward economy, such as Brazil, because of the historical association of Prussian agriculture itself with a dynamic, industrialising economy.[8]

In part, the literature utilising this concept has suffered from a certain lack of clarity around a number of essential issues. These include such matters as (1) the pre-existing conditions that provide fertile ground for the establishment of capitalist estate agriculture; (2) the significance of the social organisation of the estates for technological development in agriculture; (3) the relationship between the structure of estate agriculture and the wider economy of which it is a part; (4) the implications for society of the continued political dominance of an estate owning class, for the form of the State that will emerge, the constitution and interplay of political parties, and the development of ideology. Recently these concerns *have* been addressed, at least with reference to the classical Prussian case.[9] At this point I wish to consider what insights we might gain about this model of agrarian development from an examination of the Costa Rican experience.

9.2 THE PRECONDITIONS OF LANDLORD CAPITALIST DEVELOPMENT

Landlord capitalism in the Costa Rican context did not exactly conform to the 'classical' features associated with this model of agrarian change, at least in some respects. To begin with, historical scholarship to date has noted in such diverse locales as Chile and Prussia, the close relationship between a pre-existing feudal–like manorial economy, typically associated with a numerous rural population, and the subsequent emergence of what we have termed modern estate farming.[10] Though most of the rest of Central America conformed to this situation, Costa Rica did not. Here, those organising the initial production of coffee for the European market within the confines of estate production were faced with a sparsely settled landscape that was largely peripheral to the colonial economy of the more populous northern territories of Central America. It was there that the production of organic dyestuffs – principally indigo – evolved within the confines of precapitalist latifundia.[11]

The *tabula rasa* presented to prospective landowners in Costa Rica had several noteworthy consequences. Undoubtedly it facilitated the emergence of a sizable class of petty commodity producers engaged in coffee production which eventually came to control a larger proportion of the land in export agriculture than was typical elsewhere in the region. As we have seen the influence of small coffee farmers has at times been determinant in deciding the trajectory of Costa Rican politics. The scarcity of labour in the *Meseta Central* may have well placed limits on the size of operation that agrarian capitalists could hope to establish initially, while at a later time the shortage of good land for coffee, and the rapid valorisation of the land as a result, certainly put limits on estate expansion.

Despite these apparent constraints, a modern estate–owning class did, nevertheless, become firmly implanted here, a class that, as with Weber's Junkers, was not a rentier group but an active agent in the actual organisation and operation of the lands they owned. In this particular context, estate owners managed to bolster the influence gained from their relatively modest landholdings by monopolising processing and export activities, and providing credit to the petty commodity coffee sector.

9.3 ESTATE AGRICULTURE: A BACKWARD FORM OF DEVELOPMENT?

Regarding the question of technology, we have seen that for a long time the technical level of estate agriculture in Costa Rica was very low. The significance of the estate system was that production was organised on a enlarged scale with a substantial labour force, utilising the latest in rational and systematic methods of cultivation. Nevertheless, these agricultural techniques were employed within a labour–intensive and land–extensive production process. With respect to the employment of technology then, and in terms of the basic social organisation of the estates as well, the Costa Rian situation would reinforce the thesis that landlord capitalism is a retrograde form of economic development.[12]

If estate agriculture is initially a backward form of capitalist development in the countryside, the question remains whether it typically continues to be so. Does an estate economy pose insurmountable obstacles for the organisation of a modern, capitalised and intensive agriculture? Definitive answers to this question are not likely to be forthcoming until more historical studies of estate dominated economies in different parts of the world have been completed. Nevertheless, there is some evidence to suggest that it need not pose such an obstacle. The case of Prussia is itself illustrative. Towards the end of the nineteenth century a transformation in the organisational structure of the large estates was taking place there. The old estate system, which had tied its permanent labour force to the estate by granting individual plots of land was increasingly abolished, the land incorporated into commercial estate production, and the former permanent estate workers reduced to the status of a rural proletariat.[13]

Various circumstances put pressure on the incomes of the Prussian landowners, impelling them to seek out new ways to raise estate revenues. A key factor was certainly the stiff competition they faced from low cost grain production in the New World that entered the world wheat market at this time.[14] Other factors existed as well, including the valorisation of land which made take-over of the subsistence plots of the permanent labourers particularly attractive, and the fact that for various reasons, the permanent worker was not providing the same quantity of family labour to the estate owner *gratis*, as had previously been the case.[15]

In the context of these various pressures operating on the estate owners, it would appear that one particular structural change in the wider economy greatly influenced the kinds of solutions pursued by the large agriculturalists to confront the crisis facing them. This was the growing presence of a local surplus population of migrant labour. Despite the different explanations as to the origins of this surplus migrant population,[16] its existence would seem to have provided landowners with the requisite structural precondition to embark on new entrepreneurial strategies to bolster their sagging fortunes. Principally, this involved the introduction of machinery such as steam threshers, and the increasing change–over to intensive cultivation of root crops – sugar beets and potatoes. Both strategies exacerbated the seasonal demand for labour, at the expense of permanent labour – and were therefore predicated on having a supply of migrant labour at hand for those periods of intense labour demand.[17] This whole process entailed a veritable reorganisation of Prussian estate farming, involving the intensification of cultivation, the increasing use of machinery and fertilisers, and accompanying these changes, the tranformation of labour relations on the estate as permanent workers previously tied to it were replaced by wage workers hired on a seasonal basis. As one observer has written, there developed 'the strengthening of the cash nexus for labour contract and a more complete utilisation of labour power purely for the benefit of the main estate.'[18]

This change in estate organisation marks the shift between what Marx referred to as the formal and the real subsumption of the labour process by capital.[19] The latter denotes a further stage of the capitalist development of estate agriculture, the diffusion of the wage relationship and with this the foundation was laid for the further intensification and capitalisation of the enterprise. It was a reorganisation with consequences of a profound social, and ultimately political nature as well, and indeed contemporary observers, including Max Weber were acutely concerned that this transformation would have implications far beyond the local level, to the point where it would affect the very political fabric of the German nation state.[20]

Was the reorganisation of modern estate agriculture in Prussia an historical anomaly, or will it serve as an archetype for considering the historical development of landlord capitalism elsewhere in the world? This question is not easily answered because of the dearth of in-depth studies of estate farming in other locales. What can be said is that in some countries, at least, where estate agriculture predominates, there is evidence of a more contemporary phase of structural reorganisation. The Central American countries are a case in point, and not only in Costa Rica, to which I shall return below.

The emergence of modern estate-type agriculture in Guatemala, El Salvador and Nicaragua late in the nineteenth century has received some attention already.[21] Of particular relevance to this discussion are studies which have pointed to contemporary structural changes in Central American agriculture. These changes are specific to the post-Second World War period, indicating the very late development of landlord capitalism here, certainly relative to Eastern Europe. The particular forces that would seem to have impelled these changes appear to be specific to this context, and included such factors as the spread of social legislation involving minimum wages, social security and the like to agriculture, and also the threat posed by labour unions and their attempts to organise the permanent workforce on the estates.[22] Significantly, from the point of view of understanding the dynamics of estate farming in general, there is evidence here as well that a key structural determinant of landowners response has been the appearance of a new and growing surplus population of landless labourers, at least by the 1960s, in those areas where commercial export agriculture predominates.[23]

The growth of the landless rural population has allowed the large coffee growers, for instance, to divest themselves of their permanent workers – those most likely to be organised and to be granted the benefits of new social legislation – as much as possible. Their labour was substituted, not so much by machinery in the case of coffee, but by such capital inputs as herbicides that drastically reduce the labour requirements for necessary weeding operations. This, plus the increasing recourse to hiring outside labour on short–term contract, had reduced their permanent workforce very substantially by the 1970s. Subsistence plots previously retained by the permanent workers have been shifted to commercial estate production, with those permanent workers remaining being converted to the status of landless wage labourers.[24]

How, then, does the Costa Rican experience fit into this pattern of agrarian change? In the first place, the *cafetaleros* of Costa Rica were not in the process of being rapidly pushed out of a world market because of the high costs of production on their estates relative to producers elsewhere, such as occurred with capitalist grain farmers in Prussia. Costs of production were historically higher in Costa Rica, which likely worsened the structural crisis of this class, but this was a longer term problem and did not force an immediate adjustment of estate economy, or of the rest of society. The *cafetaleros* no longer had the political influence after the 1940s to force adoption of another measure that had been favoured by the coffee oligarchy in other countries – the devaluation of local currency and the subsequent increase in all manner of consumer goods that this would have provoked. Such a 'solution' would not have overcome problems that were really structural in nature, but would rather have attenuated them, and at the expense of the rest of society.

Another characteristic of the Costa Rican situation was its very backward state, even by the post-Second World War period, relative to the more advanced Latin American countries. Little notable industrial expansion and the urban growth that this implies had taken place. Investment in land for speculative purposes did not, therefore, produce income comparable to that which could be had by putting land into coffee production. In addition, State credit policies which discouraged the extension of farms and strongly favoured the intensification of cultivation on them encouraged productive investment activity on the part of agrarian capital. Unlike in Argentina, for instance, speculative rent was not a major obstacle to raising agrarian productivity, despite the reasonably high levels of land concentration in the coffee growing regions that would have made this possible.[25] Far from being a bottle–neck to a broader based economic development, the growth of agriculture during the 50's and 60's was exceptional relative to most other Latin American countries.

Given all these conditions: relatively high production costs per unit of land, lack of more lucrative fields of investment outside of coffee cultivation, a limited possibility of forcing through unpopular political measures such as devaluation, and the considerable incentives provided by State programmes for the intensification of coffee cultivation, it is apparent that the modernisation of production was the most rational response for capitalist producers.

As we have seen in previous chapters, the large Costa Rican coffee farmers, with considerable assistance from the State, were able to solve the problem of stagnation and declining incomes through a strategy involving a veritable 'green revolution' in this sphere of agriculture. A combination of new varieties, new planting techniques and a technological package of agro–chemicals and fertilisers boosted the productivity of the coffee sector very considerably by the 1970s. It is also clear that we are speaking of fundamental structural changes as well in the organisation of the coffee estates. As elsewhere in Central America, the traditional permanent labour force retaining their own plots of land on the estate was increasingly displaced, either by short term contract labour or, as in the less populous river valleys on the Atlantic slope, by permanent wage labour without the traditional rights of access to estate lands.

What is not so clear is the extent to which the development of a 'surplus' population of landless and/or semi–proletarian labour on the margins of the estates was crucial to the contemporary modernisation of the large coffee farms. Most evidence would point to the availability of such labour willing to be hired on a contractual basis in recent times for most of the capitalist coffee farmers, and here the fact that coffee is generally cultivated in close proximity to the areas of highest population density in the country may have been a crucial factor in solving the landowners particular labour requirements under the new system of cultivation. This conclusion is supported by the fact that in the outlying areas of coffee production where population density was much lower, a substantial wage labour force had to be maintained on the estates throughout the year, even under the more modern and capital intensive system of cultivation.

Regardless of the particular way in which the problem of labour recruitment was solved however, the experience of Costa Rica provides further evidence that the continued survival of estate farming should not be seen as providing an insurmountable barrier to the modernisation of the agrarian sphere, at least. This conclusion holds not only for strictly agricultural activities, i.e. cultivation, but also for the agro–industrial sphere of the coffee sector, where processing operations have experienced technological advancement together with the clear cut concentration and centralisation of capitals typical of the process of capitalist development in its most modern forms.

9.4 ESTATE AGRICULTURE AND UNDERDEVELOPMENT

These developments occurring after the Second World War do not change the fact that in Costa Rica, as elsewhere, estate agriculture was for a long time associated with a broader process of underdevelopment. This was despite the fact that certain structural features of this economy offered potential for local industrial expansion. A sizable segment of small farmers were engaged in commodity production, even before the turn of the century, so that a money economy had taken hold in the countryside thereby supplying a crucial prerequisite for the development of local demand for consumption goods. But such demand could not expand beyond a certain point, because the oligarchy's monopolisation of the spheres of processing, credit and marketing severly restricted the accumulation possibilities of small coffee farmers. Neither was much of a demand for consumption goods provided by the significant estate labour force because the social organisation of these estates at this time kept the permanent worker's cash income at a very low level.

As for the local market for production goods – commodities used in the cultivation and processing of coffee – we have seen that the estates, which were the most advanced coffee farms technically speaking, organised production on what was essentially an *extensive* basis. This provided little of the demand for production inputs such as chemical fertilisers, agro–chemicals, irrigation equipment and assorted farm machinery that today is associated with intensive coffee production. A potential demand for other types of production goods *did* exist, however. In the processing sphere, productive consumption by agrarian capitalists was much more substantial. The problem here was that such machinery as was needed generally could be procured most cheaply from the more advanced nations. As long as the *cafetaleros* were able to maintain a policy of free trade and forstall the passing of the protectionist legislation needed by the nation's embryonic industry, most of the benefits provided by the existing local demand accrued to manufacturers elsewhere, notably in Europe.

9.5 LANDLORD CAPITALISM AND DEMOCRACY: COMPARATIVE PERSPECTIVES

A most interesting, and possibly the most difficult, question posed by the dominance of the large estate owners in society is related to their impact in more clearly political terms – how they shape the characteristics of the political parties that will emerge, the form of the State that will prevail, and the development of ideology. For if landlord capitalism does not appear to constitute an insurmountable barrier to progress at the level of the production process, there is less evidence to indicate that this path of agrarian development is compatible with the democratisation of politics. Indeed, it may be seen as fundamentally inimical to such a process.

Historically, there has been a strong association of estate agriculture with political systems of a profoundly authoritarian content. The minimal development of political parties and the highly personalistic nature of estate organisation[26], where landowners and their local judicial representatives serve as paternalistic gatekeepers to material resources, ensures the exclusion of the bulk of the population from effective political participation. This has been true even where governments in such contexts have adopted a more or less modern republican form. Nevertheless, economic development, though constrained by a retrograde form of agrarian capitalism, still nurtures some new economic activities and thereby promotes the expansion of social classes and groups that see their interests as lying outside the traditional agro–exporting system of the landowning oligarchy. When this happens, new political projects are given birth, projects that necessarily challenge the traditional political supremacy of the oligarchy. The outcome is certain to be volatile.

The historical experience of Germany shows in a very sharp way the kinds of pressures that can be brought to bear. The unification of Germany under Bismarck had placed a modern industrialising region with an emerging industrial bourgeoisie and a rapidly growing and well-organised proletariat within the same national-economic space as a powerful estate owning class – the Prussian 'Junker' landowners. Here, new economic developments abroad towards the end of the nineteenth century increasingly tied the survival of these landowners to protectionist policies that were antithetical to the interests of other major classes in this society – notably the urban proletariat and to a lesser extent the small peasantry of the West. The survival of the Junkers thus became more and more incompatible with the continual strengthening of liberal democratic political structures, because of the possibility this would allow for other groups to block an agrarian policy aimed at saving the Junkers at their expense. The so–called 'solidarity bloc' which the estate owners were able to forge with the powerful interests representing heavy industry – the so–called 'marriage of iron and rye' – removed the most important obstacle to a Junker inspired agrarian policy. The alliance they were able to establish with sections of the peasantry in the West, furthermore, gave the large landowners the political strength needed to put the draconian measures into practice.[27]

The success of the Junkers in resisting the challenge to their influence did more than simply thwart the economic interests of other classes in German society, of course. They were able to firmly establish their ideological hegemony within the nation state, to 'insinuate their values, their style of life and thought, into a broad segment of the classes whose interest diverged from theirs'.[28] Over time, this subordination to the political ideology and culture of the Junkers had as a result the slow but steady emasculation of the centrist bourgeois and petit bourgeois parties in Germany. This reached the point where,

> By the end of the century, after decades of unprecedented economic growth and modernisation, Germany was essentially governed by one upper stratum – an uneasy amalgam of different classes and different interests, subordinated to the pseudo aristocratic values of the past and pledges to the common defense of privilege, which stance was defined as national virtue.[29]

It is not surprising that this led to the gradual evaporation of the 'middle ground' between the political project of Social Democracy and the reactionary Conservative Party of the Junkers. Such a development could not help but undercut the possibility of incorporating an increasingly restive working class in a reformist rather than a revolutionary direction. When this discontent was aggravated by the strongly anti-popular economic policies favoured by the Conservative Party,[30] and the structural crisis of high-cost Junker agriculture advanced, the ground work had already been prepared on the ideological terrain for political solutions of a profoundly authoritarian nature. Indeed, it has been argued that elements of the Nazi world view, 'can be perceived in the policy of an agriculture politically and spiritually dominated by the aristocratic landowners in the eastern half of the German Reich'.[31]

This necessarily brief overview of the role of the Prussian Junker class in Germany cannot detail the manifold ways in which this group shaped the modern social and political order of that country. At the most it may serve to highlight a dimension of the problem posed by the continual dominance of an estate-owning class in the life of a society. In very general terms, the German experience suggests that the preservation of the landed oligarchy's economic interests may be, and likely will be, at odds with the advancement of other social classes taking shape in a developing capitalist society. Moreover, as this antagonism matures, a strong dynamic is set in motion that requires – from the oligarchy's point of view – the thwarting of pressures towards the extension of civil and political rights to a broader spectrum of the citisenry. In other words, the political conditions for preserving the oligarchy's economic position will likely at some point require new authoritarian structures which, as politics becomes less a local and more a regional and national affair, requires that these structures of domination be elaborated at this level. If at one point the interests of estate owners can be maintained by a small rural police force, at another point in time, this same task will require the resources of the modern police *state*.

The Argentine experience suggests another type of economic and political evolution of society in which capitalist landowners constitute the leading fraction of the dominant class, though this time in a relatively more backward social formation. Here we find a landowning oligarchy ceding to and even helping to sponsor a programme of industrialisation, once the Great Depression put into jeopardy the old agro–exporting scheme. This event stimulated the emergence of a new configuration of social forces that began to form the basis for populist politics that would reorient State policies away from the large agrarian interests.

In Argentina under Perón landowners were displaced from their former position of prominence in the government, but managed to maintain their economic position, with the exception of the strictly rentier fraction of this class . Initially State policies under Perón took on a very pro–industrialisation character oriented more to redistribution of the agrarian surplus without much concern for the agrarian interests or with raising agricultural productivity. Later, when stagnation in the countryside became the bottle neck of economic expansion, structural obstacles – the possibility that the concentration of land in a few hands allowed for the appropriation of speculative rent – meant that standard efforts to stimulate agriculture through price supports would fail. Even worse, such policies undermined the material standards of the urban social base of the regime through inflation, thereby helping to create a polarised political climate. As the political contradictions sharpened, the options were limited and fairly clear-cut. Either carry out a restructuring of the agrarian sphere through a substantial reform thereby laying a firmer economic base by making agriculture a dynamic sector, or avoid reform and contain popular pressure for change through repression. As it turned out, the role of the landowners was crucial in sponsoring the 1955 rightist military *coup d'état* that would intiate the second option, one which subsequently proved to entail long term economic stagnation.

This experience demonstrated once again the incompatibility of bourgeois democracy with the survival of a landowning oligarchy particularly if the viability of the latter was tied to an economic programme inimical to the interests of other major class forces in society. As I have noted in Chapter 1, some analyses of events leading up to Castello Branco's 1964 coup in Brazil [32] suggest that similar lessons *vis-à-vis* the large landowners have emerged from this experience as well.

9.6 COSTA RICA: ONE SOLUTION TO THE DILEMMAS OF LANDLORD CAPITALISM

What kinds of insights and lessons with respect to the relationship of capitalist landowners to the State does my previous discussion of Costa Rican development suggest? Certainly in some important respects it represents an anomalous situation relative to those cases just considered. So too has Costa Rican social development moved along a different trajectory from that of its Central American sister states. The latter have in a number of ways shared the economic and political history of Costa Rica, particularly since mid-nineteenth century with the expansion of coffee and the upsurge of a coffee bourgeoisie as a leading force in the economic and political life of these societies.

From 1950 or so the failure of progressive movements in these northern countries has inaugurated a period of economic modernisation in which the interests of agrarian capitalists have been upheld at the expense of most other classes in society, and especially the poorer peasantry and the rural proletariat. This has increasingly required the full force of the State, in which the military, as it becomes more central to the co-ordination and functioning of these regimes, has become a major actor in national politics. Landlord capitalism here has thus meant the modernisation of estate agriculture to some extent, to be sure, accompanied by an initial phase of import substituting industrialisation. The unchecked rule of agrarian based capitalists has also, however, led to a virtually complete emasculation of even the feeble beginnings of liberal democracy that once existed and the individual liberties associated with it. In the Central American context the continuing influence of the landed oligarchy has, it must be noted, usually been secured with assistance, crucial at times, from friendly regimes elsewhere in the region, and at times with the critical aid of the United States.

In Costa Rica the basis for an alternative route out of the classical dilemmas posed by the dominance of capitalist landowners in society was being laid certainly by the early 1940s, and in some important respects even before. The presence of a fairly numerous class of formally independent petty commodity producers in the countryside that could constitute a political counterweight to the landowning oligarchy in the early part of the century was one important feature. It helped contribute to the development of a somewhat less exclusionistic oligarchic state in the first part of the present century. Also significant was the fact that the establishment of estate agriculture proceeded essentially by a process of colonisation of empty lands, rather than by a process of primitive accumulation more typical of those other Central American countries where a dense indigenous economy already existed. This meant that the semi–servile mechanisms for incorporating a displaced indigenous population, so typical of the early phase of modern estate farming in the northern countries, did not develop in Costa Rica. Consequently, force was much less integral to the reproduction of estate economy here. In this key respect, social relations on the Costa Rican estates were more akin to those that developed on the capitalist estates of Brazil or Argentina.

These factors undoubtedly played their part in determining a more democratic solution to the political crises of the agro–exporting scheme of the oligarchy. There were other circumstances of a more conjunctural nature that took on considerable historical importance. The Calderon-Vanguardia Popular alliance not only put the oligarchy into political disarray, it created the conditions for a stalemated struggle between the oligarchic forces and the progressive Government alliance. This alliance contributed to the historical division of the progressive forces in Costa Rican society, opening the way for a temporary alliance of the reformist *Partido Social Democrata* with the oligarchy. Once Figueres and his forces had made the crucial move and taken power through armed struggle, this configuration of the chief political actors made it possible for Figueres to take the course of expediency and proscribe the Communist Party, an action dictated by wider geo–political considerations detailed in Chapter 4.

This stalemated struggle was itself a basic condition for the emergence of Figueres and the PSD in what I have argued was essentially a Bonapartist type of situation. Thus, specific objective conditions, partly structural and partly conjunctural, opened the way for a development which gave greater autonomy to the State *viz-à-viz* those traditionally powerful private interests in society. After this point the State itself came to constitute a social force promoting the reorganisation of the economy. As I have shown, there was initial resistance to the modernisation project of the State, which was without a doubt significant because it came from the most influential group related to the coffee economy – the producer–processors. In Costa Rica the historic cleavage between these *beneficiadores* and small and medium cultivators, however, prevented the solidification of an 'agrarian bloc' to oppose the policy to rechannel part of the agrarian surplus for development purposes. Had such a political bloc been formed, it is likely that a cornerstone of the development project of Figueres and his forces would have floundered, and that the influence of *Liberación Nacional* in the restructuring of Costa Rican society would have been much reduced, if not placed into jeopardy altogether. As it turned out, the PLN programme found a resonance with the rural smallholders of the *Meseta Central*, an event considerably facilitated by Figueres' own personal attraction as a figure whose steadfast claims to rural roots and humble *campesino* origins gave him an appeal that could never have been his had he been identified with 'los ricos'.

Displacing the oligarchy as a political stratum in Costa Rica – over the longer term – was not simply a matter of clever political manoeuvring and the success or failure in forming effective political alliances. Much credit is due to the ability of Figueres and *Liberación Nacional* to also displace the ideological–discourse of the oligarchy from national politics, infused as it was with liberal economic doctrine, and replace it with an alternative political discourse based on the elements of an 'active' State, developmentalism, and ameliorative social reforms. In other words, Figueres and his forces did not simply create a 'breathing space' for the warring factions in civil society; their historical role was more significant than this. Not only did they put an end to the stalemated struggles which paralysed the national political scene during the late 1940s, but they took power with a programme that had been worked out in advance and which proved to be appropriate for the times, in terms of both the internal and the international economic and geopolitical situation. Needless to say, not all comparable political movements in the region have been so fortunate.

The reorganisation of Costa Rican society took various forms, but of particular importance was the new relationship forged between the State and the oligarchy. This new relationship had several aspects. In the first place, the State gained control over a part of the agricultural surplus previously the domain of the capitalist class, and the large coffee producer-processors especially. In the second place, the State utilised this surplus to create the conditions for the modernisation of coffee production – the most significant productive activity – through the creation of essential infrastructure and credit policies tailored to this end. Somewhat later other activities, agricultural and industrial, were also promoted to provide a broader basis for economic expansion and, presumably, to lessen the State's dependence on the surplus generated by coffee producers.

We can now assess the result of this development in the light of some of the other historical cases considered. Firstly, the most important economic sphere of the economy in Costa Rica was transformed from a very backward technical basis to one of the most technically advanced coffee economies anywhere in the world. This involved a relatively broad spectrum of producers, including small capitalist and family units of production, and to some extent even the smallest farms, the "sub–family" units. Given the greater weight of small capitalist and family size coffee enterprises in the Costa Rican countryside relative to other coffee economies, a more broadly based modernisation obviously had important economic advantages for the State over one which favoured large capitalist units alone, in addition to political advantages to the ruling party.

It was, as I have argued, a strategy based on a certain degree of autonomy from the large agrarian interests. Nevertheless, economically speaking, it is clear that the capitalist coffee sector did emerge out of this experience fortified as a class. This does not deny that many individual members of this class were not unscathed by this process of rationalisation. Quite the opposite, in fact, was indicated by my consideration of the coffee processing sphere where, since the early 1950s, a high proportion of producer–processors disappeared as independent capitalists. The data on coffee farms suggests a similar if not so dramatic decline also occurred with respect to large estate owners since mid century.

It must be mentioned that this conclusion is at odds with those of perhaps the best known observer and historian of the nation's coffee oligarchy. In his *La Dinastía de los Conquistadores*, Samuel Stone argues that the impact of redistributionist programmes of the post-1950 state in Costa Rica – taxes on producers, social security and minimum wage legislation, the *aguinaldo*, *etc.* – have not only produced a deterioration in the position of the coffee *peon* by destroying 'the functional relations between *peon* and *patrón*', but have produced a crisis of profitability for the coffee estate owners and thereby destabilised the nation's most productive activity.[33] My own interpretation of this process leads me to a rather different set of conclusions.

One of the reasons I believe this is so has to do with understanding the specific role of the State since 1949. In my view, it would be a mistake to conceive contemporary State intervention in this social formation as wholly, or even primarily redistributive in character. Not only would this, in practice, run counter to the political doctrine of the early PSD and later the PLN, the ruling party of this period, but it also obscures a whole range of State activities that had little to do with income redistribution but much to do with promoting the modernisation of specific economic groups in the countryside, activities which in fact served to exacerbate previous inequalities. Furthermore, Stone's discussion would seem to be based substantially on generalisations made from several case studies, which is problematic if not viewed alongside data that provides more of an overview of the entire sphere of activity. For there is no doubt that at the level of some individual producers, even with the capitalist estate owners Stone is concerned with, the contemporary process of modernisation and rationalisation of production may be seen as having had a very negative impact. This is not the same as arguing, as Stone does, that the impact of this process on a specific class of producers has been wholly or even largely negative. My own interpretation tries to pay some attention to empirical evidence of the performance of aggregates of producers distinguished along class lines. This kind of analysis suggests that after a considerable restructuring of producer-processors in the 1950s and 1960s, the economic nucleus of capitalist coffee growers emerged basically strengthened as a class, in comparison with its position at the beginning of this period. This is not to say that a considerable 'weeding out' of smaller and inefficient members less able to adapt to the present exigencies of this industry did not take place, and that for a significant number recent State policies have indeed been anathema to their survival.

In my view, then, Stone's argument is mistaken on two grounds. First, one is left with the impression that coffee production as a whole, and specifically that conducted on a larger scale, is in a state of decline and disarray. Here I feel he has confused the inevitable destruction of individual capitals that comes with competition and expansion, a "natural" state within a capitalist economic system, with general economic decline. Secondly, his argument that the interventionist State has been the enemy of the old coffee oligarchy and has figured in their contemporary economic as well as political decline, is only half true. It can be said that the State has been an enemy of this class as it was previously constituted, both economically and politically. However, there is much less support for the view that the State has opposed the maintenance and expansion of agrarian capital that has been willing and able to adapt to a new economic order. In fact, my analysis suggests the very opposite. As a twentieth century Bonaparte, Figueres and the *liberacionista* forces were of some historical consequence precisely because they had broken the political power of the agrarian bourgeoisie, and continued to do so. On the other hand, though adversaries of oligarchic political rule, to be sure, by protecting the material base of this class, and by 'organising' the rationalisation of this sphere of production, they in fact generated its economic power anew. Even more than this, the State has promoted the emergence of new capitalist fractions in agriculture with the mushrooming of such activities as beef ranching, not to mention efforts made to stimulate the expansion of industrial capitalists through protection, expansionary credit policies, guarantees and an assortment of other incentives.

In reality, *Liberación Nacional* has been the best representative of the most modern elements of capital, be it local or multinational – elements that look to the future and not the past for solutions to contemporary problems. Figueres himself was to have remarked that only 'communism' and *Liberación* have had real proposals about how to solve the problems of contemporary Costa Rica.[34] Each had been the author of a distinct social and economic project. The repression unleashed by the Junta of 48 against *Vanguardia Popular* demonstrated that the victory of one force required the negation of the other. This action was the first signal of the class character of *Liberación Nacional*. Subsequent history has only confirmed that this is where the predominant instincts of this political movement lie.

7.7 THE COSTA RICAN MODEL AND THE CENTRAL AMERICAN CRISIS

One final issue remains outstanding. What does the analysis presented above suggest about the suitability of the Costa Rican model as a solution to the advanced crisis in other Central American countries, in particular El Salvador and Guatemala? To begin with, a number of circumstances favoured the initial establishment of the Junta of 1948, and the subsequent democratisation of politics which do not exist any longer, if they ever did, elsewhere in the region. It must not be forgotten that even in Costa Rica, a break with past political practices and economic policies *did* require an armed struggle, however brief, by a force that represented an alternative to the system of the oligarchy, on the one hand, and solutions offered by the left as represented by *Vanguardia Popular*, on the other. Several factors contributed to the success of Figueres and his army in the short run. Chief among these was the fact that the oligarchy itself had become disorganised politically during the 1940s, and their control of the State was no longer as secure as it customarily had been. Despite their initial alliance with the movement led by Figueres, the traditional coffee oligarchy did not have a *hegemonic* role in this power bloc. They were not able to establish their hegemony even when formal political power briefly returned to a government supportive of their interests under Ulate in 1950. Moreover, given the historical schism between the progressive forces in Costa Rica, Figueres was able to quickly distance himself from the Communist left, thereby disarming the real threat of external intervention on the part of the US to re-establish the *status quo ante*,[35] or at least some arrangement more amenable to the interests of the oligarchy.

Does a third force encounter such favourable conditions today elsewhere in Central America? The answer must surely be that it does not. Since the aborted attempts at reform in the 1950s, the regional oligarchies have been reinforced through the militarisation of the State apparatuses of their respective countries.[36] These reinforced and modernised military regimes have, with few exceptions, proven a staunch defender of the landed oligarchy's economic interests. Today it stands as a major obstacle to any real modification of the *status quo*, one that has proven intransigent in both Guatemala and El Salvador even to considerable political and economic pressure of the United States itself.[37] Events have proven that for some time now there has been very little political space between the dictatorship of the oligarchy, and those forces favouring armed struggle to bring about change. The experience of El Salvador's Christian Democratic movement in the late 1960s and early 1970s is a case in point. Representing a reformist option, the Christian Democrats favoured a direction that has been described as 'neither communist nor capitalist but, rather, a third autonomous path to development, one which would be scientifically and technically planned . . . to ensure social justice and a decent living standard for all Salvadoreans.'[38]

The rise of Christian Democratic influence was part of a general liberalisation that saw increasing activity on the part of different social sectors, from students to peasants, in pressing for change in the existing system. The Christian Democratic party itself had used its electoral successes in the 1960s to press for more administrative efficiency and honesty, and urban renewal projects. When the reformist movement it led began to pressure for a reform of the nations highly inequitable landholding system – a matter that went to the heart of oligarchic privilege, the latter and its military representatives did not wait long in organising a reply. The elections of 1972 were marked by fraud that denied the Christian Democrats a victory in favour of the candidate of the traditional ruling party – the military's Party of National Conciliation. Not long afterwards extensive repression was unleashed against the Christian Democrats, and its leader, José Napoleon Duarte, who was jailed, tortured and exiled to Guatemala. This decisive blocking of reform via the existing political process through a reversion to the long entrenched fraudulent practices of the oligarchy's representatives in power saw much of the rank and file of the reformist coalition, including Christian Democrats, move towards the popular organisations associated with the different revolutionary armed forces that were beginning to take shape in the country.[39]

Politics in Guatemala since the US sponsored counter–reform of Castillo Armas in the mid 1950s has provided even less manoeuvring space for the proponents of non-violent change than has been the case in El Salvador. Continuous electoral fraud and terror campaigns orchestrated by both Government security forces and para-military death-squad type organisations against labour unions, centrist and centre-left political parties, university students and rank and file clergy struck down both the hope of peaceful change, and the possible agents of such a process. As one observer has written,

> By the early 1980s the majority of people and organisations in opposition to the government and advocating significant structural change were in exile. They represented a broad cross–section of the Guatemalan population and had begun to link together into a consolidated front opposing the government.[40]

An historical perspective on Central America shows that a policy of supporting centrist and centre–left political organisations favouring *reform* has at times been part of the rhetoric of US foreign policy makers, but has not been their first priority when it came to translating policy into practice. This has consistently been the case through Democratic and Republican administrations. And while at one time the rhetoric *might* have become a reality in some countries of the isthmus, much too much has changed for this to be the case anymore. Even in Costa Rica, as we have seen, under perhaps the most favourable conditions, liberal democracy came into existence through force of arms. Such favourable conditions no longer exist, while those forces in Central America who see a political system *à la Costa Rica* as the ideal have for some time now lost the initiative to a coalition of popular organisations and revolutionary groups on the left.

As a 'revolution' of an incipient middle class, the Costa Rican model proved at least moderately successful in delivering the bulk of its benefits to elements of this class and modernising elements of the oligarchy. The shift in organisational strength and initiative to a broader segment of the dispossessed population has already proven in Nicaragua to require a new model of development to accommodate the present constellation of oppositional forces that have emerged in the last decade to oppose the local oligarchies and their foreign backers. The old models will not do for the present realities of Central America.

Today in much of the region, particularly in Guatemala and El Salvador, we are reminded of the words of Alexander Gerschenkron, quoted at the beginning of this chapter. As a perceptive observer of the role of a powerful landowning class in German society and politics, he came to the conclusion that the forces organising post-war reconstruction either had to deal with this class once and for all, through a radical agrarian reform, 'or embark upon a policy of ruthless and lasting oppression of the German nation, for only this would enable the world to escape the horrors of a third German aggression, of a third world war, after a breathing spell of one or two decades'.[41] In Central America, nations organised by and in the interests of a landed oligarchy had never been able, in previous times, to threaten the interests of nations much beyond their own borders, as Germany had done in a previous age. And yet, now they *are* proving to be an arena for superpower confrontation in a world continually under the threat of global nuclear war. Viewed from this perspective, the fate of the remaining Central American landed oligarchies can be seen as an issue of some considerable importance for the peace and security of peoples and nations not only within the region, but perhaps well beyond it.

178 *Coffee and Democracy in Modern Costa Rica*

Notes

1. This process in disparate regions of the globe is described in the following studies: David Brading, 'Hacienda Profits and Tenant Farming in the Mexican Bajío, 1700–1860' in Duncan and Rutledge (eds.) *Land and Labour in Latin America*, (Cambridge University Press (1977); Warren Dean, *Rio Claro: A Brazilian Plantation System, 1820–1920*, (Stanford University Press, 1976); Marco Palacios, *Coffee in Colombia, 1850–1910*, (Cambridge University Press, 1980); Robert A. Dickler, 'Organisation and Change in Productivity in Eastern Prussia' in W. Parker and E.L. Jones (eds) *European Peasants and Their Markets*, (Princeton University Press, 1975); and Alan Richards, 'The Political Economy of *Gütswirtschaft*: A Comparative Analysis of East Elbian Germany, Egypt, and Chile', *Comparative Studies in Society and History*, *21*, (1979).

2. See, for example, Max Weber, 'Developmental Tendencies in the Situation of East Elbian Rural Labourers' *Economy and Society* 8, 2 (1979).

3. Richards, 'The Political Economy of *Gütswirtschaft*.'

4. Cristobal Kay, 'Comparative Development of the European Manorial System and the Latin American Hacienda System' *Journal of Peasant Studies 2*, 1 (1974).

5. V.I. Lenin, *Collected Works* vol.13, (Moscow: Progress Publishers, 1962).

6. Roger Bartra *Estructura agraria y classes sociales en Mexico*, (Mexico: Era, 1974).

7. Agustin Cueva, *El Desarrollo del Capitalismo en America Latina*, (Mexico: Siglo Veintiuno Editores, 1977).

8. Teresa Mead, 'The Transition to Capitalism in Brazil: Notes on a Third Road' *Latin American Perspectives V*, 3 (1978).

9. See Miguel Murmis 'El Agro Serrano y la Via Prussiana de Desarrollo Capitalista' in *Ecuador: Cambiós en el Agro Serreno*, (Quito: FLACSO/ CEPLAES, 1980).

10. Richards, 'The Political Economy of *Gütwirtschaft*'.

11. Torres Rivas, *Interpretación*, p.51.

12. For a more general discussion of the question of estate agriculture and technological development, with particular reference to the case of Prussia, see Winson 'The "Prussian Road" of Agrarian Development'. The social aspects of estate agriculture are dealt with by Weber, 'Developmental Tendencies'; Richards, 'The Political Economy of *Gütswirtschaft*'; and Keith Tribe, 'Prussian Agriculture – German Politics: Max Weber 1892–7' *Economy and Society 12*, 2 (1983).

13. Weber, ibid., p.184, 191.

14. Harriet Friedmann, 'World Market, State, and Family Farm: Social Bases of Household Production in the Era of Wage Labour', *Comparative Studies in Society and History 20*, 4 (1978), pp.574–5.

15. Weber, ibid., pp.191–3.

16. Differing explanations are offered in Tribe, 'Prussian Agriculture', p.193 and Winson, 'The "Prussian Road" of Agrarian Development: A Reconsideration' *Economy and Society 11*, 4 (1982), p.395. The former

lays stress on the switch over to intensive root crop cultivation as having created conditions for the development of such a surplus population. The latter paper argues that the existence of such a population was a precondition for more intensive cultivation, and was created by the internal dymamics of estate agriculture, together with normal demographic increase and the improved possibilites of recruiting labour from eastern regions. This question is a thorny one for the political economy of estate agriculture in general, for it would seem to be essential for understanding the process whereby estate organisation undergoes a structural transformation, accompanying the capitalisation and intensification of production.

17. As Weber notes with respect to the reorganisation of the estates, 'the condition for this of course was naturally that seasonal workers were freely available, which was not the case in the traditional organisation of farming', 'Developmental Tendencies', p.192.

18. Werner Conze, 'The Effects of Nineteenth Century Liberal Agrarian Reforms on Social Structure in Central Europe' in F. Crouzet (ed.) *Essays in European Economic History, 1789–1914,* London: Edward Arnold, 1969).

19. See Chapter 2, p. 20.

20. Weber wrote – 'I regard the "rural labour question" here completely as one of *Stäatraison . . .* The state interest in the rural labour question of the East is solely to be found in the question of the condition of the foundations of social organisation – can the state rely on it in the long run to solve the political tasks which exist in the East. In my opinion the answer is no.' Cited in Tribe, 'Prussian Agriculture', p.208.

21. See Torres Rivas, *Interpretación,* for the most comprehensive treatment. Jaime Wheelock's *Imperialismo y Dictadura: Crisis de una Formación Social,* (Mexico: Siglo Veintiuno Editores, 1975) provides an essential study for Nicaragua. For Guatemala, see Sanford Mosk, 'The Coffee Economy of Guatemala: 1850–1918' *Inter-American Economic Affairs IX,* Winter (1955), David McCreery, 'Coffee and Class: The Structure of Development in Liberal Guatemala' *Hispanic American Historical Review 56,* 3 (1976), and for a regional overview see my 'Class Structure and Agrarian Transition in Central America', *Latin American Perspectives 5,* 4 (1978).

22. See C. Bataillon and I. Lebot, 'Migración interna y empleo agricola temporal en Guatemala', *Estudios Sociales Centroamericanos V,* January–April (1976), p.53.

23. See ibid., and L.B. Fletcher's, *Guatemala's Economic Development: the Role of Agriculture* Ames: Iowa State University Press (1970), for Guatemala and Torres Rivas, *Interpretación,* p.230 for El Salvador. The phenomenon of migrant labour in Nicaragua is dealt with by Orlando Nuñez, *El Somocismo y el Modelo Capitalista Agro-exportadora,* Managua: Dept. of Social Sciences, UNAN (1978), for example.

24. See Bataillon and Lebot, 'Migración interna', p.53; Peter Dorner and Rodolfo Quiros, 'Institutional Dualism in Central America's Agricultural Development', *Journal of Latin American Studies V,* November (1973), p.225 and Lester Schmid, 'The role of Migratory Labour in the

180   *Coffee and Democracy in Modern Costa Rica*

Economic Development of Guatmala', unpublished Ph.D. dissertation, Madison: University of Wisconsin (1967), pp.338–9.

25. Edelberto Torres Rivas, 'Las contradicciones en la transformación de la estructura espacial rural en centroamerica', paper presented at the Universidad Central de Venezuela, mimeo (1975), p.16.

26. One historian has summed up the social milieu of the estates in Prussia as follows. "The social and political position of the great landowners in the local communities of the East gave them such control over the lives of the poverty stricken agricultural workers and peasants that these classes, though legally free, were actually in the state of semi-bondage as long as they remained on the remote, isolated estates.' Sarah R. Tirrel, *German Agrarian Politics After Bismarck's Fall* (New York: Columbia University Press, 1951), p.67.

27. See Alexander Gerschenkron, *Bread and Democracy in Germany* (New York: Howard Fertig, 1966), p.53.

28. Fritz Stern, 'Prussia' in David Spring (ed.) *European Landed Elites in the 19th Century*, (Baltimore: Johns Hopkins, 1977), p.48.

29. Ibid., pp. 47–8.

30. Alexander Gerschenkron, p.53.

31. Ibid.

32. See José Nun, *Latin America: The Hegemonic Crisis and the Military Coup* Berkeley: Institute of International Studies, University of California (1969) and Celso Furtado, 'Obstacles to the Political Development of Brazil' in Claudio Veliz (ed.) *Obstacles to Change in Latin America* (New York: Oxford University Press, 1969).

33. Stone, *La Dinastía, pp. 133–47.*

34. Delgado, *El Partido*, p.170.

35. See Chapter 4. The *status quo ante* was undoubtedly a less than appealing option in itself for the United States, given the prominent role of *Vanguardia Popular* in the previous administration. The long-term breakdown of oligarchic rule here beginnng in the early 1940s, made the sponsoring of a counter-reform less of a clear cut option for the United States than was the case in Guatemala, for example, some years later.

36. This process is detailed by Andrea Brown, 'CONDECA: Integrating the Big Guns' in S. Jonas and D. Tobis (eds) *Guatemala*, (Berkeley: NACLA, 1974) and NACLA, *Latin American and Empire Report*, 7, 5 May–June (1973), p.22 and Tom Barry, Beth Wood, and Deb Preusch, *Dollars and Dictators*, (Albuquerque: The Resource Centre, 1983), pp.117–23.

37. Witness the limited impact of the banning of arms shipments to the Guatemalan dictatorship under the Carter Administration. However, in part this may be explained that arms shipments arranged earlier continued under this administration, while other nations such as Israel stepped in to meet the needs of the military through the establishment of a munitions and small arms plant, by training military personnel and by establishing sophisticated electronic monitoring equipment in Guatemala. See Barry *et al.*, ibid., and *Latin American Weekly Report* (Nov. 22, 1985), p.10 and Cheryl A. Rubenberg, 'Israeli

Foreign Policy in Central America', (*Third World Quarterly*, 8, 3, 1986).
38.   Lisa North, *Bitter Grounds: Roots of Revolt in El Salvador* (Toronto: Between the Lines, 1981), p.67.
39.   Ibid.
40.   Jim Handy, *Gift of the Devil: A History of Guatemala*, (Toronto: Between the Lines, 1984), p. 230.
41.   *Bread and Democracy* (1943), p.173

Appendix

Table A.1 Costa Rica: distribution of coffee farms by number, 1950–5, 1963, 1973

Category		1950–5	(%)	1963	(%)	1973	(%)
.69 – 3.9	ha.	6970	(32)	11280	(38)	17072	(53)
4 – 9.9	ha.	6003	(27)	6601	(22)	6256	(19)
10 – 19.9	ha.	3114	(14)	4242	(14)	3485	(11)
20 – 199.9	ha.	4947	(23)	6390	(22)	4668	(14)
100 – 199.9	ha.	550	(03)	747	(03)	521	(02)
200 – 999.9	ha.	330	(02)	462	(02)	316	(01)
1000 +	ha.	44	(.2)	53	(.2)	32	(.1)
Total[*]		21988	(100)	29775	(100)	32353	(100)

[*] percentages may not add to 100 due to rounding.
Source: Censo agropecuario, 1950–5, 1963, 1973.

Table A.2 Costa Rica: distribution in coffee farms by area, 1950–5, 1963, 1973

Category		1950–5	(%)	1963	(%)	1973	(%)
.69 – 3.9	ha.	6713	(10)	11005	(14)	13536	(17)
4 – 9.9	ha.	12435	(18)	12959	(16)	14909	(18)
10 – 19.9	ha.	9036	(13)	11228	(14)	11231	(14)
20 – 99.9	ha.	26276	(38)[**]	24487	(31)	23520	(28)
100 – 199.9	ha.			6102	(08)	6056	(07)
200 – 999.9	ha.	12758	(18)	11226	(14)	9885	(12)
1000 +	ha.	2618	(04)	3293	(04)	3372	(04)
Total		69836	(100)	80300	(100)	83407	(100)

[*] percentages may not add to 100 due to rounding.
[**] area in farms reported only for 20–199.9 ha. in this census.
Source: Censo agropecuario, 1950–5, 1963, 1973.

Table A.3   Costa Rica: total coffee production and productivity, by size categories 1950–5, 1963, 1973

Category	Total Production (kg)			Productivity (kg/ha.)		
	1950–5	1963	1973	1950–5	1963	1973
.69 – 3.9 ha.	9 128 960	28 871 936	52 295 537	1360	2624	3863
4 – 9.9 ha.	16 955 392	36 313 344	60 509 222	1364	2808	4059
10 – 19.9 ha.	13 210 368	34 592 256	47 107 541	1462	3081	4194
20 – 99.9 ha.	34 240 256	85 848 320	113 625 031	1677**	3506	4831
100 – 199.9 ha.	9 815 547	28 047 872	32 246 004		4597	5325
200 – 999.9 ha.	27 136 000	45 621 248	49 913 685	2127	4064	5196
1000 + ha.	4 986 368	11 260 160	11 859 901	1905	3419	3517
Total	114 134 270	274 388 990	369 205 120			

* Hectares per category taken from Table 6.4.
** Area in farms only reported for 20–199.9 ha. category.
Source: Censo agropecuario, 1950–5, 1963, 1973

Table A.4 Value of coffee exports as a percentage of all export earnings, 1976

Country	Coffee exports as a % of all exports
Burundi	86.1
Uganda	85.8
Ruanda	77.9
Ethopia	55.9
Colombia	57.7
El Salvador	53.5
Haiti	36.8
Ivory Coast	34.0
Guatemala	32.0
Tanzania	32.0
Costa Rica	27.6
Kenya	27.0
Angola	26.7 (1973)
Honduras	25.6
Cameroon	24.0
Brazil	23.7
Central African Rep.	23.2
Madagascar	22.3

Source: *Quarterly Statistical Bulletin on Coffee,* vol. 2, no. 2 (April–June) 1978.

References

1. Newspapers and Journals

Diario de Costa Rica, San José, 1950–3.
Latin American Weekly Report, 1985.
La Nacion, San José, 1950–80.
La Prensa Libre, San José, 1949–80.
La Republica, San José, 1950–80.
El Agricultor Costariccense, San José, 1962, 1978, 1979.
Surco, San José, 1942–3.
La Gaceta. San José, 1952, 1957.
Memoria Anual, Banco central de Costa Rica, 1959, 1961.
Revista del Instituto de Defensa del Café, San José, 1932–46.

2. Official Publications

Anuario Estadistico de Costa Rica, (1974) San José, Dirección General de Estadisticas.
BANCO ANGLO COSTARRICENSE. (1954) *Programa para la Rehabilitación de Cafetales.*
BANCO CENTRAL DE COSTA RICA (1958) 'Reduce Impuesto de Importación de Abonos Arancel de Aduanas, Ley no. 1738 de 31 Marzo de 1954', *Memoria Anual.*
—— (1972, 1973) *Informe Sobre la Politica de Credito a la Actividad Cafetalera Durante 1979*, (San José).
—— (1972, 1973) *Politica Creditica en Relación con la Actividad Cafetalera*, (San José).
—— (1976). *Programa Nacional de Credito para Abonamiento de Cafetales*, (San José).
DEPARTMENT OF OVERSEAS TRADE (1934. *Ecomomic Conditions in the Republic of Costa Rica*, (London: HMSO).
DIRECCIÓN GENERAL DE ESTADISTICAS, *Censo agropecuario*, (1950, 1955, 1963, 1973) Dirección General de Estadistica, (San José).
DIRECCIÓN GENERAL DE ESTADISTICAS, 1974 *Anuario Estadistico de Costa Rica*, San José: Dirección General de Estadisticas.
ECLA (1958) *Coffee in Latin America: Vol.I, Colombia and El Salvador* (New York).
—— (1958) *Coffee in Latin America: Vol.II, Brazil (New York).*
—— *(1956, 1957, 1958) Economic Bulletin for Latin America*, vols. 1–3 (Santiago).
—— (1975, 1976) *Economic Survey of Latin America.* (Santiago).
ECLA (1973) *Tenencia de la Tierra y Desarrollo Rural en Centroamerica*, (San José: Editorial Universitaria Centroamericano).

INSTITUTO INTERAMERICANO DE CIENCIAS AGRICOLAS (1950) 'Los Salarios en Café no Cobren el 38% de las Necesidades de los Trabajadores' (Resumen de Seminario, 28 August).

INSTITUTO INTERNACIONAL DE AGRICULTURA (1935) *El Café en 1931 y 1932: Questiones Economicos y Tecnicos* (Rome).

MINISTERIO DE AGRICULTURA E INDUSTRIAS (1953). 'El Abonamiento del Cafeto' (Boletin Divulgativo no. 18. San José).

OFICINA DE PLANIFICACIÓN SECTORIAL AGROPECUARIO (1979) *Programa de Mejoramiento de la Producción de Café de Costa Rica,* (San José).

OFICINA DEL CAFÉ (1959) *Plan de Abonamiento Intensivo,* (San José).

—— (1975, 1976) *Informe de Labores,* (San José).

—— (1979) *Informe Sobre la Actividad Cafetalera de Costa Rica,* (San José).

—— (1978) *Manual de Recomendaciones Para Cultivar Café,* (San José).

OVERSEAS ECONOMIC SURVEYS (1950, 1954) *Costa Rica: Economic and Commercial Conditions,* (London: HMSO).

UNITED NATIONS (1938–61, 1963, 1972, 1973) *The Growth of World Industry,* (New York).

—— (1958) *Yearbook of National Accounts,* (New York).

3. Unpublished Theses

ARCE, Antonio M. (1959) 'Rational Introduction of Technology on a Costa Rican Coffee Hacienda: Sociological Implications'. Ph.D. thesis, Michigan State University.

BOLAÑOS ARQUIN, Margarita and Nancy CARTIN LELVA (1979). 'Obstaculos Ideologicas al Desarrollo de Organizaciones Reinvindicativas de Clase en el Proletariado y Semi-Proletariado del Café, Department of Anthropology, University of Costa Rica.

CAMPANARIO S., Roberto (1978) 'Los Clases Sociales en el Agro en Costa Rica', Thesis for the Licenciatura, University of Costa Rica.

CARTAY ANGULO, Rafael (1969) 'La Comercialización de Café en Costa Rica a traves de Cooperativos', Masters of Science thesis, Instituto Interamericano de Ciencias Agricolas.

GARITA BONILLA, Nora C. and LEON QUESADA, Ma. del Rosario (1977) 'Diferenciación al Interior del Bloque Cafetalero', Thesis for the Licenciatura, University of Costa Rica.

PETERS SOLORZANO, Gertrud. 1979. 'La Formación Territorial de las Grandes Fincas de Café en la Meseta Central; Estudio de la Firma Tournon (1877–1950)', Thesis for the Licenciatura, University of Costa Rica.

QUIROS GUARDIA, R.E. (1971). 'Agricultural Development and Economic Integration in Central America', Ph.D. thesis, University of Wisconsin.

ROJAS BOLAÑOS, Manuel. (1977). '*Clasey lucha de Clases en Costa Rica:* 1940–1948', Ph.D. thesis, National Autonomous University of Mexico.

SCHMID, Lester (1967) 'The Role of Migratory Labour in the Economic Development of Guatemala'. Unpublished Ph.D. dissertation, University of Wisconsin, Madison.

ZUÑIGA OREAMURO, D. (1971) 'El Café: Su Imperativa Economica, Politica y Social en Costa Rica', Thesis for the Licenciatura, University of Costa Rica.

4. Books and Articles

AGUILAR, Justo, Carlos BARBOZA and Jorge LEON (1981) *Desarrollo Tecnologico del Cultivo del Café*, (San José: Consejo Nacional de Investigaciones).

AMERINGER, Charles D. (1978) *Don Pépé: A Political Biography of José Figueres of Costa Rica*, (Albuquerque: University of New Mexico Press).

AMERLING, Raymundo (1939) *Estudio Sobre las Condiciones Agricolas del Distrito Cafetalero Uruca* (San Pedro: Facultad de Agronomia, University of Costa Rica).

ANDRADE M., Eduardo (1979) *Recursos de los Paises Para Transferencia de Tecnología en Café*, San José: Instituto Interamericano de Ciencias Agricolas).

ARÍAS SANCHEZ, Osar (1979) *Nuevos Rumbos Para el Desarrollo Costarricense* (San José: Editorial Universitaria Centroamericana).

BANAJI, Jairus (1977) 'Modes of Production in a Materialist Conception of History', *Capital and Class*, no.3 (Autumn).

BARRENECHEA CONSUEGRA, Ferrando (1956) *Una Organización Para Empresarios del Café*, (San José: Escuela Superior de Administración Publica).

BARRY, Tom, Beth WOOD and Deb PREUSCH (1983). *Dollars and Dictators* (Albuquerque: The Resource Centre).

BATAILLON, C. and I. LEBOT (1976) 'Migración Interna y Empleo Agricola Temporal en Guatemala', *Estudios Sociales Centroamericanos*, 13.

BELL, John P. (1971) *Crisis in Costa Rica*, (Austin: University of Texas Press).

BRENNER, Robert (1977) 'The Origins of Capitalist Development: A Critique of Neo-Smithian Marxism'. *New Left Review*, No. 104, July–August.

BROWN, Andrea (1973) 'CONDECA: Integrating the Big Guns' in S. Jonas and D. Tobis (eds.) *Guatemala* (Berkeley: NACLA).

BUARQUE DE HOLLANDA, Teodoro and Carlos RABBE (1975) 'Costa Rica: Migración Rural – Rural y Estructura Agraria en el Periodo 1950–1963', *Estudios Sociales Centroameicanos*, II.

BULGARELLI, Oscar R. (1969), *Costa Rica y Sus Hechos Politicos de 1948*, (San José: Editorial Costa Rica).

CARDOSO, Ciro (1977) 'The Formation of the coffee estate in Nineteenth-century Costa Rica' in Duncan and Rutledge (eds) *Land and Labour in Latin America* (Cambridge University Press).

CAZALI AVILA, Augusto (1976) 'El Desarrollo del Cultivo del Café y Su Influencia en el Regimen del Trabajo Agricola: Epoca de la Reforma Liberal (1871–1885)'. *Anuario de Estudios Centroamericanos* (San José: no.2).

CERDAS CRUZ, Rodolfo (1972). *La Crisis de la Democracia Liberal en Costa Rica*, (San José: EDUCA).

CENTRO DE ESTUDIOS DEMOCRATICOS DE AMERICA LATINA (1970) *Cooperativos de Cafecultores y Desarrollo de Costa Rica* (San José).

CONZE, WERNER (1969) 'The Effects of Nineteenth Century Liberal Agrarian Reforms on Social Structure in Central Europe', in F. Crouzet (ed.) *Essays in European Economic Histor, 1789–1914* (London: Edward Arnold).

CUEVA, Agustin (1978) *El Desarrollo del Capitalismo en America Latina*, (Mexico: Veintiuno Editores, 2nd edition.)

DEAN, Warren (1976) *Rio Claro: A Brazilian Plantation System, 1820–1920* (Stanford University Press).

DEL BELLO, Juan Carlos (1979) 'El Sector Agroindustrial en Costa Rica'. *Estudios Sociales Centroamericanos*, año III, no. 22,

DELGADO, Jaime Gerardo (1980) *El Partido Liberación Naciõnal* (Heredia: Editorial de la Universidad Nacional).

DE LA CRUZ, Vladimir (1978) 'Costa Rica: 100 años de Luchas Sociales, Reseña Historica'. Lecturas Complementarias no. 2, *Escuela de Historia y Geografica*, Universidad de Costa Rica.

DIAZ SANTOS, Ricardo (1976) *Datos Basicos de Costa Rica*, San José: Instituto de Investigaciones Sociales, no.14.

DICKLER, Robert (1975) 'Organization and Change in Productivity in Eastern Prussia' in W. Parker and E. L. Jones (eds) *European Peasants and Their Markets*, (Princeton University Press.)

DOBB, Maurice (1963) *Studies in the Development of Capitalism* (New York: International Publishers).

DORNER, Peter and Roberto QUIROS (1973) 'Institutional Dualism in Central America's Agricultural Development', *Journal of Latin American Studies*, vol. 5, (November).

DRAPER, Hal (1977) *Karl Marx's Theory of Revolution* vol. 1. (New York: Monthly Review Press).

ENGELS, Friedrich (1967) *The German Revolutions* (University of Chicago Press).

—— (1968) *The Role of Force in History* (London: Lawrence and Wishart).

FACIO, Rodrigo (1972) *Obras de Rodrigo Facio*, vol. 1 (San José: Editorial Costa Rica).

FLETCHER, L.B. (1970) *Guatemala's Economic Development: The Role of Agriculture*, (Ames: Iowa State University Press).

FLICHMAN, Guillermo (1977) *La Renta del Suelo y el Desarrollo Agrario Argentino* (Mexico: Siglo Veintiuno).

FRANK, Andre G. (1972) *Lumpenbourgeoisie: Lumpendevelopment* (New York: Monthly Review Press).

FRIEDMANN, Harriet (1978) 'World Market, State and Family Farm: Social Basis of Household Production in the Era of Wage Labour', *Comparative Studies in Society and History*, vol.20, no.4.

FURTADO, Celso (1969). 'Obstacles to the Political Development of Brazil.' in C. Veliz *(ed.) Obstacles to Change in Latin America*, (New York: Oxford University).

GAMBOA Marin, Ma. Paulina (1977) *Analysis Economico de La Producción del Café en Costa Rica, Cosecha 1976–77* (San José: Oficina del Café).

GEER, Thomas (1971) *An Oligopoly: The World Coffee Economy and Stabilization Schemes* (New York: Dunellen Publishing Co.).

GERSCHENKRON, Alexander (1966) *Bread and Democracy in Germany* (New York: Howard Fertig).

GRAMSCI, Antonio (1971) *Selections from the Prison Notebooks* (New York: International Publishers).

HALL, Carolyn (1978a) *El Café y el Desarrollo Historico – Geografico de Costa Rica* (San José: Editorial Costa Rica).

—— (1978b) *Formación de una Hacienda Cafetalera, 1889–1911* (San José: Editorial Universidad de Costa Rica).

HALL, Stuart (1977) 'Rethinking the "Base and Superstructure" Metaphor' in Jon Bloomfield (ed.) *Class, Hegemony and Party* (London: Lawrence and Wishart).

HANDY, Jim (1984) *Gift of the Devil: A History of Guatemala* (Toronto: Between the Lines).

HAYDEN QUINTERO, William (1970). *Relación Entre el Credito Ortogado al Café y la Expansion en Su Producción* (San José: Banco Central de Costa Rica), Series no. 5.

HILL, George. W. (1964) 'The Agrarian Reform in Costa Rica'. *Land Economics*, vol.49, no. 1.

Homenaje al Café de Costa Rica, (1933) Supplement to *La Tribuna*, October.

HOLLOWAY, Thomas H. (1977). 'The Coffee Colono of Sao Paulo, Brazil: Migration and Mobility, 1880–1930.' in Duncan and Rutledge (eds) *Land and Labour in Latin America*, (Cambridge University Press).

JIMENEZ Castro, A. (1978) *Leyes y Reglamentos Usuales Sobre Café*, (San José: Oficina del Café).

KAY, Cristobal (1974) 'Comparative Development of the European Manorial System and the Latin American Hacienda System'. *Journal of Peasant Studies*, vol. 2, no. 1.

KEPNER, D. and J. SOOTHILL (1935) *The Banana Empire* (New York: The Vanguard Press).

KRUG, C.A. and R.A. DE POERCK (1968) *World Coffee Survey* (Rome: FAO).

LENIN, V.I. (1967) *The Development of Capitalism in Russia* (Moscow: Progress Publishers).

—— (1968) *Collected Works*, vol. 13. (Moscow: Progress Publishers).

MACHADO, Absalon (1977) *El Café: De la Aparcería al Capitalismo* (Bogota).

MARX, Karl (1967) *Capital* ,3 vols (Moscow: Progress Publishers).

—— (1977) 'Results of the Immediate Process of Production', appendix to *Capital*, vol. 1. (New York: Vintage Books).

—— (1972) *The Eighteenth Brumaire of Louis Bonaparte* (Moscow: Progress Publishers).

MASSEY, D. and A. CATALANO. (1978) *Capital and Land*, (London: Edward Arnold).

McCREERY, David J. (1976) 'Coffee and Class: The Structure of Development in Liberal Guatemala'. *Hispanic American Historical Review*, vol. 56.

MERZ, Carlos (1937) 'Estructura Social y Economica de la Industria de Café en Costa Rica'. *R.I.D.C.* vol.5, 32–3.

MOORE, Barrington (1966) *Social Origins of Dictatorship and Democracy*, (Boston: Beacon Press).
MORETZHOHN DE ANDRADE, F. (1967) 'Decadencia do Campesinato Costarriquenho', *Revista Geografica*, no. 66–7, Rio de Janiero, June.
MOSK, Sanford (1955) 'The Coffee Economy of Guatemala: 1850–1918. Development and Signs of Instability', *Inter-American Economic Affairs*, vol.9, no. 3.
MURMIS, Miguel. (1980). 'El Agro Serrano y la Vía Prussiana de Desarrollo Capitalista', in Murmis (ed.) *Ecuador: Cambios en el Agro Serrano*, (Quito: Flacso/Ceplaes).
—— and Juan Carlos PORTANTIERO (1971) *Estudios Sobre los Origenes del Peronismo*, (Buenos Aires: Siglo Veintiuno).
NORRIS, Thomas L. (1953) 'A Colono System and Its Relation to Seasonal Labour Problems on a Costa Rican Hacienda', *Rural Sociology*, vol. 18, no. 4.
NORTH, Liisa (1981) *Bitter Grounds: Roots of Revolt in El Salvador* (Toronto: Between the Lines).
NUN, José (1969) *Latin America: The Hegemonic Crisis and the Military Coup* (Berkeley: Institute of International Studies).
NUÑEZ, Orlando (1978) *El Somocismo y el Modelo Capitalista Agro-exportadora* (Managua: Dept. of Social Sciences, UNAN).
PALACIOS, Marco (1980) *Coffee in Colombia, 1850–1970* (Cambridge University Press).
PEREZ BRIGNOLI, Hector (1980) 'The Economic Cycle in Latin American Agricultural Export Economies (1880–1930): A Hypothesis for Investigation', *Latin American Research Review, 15*, (2).
RICHARDS, Alan (1979). 'The Political Economy of Gütswirtschaft:
A Comparative Analysis of East Elbian Germany, Egypt and Chile.', *Comparative Studies in Society and History*, vol. 21.
SALAZAR, José *et al.* (1978) 'Costa Rica: una Politica Agraria Innovadora.' *Estudios Sociales Centroamericanos*, no. 20.
SANDNER, Gerhard (1961) *Agrar kolonisation in Costa Rica.* (Kiel: Schmidt & Klaunig).
SCHIFTER, Jacobo (1979) *La Fase Oculta de la Guerra Civil en Costa Rica*, (San José: Editorial Universitaria Centroamericano).
SELIGSON, Mitchell A. (1980) *Peasants of Costa Rica and the Development of Agrarian Capitalism* (Madison: University of Wisconsin Press).
—— (1975) *Agrarian Capitalism and the Transformation of Peasant Society: Coffee in Costa Rica* (Buffalo: Council on International Studies, SUNY).
SOLLEY GÜELL, Tomas. (1940) *Compendio de Historica Economica y Hacendaria de Costa Rica*, (San José: Editorial Soley y Valverde).
STEIN, Stanley J. (1970) *Vasssouras: A Brazilian Coffee County, 1850–1890* (New York: Atheneum).
STERN, Fritz (1977) 'Prussia', in David Spring (ed.) *European Landed Elites in the 19th Century* (Baltimore: John Hopkins University Press).
STONE, Samuel (1975) *La Dinastía de los Conquistadores* (San José: Editorial Universitaria Centroamericana).
—— (1976) 'Costa Rica: Sobre La Clase Dirigente y la Sociedad Nacional'. *Revista de Ciencias Sociales*, San José, no. 11).

TAKAHASHI, K. (1976) 'A Contribution to the Discussion' in R. Hilton (ed.) *The Transition from Feudalism to Capitalism* (London: New Left Books).

TIRREL, Sarah R. (1951) *German Agrarian Politics After Bismarck's Fall.* (New York: Columbia University Press).

TORALES, Ponciano. (1978) *Reseña Historia del Sindicalismo en Costa Rica,* (International Labour Organisation, Costa Rica).

TORRES RIVAS, Edelberto (1978) *Elementos Para la Caracterización de la Estructura Agraria de Costa Rica* (San José: Instituto de Investigaciones Sociales, Universidad de Costa Rica).

—— (1973) *Interpretación del Desarrolla Social Centroamericana* (San José: EDUCA).

TRIBE, Keith (1983) 'Prussian Agriculture – German Politics: Max Weber 1892–7' *Economy and Society,* vol. 12, no.2.

VIQUEZ, Gerardo and Leonidas LOPEZ (1971) 'Informe de Costa Rica', *Café y Cooperativismo en America Latina,* San José: CEDAL, No. 40.

WASSERSTROM, R. (1975) 'Revolution in Guatemala: Peasants and Politics under the Arbenz Government', *Comparative Studies in Society and History,* vol. 17, no. 4.

WEBER, Max (1979) 'Developmental Tendencies in the Situation of East Elbian Rural Labourers', *Economy and Society,* vol. 18, no. 2.

WHEELOCK, Jaime (1975) *Imperialismo y Dictadura: Crisis de una Formación Social* (Mexico: Siglo Veintiuno Editores).

WINSON, Anthony (1978) 'Class Structure and Agrarian Transition in Central America', *Latin American Perspectives,* vol.5, no.4.

—— (1982) 'The "Prussian Road" of Agrarian Development: A Reconsideration', *Economy and Society,* vol. 11, no. 4.

—— (1983) 'The Formation of Capitalist Agriculture in Latin America and Its Relationship to Political Power and the State', *Comparative Studies in Society and History,* vol.25, no. 1

WOLF, Eric and E. HANSEN (1967) 'Caudillo Politics: A Structural Analysis', *Comparative Studies in Society and History,* vol. 9, no 2.

ZELAYA, Chester *et al.* (1979) *Democracia en Costa Rica,* 2nd edn (San José: Editorial Universidad Estatal a Distancia).

Glossary

adicionales   extra workers hired on by planters on a short-term contractual basis

beneficio   coffee processing plant

beneficiador   owner of coffee processing facilities

cafetal   land planted in coffee trees

colono   a permanent coffee estate labourer who was responsible for the care of a small area planted in coffee (colonia). Colonos typically were given a garden plot and some pasture to cultivate for their own use. This type of permanent coffee estate labourer was only prevalent in a few areas.

fanega   unit of measurement equivalent to 256 kilograms

finca   a small or medium size farm

jornaleros   landless labourers on the coffee estates

manzana   unit of area equivalent to 0.69 hectares, or 1.7 acres

Meseta Central   inter-montain valley of central Costa Rica

mild coffees   a high quality Arabian coffee that generally commands better prices than Brazilian and robusta coffees.

robusta coffee   a species encountered in the Congo by Emil Laurent in 1881. A larger variety than the *arabica* coffee tree, it produces a lower quality coffee that consequently commands a lower price on the world market.

unwashed coffee   coffee that is dried in the sun without being depulped beforehand. The dried pulp is later removed by a machine. Also known as 'dry hulled' coffee.

washed coffee   coffee beans that are depulped by machine and via fermentation in water before being dried. Usual method for processing coffee in Costa Rica.

Index

Acción Demócrata, 45, 52
ad valorem tax, 84–6
aguinaldo, 70
Alajuela, 16
Allende, 1
Ameringer, Charles, 61, 66, 69
Arbenz, Jacobo, 3
Arce, Antonio Manuel, 124–5
Arevalo, Juan José, 3
Argentina, 4, 164, 168–9
Association of Small Producers, 80

Banco Anglo Costarricense, 101
Banco Nacional de Costa Rica, 108
Barrenechea, F., 128, 132
Bartra, Roger, 158
Bismarck, 167
Brazil: agrarian structure, 5,
    migration to, 15; populism in, 5,
    169; fazendas in, 13

cafetaleros, 15, 18, 23–5, 27, 40, 44
caffea arabica, 100
Calderon Guardia, Rafael Angel,
    42, 61
Calvo, Joaquin Bernardo, 15
Camara de Cafetaleros, 79–81, 87
Cardoso, Ciro, 10, 12–14, 22, 127
Carillo, Braulio, 24
Cartago, 16, 28
Castillo Armas, 52, 177
Centre for Investigations in Coffee,
    106
Centre for the Study of National
    Problems, 27, 44, 58; and co-
    operative movement, 106–7
Chile, 1, 157
coffee economy, 1; class structure of,
    15, 95–6, 114–15; polarisation
    of, 121–2; its establishment, 14;
    and land concentration, 13; and
    distribution of trees, 18; and
    repossession of land, 14; and
    size of estates, 18; and related
    industrial development, 29, 30,
    165–6; and monoculture, 30;

low technological level of, 96,
    161; and new hybrid varieties,
    101; yields, 109; and role of
    fertilisers, 116–17; and
    productivity of farms, 119–21
coffee estates: internal organisation,
    18–19, 122–7; modernisation of,
    122–7; labour force on, 19–20,
    30, 42; technological
    development of, 20–1, 161
coffee exports, 16, 40, 41
coffee oligarchy, 2–3; and free trade
    ideology, 31; the organic crisis
    of, 41, 43; and control of
    processing, 22–3, 79–85, 87, 96
coffee processing: early
    development, 21–3; by the 'wet
    method', 35–38, and co-
    operatives, 106–8, 133–5; and
    concentration of firms, 128–31;
    and agricultural credit, 135–6
Colombia, 95
communal Indian land, 12
Communist Party, 41–43
co-operative movement, 106
Costa Rica: liberal democracy in, 1,
    6; state autonomy in, 7, 50;
    model of development in, 7;
    social reforms in, 25;
    nationalisation of banks in, 62
Costa Rican Confederation of
    Democratic Workers, 72
Costa Rican Institute of Electricity,
    63
Cuba, 1
Cueva, Agustin, 158–9

Department of Agriculture: and the
    revitalisation of coffee, 101–2
Department of Co-operatives, 107
Diario de Costa Rica, 46, 78, 82, 88,
    diversification: agricultural,
    147–8; industrial, 149–54
Dreyfus movement, 57
Duarte, José Napoleon, 176

193